From Dún Síon to Croke Park

From Dún Síon to Croke Park

The Autobiography

MICHEÁL Ó MUIRCHEARTAIGH

PENGUIN
IRELAND

PENGUIN IRELAND

Published by the Penguin Group
Penguin Ireland Ltd, 25 St Stephen's Green, Dublin 2, Ireland
Penguin Books Ltd, 80 Strand, London WC2R 0RL, England
Penguin Group (USA) Inc., 375 Hudson Street, New York, New York 10014, USA
Penguin Books Australia Ltd, 250 Camberwell Road, Camberwell, Victoria 3124, Australia
Penguin Books Canada Ltd, 10 Alcorn Avenue, Toronto, Ontario, Canada M4V 3B2
Penguin Books India (P) Ltd, 11 Community Centre, Panchsheel Park, New Delhi – 110 017, India
Penguin Group (NZ), cnr Airborne and Rosedale Roads, Albany, Auckland 1310, New Zealand
Penguin Books (South Africa) (Pty) Ltd, 24 Sturdee Avenue, Rosebank 2196, South Africa

Penguin Books Ltd, Registered Offices: 80 Strand, London WC2R 0RL, England

www.penguin.com

First published 2004
I

Copyright © Micheál Ó Muircheartaigh, 2004

The moral right of the author has been asserted

Set in 12/14.75 pt PostScript Monotype Bembo
Typeset by Rowland Phototypesetting Ltd, Bury St Edmunds, Suffolk
Printed in Great Britain by Clays Ltd, St Ives plc

A CIP catalogue record for this book is available from the British Library

ISBN 1–844–88044–3

I have always been conscious of indebtedness to the many players I have met and spoken about in the course of my broadcasting career. I dedicate this book to them and in particular to a most worthy representative of them all: the late Cormac McAnallen of Tyrone.

I knew him from his minor days in the 1990s and discovered early on that the Eglish clubman was no ordinary player or person. He excelled as a footballer and made a huge contribution to his county's historic All-Ireland win of 2003. Yet I was even more impressed by his absolute commitment to serve the GAA in every aspect of the association's programme.

He asked for nothing in return, and his untimely death in March 2004, at the age of twenty-four, robbed sporting Ireland of a born and most genuine leader.

Micheál Ó Muircheartaigh

June 2004

Chapter One

Is buachailín mise do shiúlaigh a lán
Ag cur tuairisc' na h-áite is fearr ionad.

I was born on 20 August 1930, at home, in Dún Síon, Dingle, Co. Kerry. The late Princess Margaret was born on the same day – at home as well, I presume, though I never met her to confirm the coincidence. I did interview her nephew Prince Edward for RTE Radio Sport years later, but we were too taken up with greyhound conversation to digress into the area of his famous aunt's birth.

My parents often said that I nearly passed away during the early weeks of my life, after contracting pneumonia. In later years my godmother and neighbour Mary Quinn confirmed the story, and described how she wrapped me up cosily for the three-mile trip by horse cart into Dingle for baptism.

It was a good time to be born: Kerry had just won the Munster football title on the way to a second All-Ireland on the trot – halfway to the county's first ever 'four-in-a-row'. Classics were introduced into greyhound racing that year, and Derbies were run for the first time. But nobody could have known then how important those two sports would be to my life.

Dún Síon was farming country, good land in an idyllic setting. The great Atlantic Ocean was less than a half-mile to the south and east of our house, and directly to the north we had a perfect view of the mountain range that incorporated Brandon, the Conor Pass and Strickeen. Eight families lived in the village: Kennedys, Kevanes, Griffins, Quinns, two families of related Farrells, our cousins the Lynches and ourselves. Speaking Irish was as normal as speaking English: Dún Síon was classed as a '*Breac-Ghaeltacht*', or bilingual area.

My father, Timothy, or Thady as he was known, was of the third generation of Moriartys in Dún Síon since the clan moved west from Anascaul, victims of an eviction in 'bad times'. My mother, Catherine, or Katie, Quinn, came from the smaller community of Coum Bowler, an Irish mile from Dingle town along the road that heads for the Conor Pass. She was always known by her maiden name, as was the norm then for housewives throughout all of what Daniel Corkery described as the 'Hidden Ireland'.

I was the fourth in a family of eight. Padraig was the eldest, followed by Eileen, Náis, myself, Dónal, Máire, Siobhán and finally Kathleen.

There was one more, a brother who died at birth. I remember the small body in a cradle or cot before burial in a non-consecrated pre-Christian graveyard that harbours a magnificent collection of Ogham stones. My father and our neighbour Peter Farrell attended the burial, but the rest of us witnessed it from high up in Gort na Druinne. The place and others like it in the locality have all been consecrated since by Monsignor Padraig Ó Fiannachta, the enlightened Dingle parish priest of the present time.

I and most members of my own family stood on that spot as we waited for the rising of the sun over Kinard Hill on the morning of the new millennium, 1 January 2000. I thought it was a most fitting place to celebrate a special dawn, among the Ogham stones and remains of the innocent and unbaptized of countless generations from the area where I grew up.

When the first rays of the millennium sun edged upwards behind the hill the atmosphere was absolutely still and silent, reminding me of lines from Seán Ó Coileáin's poem 'Tigh Molaga':

> Ni raibh gal ann de'n ghaoith,
> A chroithfeadh barr crainn ná bláth.

I have an early recollection of the wake of a neighbour, Mrs Kennedy, or Mag Sheehy as she was known. Náis, who is a great man on dates and details, tells me she passed away when I was aged three. Anyway, I remember going towards the wake house with

Náis and seeing clay pipes on the window sill outside. People would take a pipe and light up as they arrived. The power of imitation is strong in children: some of us had our first smoke that day and, still copying the elders, prayed 'May the Lord have mercy on the dead.'

When I was five my grandmother Kate Lynch died. I remember that well, as I do the day when my pullover, or *geansaí*, caught fire. It happened quite simply. Like most farmhouse kitchens, ours was large and had a steel-range fire at the gable end. For some reason that I could never fathom it had a six-inch step right in front of the fire: what better place for me to settle myself one cold day?

I can still see myself sitting there, looking towards the door with my back to the fire. The heat soon became too much and I decided to make a run for it, out into the open air and up the back garden. Fortunately Náis, who was only a little over a year older, spotted me in my blazing *geansaí*. Somehow he managed to put out the fire and remove the garment in record time. I can still see that blue-and-white knitted jumper with most of the back completely gone up in smoke, but miraculously as far as I know I didn't have a trace of a burn. *Buíochas le Dia*, that type of luck was always with me.

I had a fascination for the open air from early childhood, with a belief that no known roof was as beautiful as the sky above. We roamed the village and fields from a very early age. Náis and I, and our neighbour Donnchadh Quinn, marvelled at times at the knowledge of the older Tom Kennedy as he spoke to us about the mysteries of the sky. He would talk about the Milky Way, the North Star, the Plough, the moon and even the unseen planets. To our young minds he was a natural genius with a gift for many things, and we used to hear the wise elders say that the 'brains' were always in that family. Hadn't he an uncle a priest in America!

We were familiar with the names for all the fields thereabouts, mostly in Irish: An Fearann Dubh, Gort an Aitinn, Gort na Druinne, An Pháirc Chaol, Gort A' Leasa, Páirc A' Róis and so on. Most houses had children of varying ages, and there was no shortage of company. Every house was a 'rambling house' at some stage, with card playing well into the night.

Mary Dan, the only name we ever heard for Mrs Dan Griffin, was easily the local champion for telling ghost stories. She had spent a few years in America before returning to get married, and as children we spent many an hour gathered round her and listening to tales of ghosts galore and the fearful Headless Coach. The stories were really frightening, and it was never comfortable running the 150 yards home in the dark, our minds full of thoughts of Blackshirt or some other ghost leaping from the hedge.

Still it's a pity that the powers of electric light and television have combined to make those great characters of the world of the spirits redundant.

While nobody in our village or surrounding area was seen as 'rich' in those days, there was no shortage of food or other necessities. The land was good, and every farmer cultivated an infinite variety of potatoes – Champions, Kerr's Pinks, British Queens, King Edwards, Arran Victors, Golden Wonders . . . There was king's cabbage for certain times of the year, common cabbage that would do any time and curly cabbage that might even grow on a rock, not to speak of turnips, parsnips and onions.

Milk was considered to be wholesome food in itself. There was often a choice of white or brown hen eggs, blue duck eggs and, for those with strong stomachs, the enormous grey goose eggs. It was common practice for each farmer to cure bacon, and the killing of the pig once or twice a year was a feature in all homes. It involved help from the neighbours in the traditional team effort called a *meitheal*, and I would have witnessed it from a very early age. The various cuts of meat would be salted by hand and placed in a barrel of pickle for use when required over the coming months. Beef was always acquired from the butcher's in Dingle, and fish came directly from the sea at the doorstep or from the quayside 'in town'. The money required for other necessities came from the sale of milk to the local Dairy Disposal Creamery and year-old cattle to jobbers who came from afar.

★

There was always a great respect for education in the Dingle area, and our household was no exception. Perhaps the old tradition of hedge schools left its mark.

As only one member of a farming family could secure a job on the land, a good education was seen as a valuable passport, no matter where fate led those forced to leave. There were stories of how a Galvin man from John Street in Dingle became the first from Kerry to get into the British civil service of an earlier era. Others followed in time, and this was a fantastic boost for education in the area.

Unfortunately, most people finished up on the emigrant ship. Of the previous generation of Moriartys, all but my father, who inherited the farm, and Joe, the youngest of a large family, crossed the great pond to the United States. It was the same in the preceding generation, when all but my grandfather Aignéis left for distant corners of the world; one of his brothers got to America via Australia, though nobody is quite sure how or why he found himself 'down under' in the first place. Another brother, Tim, was an optimist, and spent most of his life prospecting for gold in Montana. The deeds of his stake are still in the family. Besides the odd trip to civilization in Chicago, New York, New Jersey and elsewhere to meet his siblings and members of the next generation from Dún Síon, he remained in hope on the mountainside.

In a way the circle of emigration in our family was broken when my uncle Joe was kept at school and eventually qualified as a teacher. He ultimately held the position of Deputy Chief Inspector with the Department of Education. He was a great inspiration to us, and took an interest in our progress at school during his many visits home. His son Iognáid is currently President of the National University of Ireland, Galway, and a great advocate of further education for as many as possible.

I was almost six years of age in May 1936 when I first enrolled in the Presentation Convent in Dingle, where both boys and girls attended classes together until first class was completed. I spent no more than a few weeks in junior infants, as the new school year began on the 1 July and I moved on to senior infants.

My first teacher was a young and handsome Sister Kevin. I learned years later that she was a Dublin girl and a member of the musical Potts family, though nobody at the time had any idea where any of the nuns or indeed the brothers came from, or who they really were. I even imagined for a while that they were a different species of being altogether and wondered whether they had to eat or not in order to survive.

I was never aware of any major hardship during my two years in the convent. That changed on transfer at the age of eight to the Monastery, as we called the boys' school, where the Christian Brothers were generally referred to as the 'monks'. We had all heard the tales of past pupils about the very strict regime that was in operation in that establishment. I have long since come to the conclusion that it was expected of the Brothers to be tough and strong on discipline, and I believe they often had the full approval of parents. But I also believe that it was unnecessary and that more sparing of the rod or leather would not have led to the spoiling of the child, as the maxim taught.

Being late on arriving in the morning was almost unforgivable unless the excuse was good, and this sometimes led to brainstorms of originality. I remember a scholar from the town being 'saved' once on saying with a degree of solemnity bordering on reverence that the family donkey had died that morning. The same animal was a key element in the finances of the family, and the sad story softened the otherwise stone-like heart of a particular Brother. The defendant would have stayed out of trouble if he had refrained from mentioning the donkey again that day, but the urge proved too powerful, and in a moment of indiscretion he announced to all and sundry that 'our donkey rose again'. He paid for that resurrection with interest.

It must be said that the Brothers did provide a good education, for which many people, including *mé féin*, are very grateful. They can claim much of the credit also for a talented bunch of Gaelic footballers that came to the fore in Dingle during the 1930s. Dingle had failed until then to capture a Kerry county championship, but under the captaincy of Jimmy McKenna the first was brought home in 1938; by 1948 five more had been added, and names such as Paddy Bawn Brosnan, Bill Dillon, Seán Brosnan, Tom 'Gega' O'Connor and Bill Casey were known throughout the land on account of their exploits on Kerry teams.

I seemed to get through school with less of the leather than the average. I went straight from third class to fifth – to balance numbers as much as anything else – and joined my brother Náis in the same class.

We generally walked to school – a mile along the road at first, then a shortcut through the Cnuicín by the side of the pre-Christian graveyard, and on to the racecourse and the Mail Road before crossing another minor hill that brought us on to the top of John Street on the brink of the town. Occasionally we might meet a few stray donkeys, and if the beasts were willing to move at an acceptable pace we would ride until we reached the edge of Dingle.

It was a great town for a bit of 'divarsion' and enterprise. I remember a massive bazaar organized by Canon Lyne to raise funds for church improvements. All the family were brought along especially to see a show of magic by a namesake of my own from Dingle town who was earning a living in Dublin from his gift of sleight of hand and as an effects man in radio plays. His stage name was Mervani, and his act was spellbinding: the children in one of his acts levitated, and he grasped bullets fired from a gun with his teeth. Nothing surprised the older generation, who knew him as a trickster pupil in the Dingle school in former years.

Confirmation was a big event in the life of our school. It took place every second year with a stately visit to the church by Dr O'Brien, the Bishop of Kerry.

Náis and I were confirmed on the same day, wearing suits made by the tailor Ferriter. The boots to match came from Dublin, where our father had spent a few days at a meeting of former Old IRA people.

Pupils from other schools received the sacrament in Dingle church on the same day, and I can still see the bishop moving from row to row and testing each individual with a question on religion.

It was a great relief to find that the answer was acceptable, though I never heard of a failure at traps.

The stations – the saying of mass in the homes of a parish on a rotating basis – is a long-established and popular custom in most parts of Ireland and remains strong in the Dingle area. It took place twice a year. Including the adjoining village, Imleach, there were eleven households in the Dún Síon station, which meant that the turn came to each home once every five or six years. The house in question would receive a complete redecoration – paint, whitewash and repairs – in readiness for the visit of the parish priest, curate and clerk.

All eleven families in our station area would come for the occasion. The kitchen, which was generally large, would be fitted out for the mass. It might not accommodate everyone, but there was no problem with listening from the back kitchen or even outside the door.

The man of the house would always be at the gate to welcome the priests. The PP usually said the first mass, while the curate would start hearing confessions in an adjoining room. That part could be an ordeal, as the confessor would be visible and sometimes close to a fire. The penitent just knelt at his side and rattled off his or her transgressions against the laws of God and man. The priests would interchange after the first mass, which was for the living; the second was for the dead of the station area.

Once mass, communion, sermon and other trimmings were over the collection of the oats money – support for the upkeep of the clergy – would begin. The heads of households went up to the priest in turn, and placed the offering on the table. The term 'oats money' dated back to the time when priests travelled on horseback. The older generation remembered Fr Tom Jones, who was champion of Ireland in handball and defeated the reigning world champion before entering Maynooth. During the stations he would remind people to attend to his horse at the gable end of the house: 'Tabhair punann eile don gcapall' – give the horse another sheaf – was a favourite phrase of his.

8

Once the liturgical elements were over everybody sat down to eat. The custom was to eat as many boiled eggs as possible, and there was always fine home-made curny cake, but drink was never part of it. A select few would be invited to dine with the priests in the parlour, where the conversation might be more formal than that flowing in the kitchen. It is a lovely custom, and in my young days it had the added bonus that you could be as late as you pleased arriving at school afterwards. First mass usually began about eight o'clock, and it was often close to midday when we would set out in a very leisurely gait on the three-mile walk to school knowing that the stations were a powerful enough answer to cover all possible questions.

The coming of World War II was significant for the people of Ireland, although the country was neutral in the conflict. Emigration to England increased, and we knew plenty of people who were 'over', including a few from our own village. The progress of the war became a constant topic of conversation, and all details were avidly read in the daily paper – the *Irish Press*, mostly. The names of Hitler, Hess, Goebbels, Goering, Rommel, Churchill, Montgomery and others became as well known as those of the Kerry team itself.

The uncertainty of the conflict created a sense of urgency: there was talk of a German invasion through West Kerry, and a battalion of the Irish Army was quartered in Dingle town in readiness. The call to join the LSF (Local Security Force) got a huge response. We were under age and could not enlist, but the Farrells, Quinns, Kennedys and Kevanes all had young men 'in green', drilling and manoeuvring.

A lookout hut was constructed on the high ground overlooking Dún Síon beach, and that was manned by a minimum of two LSF recruits each night while the war lasted. They were armed with a rifle each, and we felt we were ready for the Germans or any other invader that might decide to come at any time. Naturally the hut was a rendezvous for young people, and I recall being there with others playing cards under the moonlight and casting the odd eye over the open sea with our soldier neighbours.

Fortunately the invasion never materialized. It remained a possibility, though, and all strange-looking people who happened to arrive in the area were treated for a while as potential spies. I encountered one such person on the way home from school one afternoon with Náis and others. He was bearded and riding a donkey, with a bicycle wheel hanging on each side of the *asal*. He greeted us in an accent that was not Kerry, and I'm afraid his chances of gaining useful information – if he needed it – were slim from the start. Certainly spies did land in the south-west of Ireland, and there was speculation that a plan existed to disembark one close to Dún Síon beach.

One fine summer's evening Big Petie Farrell was saving hay in a field overlooking the sea close to a cove that was ideal for such a mission. Being a good LSF man he kept an eye on the water as well as the hay, and during one such glance he saw a submarine rise majestically above the surface. He immediately called to his brother Jamesie, but as the pair approached the cliff top the German vessel dipped and disappeared once more.

The most notable of the spies who managed to land was Walter Simon, alias Karl Anderson, who came ashore in June 1940. Lack of local knowledge led to a blunder by the German on his first mission into Dingle and almost ensured that his assignment of sending weather reports and details of British convoy movements back to base was doomed. He visited Nelligan's Pub, and in the course of drinking enquired of the woman of the house about the time of the next train to Tralee. It was a bad mistake, as the service had been discontinued in 1938; the wily Mrs Nelligan put two and two together. Before the day was out the 'tourist' was picked up on his way eastwards. He spent the remainder of the war years in the Curragh internment camp in Kildare.

The Atlantic waters to the south and west were a busy traffic lane in those days, with ships of all types heading to and from England and the Continent. These were targets for German and RAF bombers, several of which crashed into the slopes of Mount Brandon during the war years, presumably because of unfamiliarity with the area and the closeness of Mount Brandon to the sea.

The first was a German Focke-Wulf that came to grief in 1940. Two RAF bombers met the same fate in the space of four months in 1943. There was an extraordinary arrangement with the British whereby bodies recovered from the RAF crashes were handed over to RUC stations beyond the border. The German dead were buried locally in the Pauper's Grave on Cnoc A' Chairn, over-looking Daingean Uí Chúise. The same plot was the resting place for the bodies of unknown sailors washed ashore.

The sea in wartime yielded a special harvest in the form of 'wreck' – or '*raic*', as we called it. Even in peacetime storms sustain the fable that it's an ill wind that does not blow well for somebody: favourable winds often directed fine timber and other useful flotsam and jetsam into the coves, cliffs and inlets of Dingle Bay. The wartime produce was far more valuable, and bales of rubber were the very cream of the waves. Good eyesight was essential to spot the lucrative prize a distance out; bales were dark in colour and barely visible above the surface of the water as they drifted with the tides.

As Dunlop in Cork was starved of rubber in those years there was an understanding that wreck finders could sell directly to them at about £14 a bale. That was huge money at the time, and the gardaí did not interfere – in the 'national interest', I would say. A few large barrels of rum were also washed ashore, and the gardaí commandeered an odd one, but most of the liquid from the others found its way to the buckets and bottles of the community.

One day the Ferriters from the neighbouring village of Binn Báin spotted an object floating some distance out the harbour close enough to where the famous dolphin Fungie now cavorts. Father and son set out in a *naomhóg*, or currach, to inspect it – carefully at first, in case it was a mine that had broken free from its field. Once they were satisfied that it was harmless they moved in and recognized a large rum barrel. It was obviously full because it dipped well under the surface, and the problem of landing it was not an easy one. It was deemed risky to abandon the sea hunt temporarily in order to return for ropes, and so the powerfully strong father, Tomás, lay stomach-downwards in the craft before gripping each end of the large container. His son Paddy then began to row, and the battle was on.

A laden barrel is not exactly lightweight when dragged through salt water, but the strong Tomás, who sometimes in his youth imagined he held up the sky, clung on, and the dynamic duo made it to the water's edge. Their backs had been to the shore during the mission, and what a surprise awaited them there – the gardaí on duty and ready to take the booty on behalf of the state.

Situations like that tend to weaken people's regard for organized systems of government.

Lighting up the dark was a real problem in rural Ireland at the time. Electricity had not yet come, and paraffin oil, which serviced the common kitchen lamp and outdoor lantern, was stringently rationed. Of course people experimented, on the principle that necessity was the mother of invention. Somebody discovered that a piece of soft rag fixed to the top of a Brasso can absorbed the liquid and burned slowly, if not too brightly. I remember trying to do school homework under those conditions, but lack of light was an acceptable excuse for 'no eccer', especially during the busy farming months of spring and autumn. The Brother needed reminding at times in winter that darkness would already have fallen by the time we had travelled the three-mile journey home on foot at the end of the school day. Pupils from the town – where a private generator supplied electricity before the coming of the ESB – were often envious of this dispensation.

Pádógs, a simple substitute for the now unavailable candle, were sometimes pressed back into use, and I recall a time when my mother made a few. Melted animal fat was allowed reset around an elongated piece of wound cloth; when lit it supplied a dim light.

A barrel of candle wax was by far the most useful haul from the sea into the Moriarty home. It floated higher than other driftings, and my father was on hand as the barrel rolled on to Dún Síon strand. The next step was to convert the wax to candles. Náis and I used an old hacksaw to cut a section from the frame of an old bicycle as a make-do mould.

Then a string was run through a half-potato, securing it at the end with a piece of wood. Gently we pressed the mould into the potato, with the string coming out at the open end where a knot and a nail fixed the wick in a central position. Then we hacked off a lump of wax and placed it in a skillet on the hot range. As soon as it was liquefied we poured it into the mould and left it standing in cold water for about an hour. By then the wax would have attached itself to the sides of the mould, and it required a dip or two into warm water before the removal of the potato and the extraction of a finished candle. In comparision to the Brasso cans, the light it provided resembled the rising sun over Kinard Hill on a June morning.

That barrel of wax got us through most of the war.

I think it would be fair to say that a slight sympathy towards the Germans prevailed in many quarters in Ireland, particularly during the early years of the war. De Valera had declared Ireland's neutrality on behalf of the people, but that did not mean that people could not profit from England's difficulties. There was a food shortage across the water, and that brought a good rise in the price of cattle, to the great benefit of a lot of people.

I learned that at first hand one day when I was sent to the Dingle fair to sell four yearling calves, as my father and the older brothers were all down with flu. It gave me a great feeling of independence as I set out at six in the morning with a stick, a dog and four yearlings, but no knowledge of the art of selling.

My father had told me that I would do well if I got £50 for the lot, but fortunately for me there was buoyancy in the Dingle Fair Field that morning; eventually I parted with three of the beasts for £52. I was left with the worst of the four and refused all subsequent offers, as I was quite content to return home with a satisfactory sum of money and a yearling heifer to spare.

There was another source of trade that had remained untapped until then: the export of rabbits to our neighbours at war.

Hitherto rabbits had been looked upon as a nuisance; they could do a lot of damage to crops if the numbers grew too big. To keep them under control a professional trapper and great character called

Eoinín used to visit the village every few years and carry out a good cull – without ever endangering his own livelihood. But rabbits were now a commodity carrying an extraordinarily good price, and I and others quickly learned the art of setting traps and snares in the right places.

For Náis and I, and sometimes the younger Dónal, it meant several detours on the way home from school and more before bedtime to attend to our traps. There would be another inspection on the way to school if time permitted and the catch sold to middlemen en route. The rabbits were in turn collected from them by a man called Lane, who travelled the 31-mile distance from Tralee by van or horse a few times a week. (There was a good market also for fowl of all types, but people were reluctant to sell except in the case of hens that had left their best egg-laying days behind: 'Reserve her for Lane' was a phrase in common usage.) It did not take long before Dún Síon rabbits joined others from all over Ireland on the dinner tables of England. The income was certainly good – so good, in fact, that we used to hand over some of it at home.

Rabbits were bought 'dead', so we had to learn how to kill them as humanely as possible, all in the national interest of the starving British, naturally. Carcasses that showed signs of damage were not saleable, especially if there was evidence of spinal injury. But there were a few unscrupulous sellers capable of camouflaging even the severest of damage. They perfected the art of inserting a spoke from a bicycle wheel through the backbone of a substandard rabbit, thereby restoring rigidity to the corpse.

The English do not owe anything to those particular traders.

A few times a year, especially close to the season of the races, the travelling people, or tinkers as they were then called, visited in large numbers. They were decent people, with many of the men practising the ancient art of tinkering. Pots, pans and buckets that had sprung leaks would be set aside until their arrival, and it was generally no problem for a skilled tinker with 'penny menders' and some solder to restore them to full health once more. They moved about the country in horse-drawn caravans, but I never remember any of their children attending school during their stays in the vicinity. They were made feel welcome in the homes. I often witnessed members of the clan settle for the night on a makeshift or settle bed in the corner of a kitchen. As people who had travelled the country they were never short of a good story. And nobody worried whether the yarns were strictly the truth or not. Some of them were good musicians and dancers, and one great character called Danny Coffey was so lightfooted that he often boasted of being able to walk on eggs and not break them.

It would have been wrong to put him to the test.

There was Mikey Coffey and Tommy, and their womenfolk and children, and another Danny known as 'D', and the Sheridans and Noney O'Brien and her beautiful daughter Roseanne. Whenever Noney was asked would she give Roseanne to one of the locals, she always gave the same reply: 'I wouldn't give anyone even the nail of her big toe.'

There were others who travelled the country roads of Kerry and beyond, alone and on foot. One such stroller was a distinctive-looking gentleman called Con Riordan. He would call once or twice a year and stay a night or two.

Farrells' and ours were his abodes in Dún Síon. He was bearded and spoke with a cultured accent. He never begged, but sold 'fongs', or leather laces, suitable for farmers' boots; the pronunciation was that of an Etonian saying the word 'thongs'.

People bought and paid generously, and fed him while he told wonderful stories of his times in India and elsewhere; true or false, they were fantastic. He was a brilliant card player also and always carried a pack or two in the fong satchel hanging from the shoulder. Whenever he got tired of walking he had a habit of sitting comfortably by the roadside where he played cards by himself until the urge to move hit again. If we happened to come across him on the way home from school we would play with him for a while and pick up a new card trick or two before hurrying home with the news that Con Riordan was on his way. It was good news to all ears because nobody ever heard the same Con utter a bad word about anybody or any locality.

He was a very fine reader; he would oblige if asked, and sometimes he even volunteered. There was a custom then, born of necessity, that the person nearest the weak light in the kitchen would read the paper aloud for the benefit of others, particularly if it contained a famous speech from the likes of de Valera or Churchill, or the evidence given at a murder trial. There were times in Con's presence when a reader might deliberately read poorly in order to get the maestro on stage. This would drive him to exasperation, and in a loud deep voice he would say, 'Fetch *me* that paper, Farrell, and I will throw some light on it.' Of course he would be granted his wish, before proceeding to read like Richard Burton.

The countryside is poorer with the disappearance of people like him, whoever he was. Could he have been a former British Army man who really had been in India? Or a spoiled priest? I heard a few years ago that he died at an advanced age in the County Home in Killarney. My bet is that he died dealing the deck with nothing in the world on his mind but goodwill towards all mankind. *Is cinnte go bhfuil solas na bhFlaitheas ar Chonn scéalach anois.*

There were locals from Dingle who called around at fairly regular intervals, once a month or thereabouts, usually collecting potatoes that would be sold later in the town. One was known as Johnny Ate-a-Bit. He carried a ten-stone bag on his broad back, collecting a helping of potatoes in each house until the sack was full to the brim. He would spend some time with each call and invariably 'ate a bit'. He had what people referred to as a false appetite, meaning that he could eat as much as he wanted at any time of asking. He would be asked, 'Would you ate a bit, Johnny?', and the reply was always positive, even though he might have eaten his fill five minutes earlier in a neighbour's house.

He was not as good for news as other travellers, and his stock reply to 'What's the news today, Johnny?' was that an odd ship was being lost at sea all the time.

Oddly enough, it was a traveller known as Maloney who brought the news of the death of George Bernard Shaw. Maloney carried airs of a certain scholarship, and was not impressed when asked was the person he was talking about anything to the 'Shaw of the sausages'.

Chapter Two

Primary school lasted until sixth class was completed, then we went 'upstairs' to the secondary section. Here we experienced lay teachers for the first time. The number of pupils per class was greater, as the Monastery was the only secondary school for boys between Dunquin and Tralee, a span of forty miles or more. That meant that we now had classmates from the Gaeltacht area west of Dingle, others from the eastern regions of Lispole and Anascaul, and even one or two from the far side of the Conor Pass.

Padraig, who had gathered a reputation of being a fine scholar, was a few classes ahead of Náis and me. Eileen was by this time a boarder in the nearby Coláiste Íde, and our younger siblings were in primary, with the exception of the 'baby', Kathleen, who was still at home.

Everything was going along nicely until tragedy struck with the death of my mother in 1944, at the young age of forty-eight. She had been ill for a while and had made a few visits to a hospital in Tralee, but her condition was not seen as serious even when she was admitted to the Dingle hospital in January of that year.

I remember calling to the hospital during lunch break or after school, and I have a very clear recollection of our last conversation. I was too young to understand the significance of what she said as I was leaving: 'Mind your lessons, be good, and I will do all I can from above.'

She passed away unexpectedly and quietly early on the morning of 4 February, and I believe to this day that she has kept her part of the promise.

Word had not come home by the time my father left with his horse and milk tanks on the way to the creamery, and we had left for school. The first indication of something being wrong hit me as soon as I entered the school yard. Dónal, born an early riser, had got there before Padraig, Náis and me, and was coming out of the school in the company of a Brother, who had a hand on his shoulder. They came to us, and the Brother conveyed the bad news.

It was a case then of an about turn and the road home; we walked up John Street and over Greenmount, but could not bother taking the shortcut to the Mail Road. As we reached Garfinny Cross we could see Mrs Keyes leave her front door and walk slowly down the field to meet us at the fence. She had sensed something on seeing us going in the wrong direction down that road.

We eventually arrived home and waited until my father returned from the creamery. He had received the bad news in Dingle and was no sooner in the door than our neighbour Peter Farrell came rushing in. Both burst into tears. No words were spoken for a while, and it was the first occasion that I had ever seen adult men cry.

The house was full with neighbours and friends that night after the removal to St Mary's Church in Dingle, and the funeral took place to Garfinny cemetery the following day. Because it was wartime there were few motor cars on the road, and people travelled in horse carts, traps, on horseback or on foot. Two black horses pulled the hearse on the two-mile journey to the family grave in Garfinny.

My father considered that it would be unfair to take Eileen out of boarding school at that stage to tend to household work. A solution was found when Náis volunteered to forego further education and take over in the house. This he did in style, with help from Padraig when he was at home and from Eileen when she was on holidays from Coláiste Íde.

In 1945, the year after my mother's death, I sat a state examination for entry to a preparatory college for teachers. By midsummer I received the call: I would be leaving home for the first time, to become a boarder at Coláiste Íosagáin in the Cork Gaeltacht of Baile Bhúirne. Meanwhile, an aunt in New York, a sister of my father's, promised to come home as soon as the war ended and travel became normal again. True to her word, Aunty May – who had left for the States nearly half a century earlier – landed home in 1947.

She was truly a fairy godmother the likes of which rarely trod this earth. She had a passion for helping others, and provided great support to many unemployed Dingle men in New York during the days of the Great Depression. Back in Dún Síon she was a tremendous help to my father and the rest of us. Her arrival meant that Náis was free to do what he always wanted – work on the family farm, which he rightly inherited in time from my father.

I was home on holidays from Coláiste Íosagáin when she arrived, and needless to say there was great excitement. My father went to Queenstown to meet the liner – people conversant with emigration never used the name Cobh – and when he got back to Dún Síon with the 'Yank' there were trunks to beat the band. All the neighbours called that night, and despite a long absence May was able to name certain people walking along the path to the door from the sound of the steps. 'That's the strong step of Peter Quinn,' she said once. 'You could never forget it.' His greeting was in Irish as usual – 'Dé do bheatha-sa abhaile' – and everybody drank each other's health.

Aunty May was in her mid sixties at the time; she had great spirit and lived well into her nineties, returning to the States to attend a wedding at the age of eighty-four. The same trip cost me the job of being her main adviser. She had relinquished her American citizenship earlier in order to be able to vote for de Valera, and consequently needed a passport and visa to re-enter New York. I made the arrangements for her to come to Dublin, and in due course she presented herself at the Passport Office.

On seeing May's Dingle address on the application form, the official informed her that only the Cork office could deal with her case. Coming out of the office, I suggested a solution: go back the next day and give the address of her brother Joe in Dublin, with whom she was staying, as she always did on her frequent visits to Dublin.

There was no problem until we were well on our way to Kerry, complete with passport and visa, a few days later. As we came close to Kerry she hinted that my stratagem had got her a passport under false pretences and that perhaps she should go to confession in Tralee. My suggestion of St John's was accepted. She must have made a mighty story out of the episode because she arrived out of the box a long time later, more worried than ever. The priest could not forgive her: this was a matter for the bishop! He had, however, told her to 'try the Dominicans first, as they are not bound by any bishop'. It was off to the Dominicans next, where the order priest assured her that the houses of both her brothers had the same status in the eyes of God and that there was nothing that needed forgiveness. But he did ask her to drop in and see his sister in Long Island, not far from where she had planned to stay with her brother Michael while in New York.

It would make you wonder how God was able to function at times – two diametrically opposed views from experts 600 yards apart.

My aunt did manage to contact the Dominican priest's sister in Long Island. Such contacts meant an awful lot to the thousands of people who emigrated during the first forty years of the past century. Most of them never saw home again, but it would be true to say that Ireland seldom left their minds.

I got a good demonstration of this while visiting my cousins in New York one time. My uncle Michael was on the phone to a next-door neighbour from home, and he asked me to talk to Timmy Lynch, whom I had heard of but never knew. In the course of our conversation I happened to say to him that he had never been home. His reply was most revealing: 'I have indeed. Every single night before going to bed I walk out the door at home – up Bóthar na Seán and into every single field before returning home and then in my mind going to bed in Dún Síon.'

He even named all the fields. I would say that he was fifty years in the United States at the time.

I had never planned to become a teacher, but in those days one did what exams were there to be done and took the consequences. For me, going to Coláiste Íosagáin was the start of a new and exciting phase in my life.

Departure time was early September. My father saw me off to Dingle in a horse cart, complete with a large valise full of clothing and other effects as prescribed by the school.

Three other first-time prep scholars were also waiting in Dingle for the bus to Tralee, the first leg of our journey: Jim Sullivan and Mick Murphy from the west of Dingle, and Seán Ó hAiniféin from Lios Deargáin at the foot of Strickeen mountain. Those already a year or more in the college had gone back a few days ahead of the new recruits.

For some reason I did not feel lonely. The fact that I had never been on a bus before might explain the type of glee I felt; I suppose I was never afraid of the unknown. At any rate the bus trip was fantastic, though we were disappointed that Bill Dillon, holder of five All-Ireland medals with Kerry, was not on duty as conductor that day. We sped eastwards through Lispole, where Bill Casey, another 'holder of five', lived, and on to Anascaul, where Tom Crean of Antarctic fame had a pub and the home district of the great Paddy Kennedy who, strangely enough, also had five All-Irelands to his credit. Before long we were climbing Gleann na nGealt, the Glen of the Madmen, and somebody mentioned that Tim O'Donnell, a member of Kerry's four-in-a-row team of 1929–32, came from the glen to the left. His brother, John Kerry O'Donnell, was one of New York's most famous Irishmen at the time.

We were soon back to sea level once more at Camp, with the broad Tralee Bay to the left, and it is worth recalling that Camp native Charlie O'Sullivan had harvested four All-Ireland medals with Kerry.

After a journey of a little more than an hour we were in the town of Tralee. To us from the west of the county, it was on first sight an almighty metropolis. By then the train for Cork had left, and the plan was that we would stay in Tralee for the night. This was yet another extraordinary event for me – my first night ever to sleep away from home and neither kith nor kin on hand. But I was not alone: there were four of us, plus an experienced traveller from Rinn Bhuí, Lispole. Patrick Kavanagh, or simply PK, was a qualified teacher by profession, but a humorous philosopher by nature. My first night out of home was spent in this company in the Mall Restaurant in Tralee.

More joy was in store for me the next day with my first-ever train journey, steaming towards Cork. We felt we could almost dip our toes in the brown waters of the Flesk River, as we sat entranced by the splendour of the mountains, clad in hues of purple, brown and colours indescribable.

Once we left Beauty's home we were on the lookout for Mallow: 'Don't forget to change at Mallow,' my father had advised. I had often heard the words before – a constant counsel to all Dún Síon travellers from the time a local on his way to Queenstown and America failed to change at Mallow and found himself in the foreign land of Dublin instead – an alien land to a Dún Síon man, unlike New York, Boston, Springfield and a host of other places that could be reached by changing at Mallow.

We didn't forget to change at the famous junction, and from there it was downhill all the way to Cork. If Tralee was big to my eyes a day earlier, it bore no comparison with the Cork railway station. People seemed to be going and coming in all directions. The accent was different, too, and above all the din we could hear a one-syllable refrain: 'Co, Co, Co.' We were to learn later that it referred to the *Evening Echo*, Cork's own book of current psalms.

I found the excitement wondrous and felt no fear of being lost, even though I knew that we had not yet reached our destination and wasn't quite sure about the next stage: a thirty-mile journey by bus to Baile Bhúirne. I had not a clue where the departure point was located, but we had some time to spare. We ventured forth on to the streets of Cork, and got a cup of tea and something in the nature of a bun in a café – another first for us.

Anxious about the bus, we returned to the station in plenty of time; however, there was no need for worry as I soon heard, in the friendly Gaelic language, 'Tá fáilte romhaibh, tá an bus go dtí An Coláiste thíos ag an bhfalla, lean mise.' It was An Bráthair Peadar from the college, and like the Pied Piper he led us to the bus.

By then scholars other than Kerry boys were converging on the departure point, and one could say that most of the group of 1945 were together for the first time.

It was dark by the time we reached Ceann Scríbe. I will never forget my first sighting of Coláiste Íosagáin, just beyond Baile Mhic Íre. It had many windows, and all were lit up by electric light, a phenomenon that was totally novel to most of us. It cast a welcoming glow as we walked the hundred-yard passage to the front door.

An Coláiste was to be my home for the next three academic years: four was the norm, but I had already secured the Intermediate Certificate and was given a year's remission along with three others. I never looked upon it as a remission, though, as my time spent there was both pleasant and rewarding.

The college was run by the De La Salle Brothers. Irish was established as the language for sport and study 100 per cent of the time. Unlike most schools in the country at the time there was no corporal punishment. The enrolment was small by normal standards: a total of some eighty pupils divided into four classes.

Students came from all over the country: all six Munster counties, Donegal, Mayo, Galway, Kilkenny, Westmeath, Dublin; Seán Murphy came all the way from Glaslough in Co. Monaghan. This diversity of background was an immense benefit and created a unique atmosphere. All dialects of Irish were in use every day, and we compared, imitated and learned from each other. It was no trouble to say 'Conus taoi?' to a fellow Munster man, but it would become 'Cé chaoi a bhfuil tú?' if I ran into Padraig Ó Méalóid of Conamara, or 'Cad é mar a tá tú?' if it happened to be Paddy Mac Giolla Comhail from Donegal. It was in Coláiste Íosagáin, rather than in my native Kerry, that I developed a deep *grá* for the language and all aspects of Gaelic culture. There I became Micheál Ó Muircheartaigh, having grown up a Moriarty.

A carefree attitude prevailed at the school. There was no pressure to score highly in the Leaving exam because we were all guaranteed places in teacher-training college by doing 'reasonably well'. I believe it was a better education as a result: it cultivated independent minds that proved an asset in later life. Even the location of the college was providential, situated as it was in the Gaeltacht right between Baile Mhic Íre and Cúil Aodha. The locals were friendly people with open doors for the likes of us, and we felt part of the community.

A day off classes was a feature easily granted if the request for a 'Lá Saor' was loud enough and the reason for such of some merit. A Lá Saor meant rambling in Cúil Aodha, calling to shops such as Bess's or Joney's, climbing Mullach an Ois or renting a bike and crossing the hill south of the Sullane River to Inse Gíle and other places. In the college itself, Halla na Siamsaí was always available for Irish dancing and impromptu concerts.

An Bráthair Peadar was the very soul of the Irish ethos that prevailed, and he kept an open door for artists from the Gaeltacht to try out their latest compositions on us. It was in the Halla that we first heard the rousing song of 'An Poc ar Buile' composed by Seán Ó Mulláin, with its haunting chorus of 'Aililiú, Puililiú – Aililiú tá An Poc ar Buile AAA-LE-LIÚÚ tá An Poc ar Buile.' The new song was an immediate hit with us, receiving the imprimatur of millions of *aililiús* from all corners over the following days.

There were more sedate moments when the likes of An Suibhneach Meann, the Cúil Aodha Poet Laureate, would recite his latest; maybe 'An t-Emergency Léine', which highlighted the short-comings of wartime shirts due to the scarcity of cotton. The imaginative Suibhneach had no time for a shirt that failed to reach his navel, and thus in the tradition of ancient poetry the garment received condemnation in humorous verse.

The college was also a haven for wandering scholars, men who travelled in great hardship and for little reward searching for and logging old songs, tales, *piseogs* and customs of another Ireland. It was a privilege that such scholars came to see us and talk about their mission and experiences. I remember the tall and elegant Fionan Mac Colum dressed in tweeds and sporting a weather-beaten face, and a friendly wanderer from Donegal who strayed in and began his talk in the most musical of Tír Chonaill accents by setting the scene for his own home patch, 'leithinse fada caol ag gobadh amach sa bhfarraige idir Gaoth Dobhair agus Gaoth na Bráth'. It was musical and poetic to the ear without being meant as such, and my translation – a long, slender peninsula jutting out into the Atlantic – does not flow like the Gaelic did. The following day was special: we all tried to speak like that stranger from the north-west, and it was truly a Donegal day.

Invariably, talks of that kind, and more formal occasions, too, ended with a turn or two from the body of the hall. My favourite was to hear Joe Fitz from the foot of Mount Brandon recite the wonderful poem 'Gile na Gile' by the noted seventeenth-century poet Aogán Ó Rathaille from rugged Sliabh Luachra. Without fail it was delivered with perfect diction and inflection, coupled with a sense of feeling for the theme that could never be replicated. Ireland was the loser when Joe emigrated to the United States a few years later to pursue his interest in science. I wonder has he an audience for 'Gile na Gile' or other renderings in Hartford, Connecticut, where he now resides?

Dia go deo leat a Joe Fitz, cruthaíodh do ghuth le haghaidh filíochta.

The whole scene begot a wonderful education, even if it took years before we fully appreciated it. In a way, An Coláiste encompassed features of the 'Big Houses' of Celtic Ireland before the disastrous Battle of Kinsale ended an ancient manner of life on this island. There had always been a regard in those places for men and women of art, and none was ever refused refuge from weather or woe. They were given shelter, sustenance and reward, and in return performed for the chief and friends. Those Taoisigh of old might have had their faults, but let us honour their virtues – they played a noble part in keeping Irish culture alive. I have enough faith in the modern generation of Irish youth to predict confidently that they, too, will pass it on in better shape than ever to the next generation.

A typical day in the college began with morning call at about seven o'clock. The ringing of the chapel bell soon afterwards was a signal that the priest was on his way from his residence in the village. We attended mass every morning. Each of us had a Latin missal and we took turns in serving. Sunday was a special day, as we had the addition of benediction at seven in the evening. We were not a religious lot, but we looked forward to benediction, as it contained much singing that we grew to love. The roof would be almost raised in the fervour of *Tantum Ergo Sacramentum, Veneremur Cernui* and so on, and it was a suitable prelude to unscheduled recreation in the Halla before bedtime.

We had neither newspapers nor a radio in those days, television was unheard of, and the emotion of cynicism had yet to penetrate the fastnesses of the Muscraí Gaeltacht.

Only one major disciplinary incident took place during my three-year stay in the Coláiste. It occurred towards the end of my very first term. The best explanation of what happened would come from an expert on the ways of nature.

The necessary work of preparing and serving meals for growing boys was in the capable hands of female staff with good fluency in Irish and a friendly disposition. They, too, lived in the college, and the trouble was that a few students found a way of making nocturnal visits. For all we know, they might have been for recitations of some poetry.

It came to the notice of the school authorities, and before breakfast was over one morning the news spread that a pupil had been expelled. It was 8 December 1945, and it should have been a Lá Saor. There were no classes, but the usual freedom to roam was cancelled, and we gave most of the day in the church singing Latin hymns to the Blessed Virgin.

'O Maria, O Maria, sine labe concepta' are a few of the words that linger in my memory.

Of course an inquiry followed, and we had a few visits from Department of Education personnel. I suppose all those supporting the use of the Irish language will be happy in the knowledge that the inquiry was conducted in its entirety through Irish.

October was the month for the obligatory annual retreat. It involved three days of silence and meditation. While there was never a clamour to extend it to four days, neither did we resent the ritual.

The retreat was generally conducted by two 'strange' missioners, and we were all given the agenda beforehand, running something like this:

7 a.m.: *Éirí agus paidreacha* (rise and prayer)
7.30 a.m.: *Aifreann sa tseipéal* (mass in the chapel)
8.15 a.m.: *Bricfeasta*
9 a.m.: *Léacht sa tséipéal* (lecture in the chapel)
10. a.m.: *Machnamh faoin aer* (outdoor meditation)

. . . and so on until rosary time in the chapel late in the evening.

It made for a most unusual three days, with the dining room devoid of all sounds except that of knives and forks and the field full of concerned-looking individuals strolling in solitude and repenting for sins never committed. It was 'divarsion' of a kind and good material for a parody or two in the Halla once the Triduum had passed into history.

The preachers were convincing, but now and then they failed to get the point fully across. That was certainly the case with Kerry people during the retreat of October 1947. It was shortly after the All-Ireland football final in which Cavan defeated Kerry in the Polo Grounds in New York. Our friend the missioner went a little too far in his explanation of the reasons for the Breffni onslaught. He proclaimed that he had seen an action photograph of Mick Higgins, one of Cavan's heroes, and that it was a revelation.

'There he was, tearing through the defence with his jersey in tatters torn by a Kerryman, but there, too, for all to see across his chest was a sacred scapular,' he bellowed.

As there was an insinuation regarding Kerry's style of play, the students from the Kingdom could not give the power of the scapular its due recognition that afternoon. When the retreat was over and lips loosed in talk once more, innocent Kerry students surmised that 'yer man' was more likely to have a Cavan rather than a Kingdom mother.

By the way, I often meet the same Mick Higgins, mostly at

greyhound racing, and no more honourable New York–born man ever strode through a sporting arena. He's a top-class judge of a greyhound to boot, and shrewd in spotting likely winners.

As far as the students were concerned, education, culture, liturgy and all other pursuits played second fiddle to football. For a college with a small enrolment of students, Coláiste Íosagáin produced a high ratio of star players and subsequent All-Ireland medal winners. I was never one of those stars, due perhaps to a late beginning. I cannot recall even one occasion during my primary-school days when we were brought to the sports field for games. The war could not be blamed, even though de Valera extended the summer holidays by two weeks to allow the likes of us to engage in more farm work.

We had local football among ourselves in Dún Síon and once acquired a football by saving enough coupons from cocoa boxes. Our pitch was the middle of the golf links, and sometimes people from Lispole would cross over at low tide to participate in the kicking. There was never a match, but all and sundry trying for hours on end to get a few kicks at the ball.

At any rate, on arrival in Cork I was a raw recruit as far as matches were concerned, whereas many of the others were well versed in the various arts of *caid*, as we from West Kerry called football. We were organized into teams for various internal competitions; believe it or not, the winners' prize for one of the 'majors' was a few large pots of jam. I was a halfback on the winning team captained by my friend Seán Ó hAiniféin, and I was later chosen in the same position for the college junior team.

The college had a powerful senior team in the 1945–46 season. Big Diarmuid Ó hAiniféin from Fenit was the real star, a lord of midfield play. I remember a great display by him when playing against St Brendan's Seminary, Killarney, in Corn na Mumhan that year. The Sem was always rated a strong team, but our 'braves' were nearly as good that day, losing narrowly. I can still see Ó hAiniféin's rasper of a right-footed penalty crash off the crossbar and rebound at speed to where he was standing. He met it on the volley with the left and drove it inches over the bar and miles beyond the limits of the Fitzgerald Stadium.

It didn't surprise anyone that he later made the Kerry team at midfield, and won an All-Ireland medal in 1953. He would surely have added to it except for emigrating soon afterwards at the age of twenty-six.

It was by no means a one-man band. An Loinseach Mór (Muiris Lynch) from Burnham, Dingle, was goalkeeper and good enough to be selected for Munster later. He, too, eventually hoisted sail for 'Americay', where he pursued his great interest in mathematics.

Then there was Tomás Mac Aodh from Dún Garbhán, Waterford, skilful and strong enough to play anywhere, but best of all in the central roles at the edge of either square; Séamus Ó Fiannachta from Dingle, who won a minor All-Ireland medal with Kerry in 1946; Breandán Ó Sé, a Kerry senior All-Ireland winner in 1953; and the great-hearted Séamus Rhatigan from Laois, better known as 'Delaney' in tribute to the great man Bill from his own county, then among the best footballers in Ireland.

And who could ever forget the smiling, stylish John Long from Ventry, brother of Tom who won All-Irelands with Kerry and cousin of Paidí Ó Sé? John once told me that his definition of happiness was fielding a high ball, then getting both a feel and a quick look at it before dispatching it with gusto downfield. His smile was broadest as he rose to meet the ball, and 'Caith léim, a Mháirtín' was a customary roar from him when encouraging a colleague with a springy step to catapult himself into the air with a capture in mind.

No young lad ever loved football more.

There were a fair few fine players among those that entered with me. The Murphy brothers from Camp, Co. Kerry, were possibly the best of all. Padraig and Seán lined out with the Kerry junior team that won the All-Ireland of 1949. Seán went on to win a minor All-Ireland a year later, and secured the 'golden treble' of minor, junior and senior before he was twenty-one years of age when he lined out at midfield with Dermot Hanifin on the winning senior team of 1953. He won further senior medals in 1955 and

1959, and was honoured on the All-Ireland teams of the century and millennium.

Two younger Murphy brothers came to the Coláiste later, and they, too, won All-Ireland medals with Kerry – Tomás at minor level in 1950 and the late Séamus as a senior in 1959, 1962, 1969 and 1970. The latter holds a unique record in Munster finals: he was on the winning team on eleven occasions and never on a losing one.

Others among the 1945 entrants who excelled at football were Mick Murphy from Ventry, who was Kerry's full forward in the great win over Dublin in the All-Ireland final of 1955; the pole-vaulter Larry O'Donnell from Durrus in Cork; Paddy Coyle from Gweedore, a sweet footballer who played for his county and father of Colm of Meath fame; Micí Dan Ó Sé from Macroom; and one of the soundest of centre backs, Seán Ó hAiniféin from Lios Deargáin, Lispole.

There was no fancy team coach for transport to matches; players and supporters usually travelled in John Tim's lorry, which never saw either seat or bench. But it had more character than any Rolls-Royce and was really a moving theatre as it took the bends. Our 'war song' was naturally *as Gaeilge*, and if the engine of John Tim's lorry had recording equipment an authentic version would now be lying in some dump.

Fágaíg an bealach ag ridirí an uaithne
Teacht chugaibh ar sodar go cíocrach chun bua
Seo chughaibh na gaiscígh ó Ghleann Baile Bhúirne
Togha agus rogha de choláistí na Mumhan.
Gach aon fhear os na cúil 'díos na tosaigh
Fónta foirfe chun cloíte a namhaid
Colainn tréana, sprid gan traochadh
Leatar a gcáil thar na sléite anonn.
Níl in Éirinn án ná sa domhan iomlán
Dream atá i ndán sinn do chloí
Mar gur Éireannaigh agus Gaeil sinn
In ár n-anam is n-ár gcroí.

It came as no surprise to me, as I watched progress from Dublin in 1949, to see 'Baile Bhúirne' – as we often called our school, after the Gaeltacht in which it was located – make history by capturing the Munster Colleges championship and Corn na Mumhan for the first time, with Padraig Ó Murchadha as an inspiring captain.

I was gone, but one does not forget.

It was the first of seven before the doors of a beloved place were closed under different educational structures years later. I am ever hopeful that it will rise again as a beacon for further enlightenment in the field of learning – perhaps as an outpost for University College, Cork.

Chapter Three

My three years at Coláiste Íosagáin passed quickly and in early September 1948, armed with my Leaving Certificate, I was bound for Dublin to pursue a two-year teacher-training course at St Patrick's College, Drumcondra. This was another all-male boarding college, run by the Vincentian Fathers and catering for about a hundred students – about half chosen by open competition based on Leaving results, and the remainder from the prep colleges of Coláiste Éinde in Galway and Coláiste Íosagáin.

There was less emphasis on Irish as the vernacular, except for those of us on whom it had grown, and perhaps that was the reason why I felt the place had not the 'presence' of that beautiful edifice down in Cork. The daily routine was much the same. Morning call came at roughly the same time; Fr O'Neill, the Dean, entered the dormitory swiftly chanting *Benedicamus Domino* and ringing a bell as he moved along. We were all in turn expected to respond with *Deo gratias* as he passed by, and silence from any cubicle would bring him to a halt; the bell would ring louder with each extra greeting until the *Deo gratias* finally was audible. Mass followed soon afterwards and a typical college routine for the remainder of the day – lectures, meals, study, teaching practice and leisure activities.

There was freedom to leave the college on Saturdays and Sundays; the doors closed at 10 p.m. Special permission known as 'late leave' was necessary if one had reason to be out until midnight, and it was easy enough to obtain. The difficulty was that with such a variety of places of entertainment in Dublin, one could easily be delayed and find the place locked up on returning.

There could be trouble if one was not in bed and ready for the *Deo gratias* by 7 a.m. It was always managed, though; the slim students could squeeze between the iron bars of the billiard-room window, while the bigger folk had to scale a wall and jump.

I remember one dark night when a friend and I climbed to the top of the wall before contemplating the descent. *Mo chara* was first to jump, but the landing was not a soft one, and foreign sounds came from below. Naturally I hesitated, and foolishly asked my friend about the possibility of a different type of entry. He did offer to go and wake the Dean, who 'might supply a ladder'.

I had no option now but a quick *Benedicamus Domino* and a jump.

One of the great advantages of Pat's was its proximity to Croke Park, hardly a mile away. I had not long to wait for my first visit. There was neither talk nor a need of a ticket as a few of us set off to see the All-Ireland football final between Cavan and Mayo.

It was a much different Croke Park then, with standing the order of the day for more than 80 per cent of spectators. On the east side of the pitch, the tall Cusack Stand, supported by huge pillars, seated about 6,000 spectators, with standing room underneath. There were three stands on the opposite side. The Long Stand, a plain structure with a low corrugated-iron roof that gave protection from the elements, ranged from the corner flag at the Canal End to roughly midfield. It was more a barn with an opening on one side than a stand, and it was common for spectators to climb on to the roof for comfort on big days. On the other side of the broad-casting box, the Hogan Stand ran towards the Railway End; it was the fashionable area. Beyond the Hogan was the Corner Stand.

We found ourselves standing under the Cusack close enough to Hill 16, the famous terrace at the Railway End – an ideal position as events unfolded.

It was great to be in the Mecca of our dreams – the place made famous by the voice of the peerless Micheál O'Hehir. There before our eyes stood his commentary box, on stilts between the Hogan and Long stands. It was painted green and had a large window, giving us sight of him in action. Little did I know in Croke Park that day that I would be joining him in the same box before another six months had passed.

Waterford had beaten Dublin in the All-Ireland hurling final before we got to Pat's, but we had all heard Micheál talking about a Waterford midfielder by the name of Johnny O'Connor; soon we learned that he was now a senior student at Pat's. He was a powerful man who had such a spring in his step that he seemed to walk on his toes. He would become involved in greyhound racing in later years, and win the English Derby with Patricia's Hope in 1972 and again in 1973.

Meanwhile I was watching my first All-Ireland final, and that was a thrill never to be forgotten. Tyrone beat Dublin in the minor match, and Barney Eastwood was a member of the winning side. I would be telling a lie if I said I noticed him.

The minor match left one distinct memory – the class of Tyrone's centre back Eddie Devlin. He seemed the essence of composure and always in the right position as if by luck, but he was to prove in later years that this was a result of pure football intuition, rather than chance.

I met Eddie Devlin quite recently, and we recalled the details of how he was wrongly prevented from playing for Ulster in a Railway Cup semi-final one day. He was a student at University College Dublin in the 1950s, and the College team was due to play a match against Geraldine's in Belfield (before the College moved there) on the afternoon of a rugby international. Eddie had decided not to play on account of his selection on the Ulster team for the following day.

He was loyal, though, and went along and acted as linesman; when the chore was completed he hopped on his bicycle to go to Sandymount, where he was staying at the time.

The crowds were filing out of Lansdowne Road as he was going past, and who did he see but members of the Munster Railway Cup team, with Jim Brosnan of Kerry among them. They all walked together to the end of the road and parted with the words that they would see each other in Croke Park the following day. If they did it was not on the pitch: on Sunday Eddie was not handed his Ulster midfield jersey, but informed that he had been seen coming out of Lansdowne Road the previous day. The same applied to the Munster boys: the infamous ban against participation in or attendance at foreign games was still in force, and some vigilante had spotted innocent Eddie.

But he was my star of the minor final of 1948 and a really big name in football for many years afterwards.

Cavan and Mayo produced a most entertaining spectacle in that 1948 senior All-Ireland final. Accounts of the game written in retrospect ranked it as a poor exhibition of football, but nobody thought so as the battle raged.

It was a privilege to be watching the very men who wrote the most romantic chapter in the annals of the GAA when they beat mighty Kerry in the All-Ireland final a year earlier in the faraway Polo Grounds of New York. And I could now see them in the flesh, giants of the game all – the 'gallant John Joe' (O'Reilly) as captain, that shrewd mover Mick Higgins, the jinking Tony Tighe, the deep-chested prancing Simon Deignan, the balding, darting Joe Stafford, the colossal midfielder Gunner Brady, and the Babe Ruth of the Polo Grounds in the person of the sweet-kicking Peter Donohue.

Mayo had not won a Connacht title since 1937, but All-Ireland final day of 1948 revealed that a new era had begun for the cultured men of the West. A very powerful wind blew directly from the Canal goal towards its Railway counterpart, and purely by chance that made our spot under the Cusack close to the Hill the perfect viewing position. I would say that 90 per cent of the play took place in that half of the field.

The wind was in the Cavan sails in the first half, but all they had to show for it as the interval approached was two points. Then, in the closing minutes of the half the strength, skill and drive of Tony Tighe took over. I have seen him regularly in Clones over the years, and on every occasion the memory clicks: I see a clear picture of him making runs along the right wing and crashing home two crucial goals before halftime on that memorable day. The elegant Victor Sherlock got a third goal. Meanwhile, the men of the West, playing into the wind, failed to score in the first half.

That was some gale, and it blew for Mayo once the game restarted. Peter Solan, who had played in the minor final a year earlier, banged in a goal following a good point by the fair-haired Sean Mulderrig, and the margin was down to seven points.

I believe that I have never witnessed a more powerful gale at a match since then, and Cavan deserved credit for battling their way down to the Canal goal on a few fruitful missions. Donohue scored a point, Higgins – the team's saviour in many a tight battle – landed a goal, and Sherlock bore through for yet another point. Grace O'Malley, Queen of the Pirates in another age, could not have done a deadlier job on a foe; however, this time the West that once belonged to her was the victim.

Now twelve points in arrears, Mayo's position looked absolutely hopeless, even in the howling dry wind. But I am convinced that the fighting spirit displayed for the remainder of my first All-Ireland won them the titles of 1950 and 1951.

Padraic Carney and Éamonn Mongey took over at midfield, and things began to happen. Carney, a young medical student from Swinford, strode the pitch with a haughty gait. He had a commanding presence that radiates only from the greats of sport. The ball rarely if ever went beyond midfield as Mayo peppered the Cavan goal area.

Tom Acton scored two goals from close range to cut Cavan's lead by half before the angular, scheming Tom Langan was hauled down in the square just as he was about to shoot for a goal. When Carney blasted the penalty kick to the net, the West was truly awake; excitement was boundless when Mayo drew level with points in succession from Carney, Mulderrig and Mongey. If Tyrone minor Barney Eastwood was still present, he must have been hatching the first notions of bookmaking at that juncture, considering the many swings of fortune that had taken place so far in an extraordinary game.

But the best was still in store. Against the wind Cavan made a rare foray into the southern region of the pitch and won a free. It was clockwork then for Peter Donohue to put the Breffni men a point ahead once more.

The ending was both dramatic and controversial; this is how I recall it, and indeed often see it unfolding as follows with the inner eye:

SLIDE 1

A foul on a Mayo player.

SLIDE 2

Padraic Carney standing with his hands on hips and preparing to start his run-up to take a fourteen-yard free.

SLIDE 3

The position is a little to the Cusack side of centre; the goal line is well covered with Cavan players, and isn't that forward Mick Higgins in there among them?

SLIDE 4

Carney is moving, and now kicking, and the Cavan men are still on the line.

SLIDE 5

All except one are still on the line – the exception is Higgins, and he is attempting to block the ball.

SLIDE 6

He is now in possession; the game is over and Cavan have won their second consecutive All-Ireland.

I think I can explain Higgins's dramatic rescue. He had learned from the greyhounds that perfect timing from the trap wins many a Derby: too early and the dog bounces his head off the bars of the trap, too late and the race is over. Higgins got it dead on – all a matter of masterly timing.

Naturally Mayo inner eyes see different pictures, with Garda Higgins perhaps too close to the ball at the critical moment.

And so ended the first All-Ireland football final that I witnessed – the first of fifty-five to date.

Seán Purcell of Galway – the greatest footballer that I have ever seen – was present at that final. I know it because he was a fellow student in Pat's at the time. He was a year ahead of us Hedgers, as first-year students were known, and was thus one of the Gents, the curious title appended to final-year students.

As the fortunes of the game billowed and flowed, I am sure that Purcell reminded himself that he could easily have been out there on the field rather than in a spectator's role. His Galway had held Mayo to a draw in the Connacht final, and were still level with them at the end of the replay before Mayo won by three points in extra time.

If only that free went in . . .

If only the ref saw such and such . . .

Wherever Purcell went an enormous reputation accompanied him. He was one who never sought the limelight, but the light always followed him. He attended St Jarlath's College of Tuam and was sensational in competition at that level. His initial coaching in the game came from a nun.

Jarlath's and St Patrick's of Armagh clashed in the first All-Ireland college final in 1946, and again in 1947. The Armagh side won the first, and Tuam took the Croke Cup at the second attempt, but the most important outcome was the impact the games made on adult minds. Henceforth the names of Iggy Jones of Dungannon and Seán Purcell of Bishop Street, Tuam, looked destined for real fame.

Purcell was a fixture on the Galway senior team by the time he came to Pat's in September 1947, and was Connacht's centre forward into the 1960s. Connacht won three of its eight Railway Cups during the Purcell era, and he was at centre forward on each occasion.

I am often asked why I rate him the best of those I have seen. It is not an easy one to answer, considering the number of players of extraordinary talent that have graced Gaelic football. Let me simply list the assets the Tuam man displayed over a long career.

He was a total master in all the skills of the game. He had style and poise in abundance. He fielded the ball well and always found room in possession. He kicked well with both feet and was proficient in the variety of kicks from hand or ground. He was a regular scorer and the perfect example of when and when not to engage in solo running. For him it was a tactic to benefit the team on certain occasions, but never to be overemployed. It was used a lot in some of the wonderful play-making between himself and Frankie Stockwell, the pair affectionately known as the 'terrible twins' of football.

I recall a fine late winning goal registered by Stockwell in Croke Park that was preceded by what looked an aimless solo run towards the corner by Purcell. What he was doing in reality was drawing the defence while Stockwell was moving into space to take a good cross in the vicinity of the goal. It was delivered with precision, and Frankie did the rest.

But what helped me in making up my mind about Seán for my number-one slot was his versatility as a team player. He was a natural centre forward, but was equally effective in any forward position and at midfield. In fact he was placed at midfield in the 1948 Connacht final in direct opposition to the feared Mayo pairing of Carney and Mongey.

And then there was his stint as a fullback in 1954. Tom Langan of Mayo was rated the best full forward in the game at the time, and was selected in that position on the Team of the Century. Galway gambled and selected Purcell for the fullback berth when lining out against Mayo in the Connacht semi-final of that year. They still talk in the West about the masterly display he put on that day, which was instrumental in Galway's surprise win.

He occupied the same position in the Connacht final, which Galway won as well. An All-Ireland semi-final against reigning champions Kerry was the next assignment for Purcell, still wearing the number-three jersey. Again he was outstanding in the role, but the Galway forwards were not making much headway, and the game looked lost for the Corrib men as the second half advanced.

It was time to gamble once more – Purcell was moved to midfield and a transformation took place that almost brought them victory.

Seán starred at centre forward on the sweet-moving Galway team that won the All-Ireland title of 1956. Frankie Stockwell set a scoring record for finals that day by scoring two goals and five points, all from play, and had the misfortune of seeing another goal that looked the best of all disallowed. That record stood until Jimmy Keaveney of Dublin and Mikey Sheehy of Kerry bettered it by a point; however, they both had scores from frees in their record totals.

I am not alone in thinking that Seán Purcell was the greatest. An apocryphal story told now and then by my friend Brian Geraghty, also of Galway fame, gives support to my view.

According to the loquacious Geraghty, Purcell was standing at a stop one night on the outskirts of Galway city, waiting for a bus that would bring him home to Tuam. Apparently it was just past the time for last buses to all termini, and only vehicles heading inward towards the night depots were to be seen. However, one driver going west spotted 'the Master' and had no hesitation in turning round and inviting Seán to sit in for a jaunt twenty miles eastwards to Tuam. They were gone some distance when a CIE inspector doing a roll call spotted the *tuplais* and flagged the driver to stop. He admitted his breach of rules, but immediately invited the inspector to have a look at the 'cargo'. The inspector did so and without hesitation promptly commanded the driver to return to the depot and get a 'double-decker'. The Master must have been the best ever in the eyes of that inspector; if the story is not true, it is about time it was converted to the truth.

In case anybody brings up the matter that we were fellow students and that such could introduce bias, I may as well give the full picture. It is true; what's more, we were paired together for teaching practice during the third term of the 1948–49 academic year, in the Central Model Schools in Marlboro Street at the very heart of Dublin city.

Chapter Four

Besides being on the same teaching team as Seán Purcell, the other major event of my stay in the teacher-training college was my introduction to broadcasting. Like many things in life it came about by sheer chance.

My prior experience was minimal. I remember an impromptu show of unorganized bedlam that developed one night in Halla na Siamsaí at Coláiste Íosagáin. I spotted a roving reporter carrying an imitation microphone with BBC written on it – possibly a prop from a school play. I felt the reporter was not doing the entertainment full justice, and I wrested the microphone from him and proceeded to give my own version.

And that was it until word came to St Pat's in early March 1949 that Radio Éireann was to conduct trials in Croke Park on the following Sunday, with a view to selecting a commentator to broadcast the occasional match in Irish. Aspirants were invited to present themselves at a certain stile at the Corner Stand side of the ground.

It was too attractive an offer to be missed – free entry to Croke Park and admission to Micheál O'Hehir's box. I treated it as an adventure and was a willing triallist along with many more. We assembled in a room underneath the Hogan Stand quite close to the famous box. Three adjudicators were present, and I ascertained later that An Bráthair Ó Flathaile and Andrias Ó Muineacháin, two famous Irish scholars, were among them. I have failed to identify the third, but he could easily have been Dominic O'Riordan of Radio Éireann.

They explained that they would have an audio link to the box during the trials, and I noticed that they were shut away completely from any view of the field.

Each of the triallists would get a few minutes describing the match *as Gaeilge*. My turn came in due course, and I climbed the steps into the box. I should have been worried because I was expected to talk about a hurling match, and it was the first I had ever seen – there was no hurling in Coláiste Íosagáin nor in Dingle, and I wasn't that long in Dublin. But I was not worried in the slightest, as I was still looking on it as an experience that was costing nothing.

That luck that I've spoken of surfaced once more, and I recognized one player, the UCD goalkeeper, Tadhg Hurley, who had attended school in Dingle, where his father was a bank manager. The family had spent some time in hurling areas and that accounted for the UCD man's proficiency in the game. He was a medical student at the time and, while he won Fitzgibbon Cup medals with UCD in and out of goal, I doubt if he ever played as brilliantly in his life as he did during my trial.

It was a help that the adjudicators could not see the pitch. I filled them in with details about his brother Bob, who was in Dónal's class in Dingle, and the sister that used to come to Dún Síon Strand. Tadhg himself saved expertly, took the frees and line balls, and generally put on a display that made all other players irrelevant – a sort of a throwback to the day when Cúchulainn had the game of his life on the journey from Cooley to Eamhain Mhacha.

The end result was that I was offered the job of broadcasting the Railway Cup football final on St Patrick's Day. In the innocence and ignorance of youth I had no qualms about accepting the unexpected offer.

I received neither guidance nor training, but somebody arranged that I would sit in the box with Micheál O'Hehir during a National League game on the following Sunday. It was the first of many meetings with him over the years, and my estimation of him did not change from day one. He was helpful, down to earth and passionately interested in the GAA, which he always placed ahead of his own interest or welfare. As there is but one Arkle in the lore of steeplechasing and one Spanish Battleship in the world of greyhound racing, I am firmly of the view that there is but one Micheál O'Hehir in the world of sports broadcasting. He did more to promote Gaelic games than anybody else and jumped his fences without the encumbrance of an ego on his back.

St Patrick's Day came quickly. It fell on a Thursday that year, and I was on duty for the second of the afternoon's matches in Croke Park – Munster against Leinster in the Railway Cup football final.

I had written home about the upcoming event and also got word to my uncle Joe, who was then a schools inspector in Portlaoise. I did a bit of homework on the teams and was fortunate to be doing the football match, as I was familiar with most of the players, especially the Munster ones.

As I hadn't been given an admission pass from any source I presented myself at a stile adjacent to the Corner Stand and informed the man in charge that I was broadcasting the second game. He looked bemused, but admitted me nevertheless. I felt lost and found cover in a room at the back of the Hogan Stand. The hurling game was on, but I did not know where I might go to see Christy Ring et al. in action, so I just remained anchored where I was.

There was a telephone in the room, and at some stage close to the end of the hurling game a man came in and dialled a number. The caller asked in a worried tone: 'Who is doing this football game? Nobody has shown up yet.' It was time then to identify myself, and as soon as the hurling game ended I was ushered into the box as O'Hehir was leaving.

He wished me luck, assured me that I would not have a problem and headed for the opening of the flat racing season at the Baldoyle track near Sutton. He did so for a long number of years as part of his work with Independent Newspapers, and consequently always broadcast the first of the St Patrick's Day finals, but never the second.

In due time I got the nod to start talking. There certainly was plenty to talk about. The Munster captain was Batt Garvey from Ventry in Dingle, and I knew that the mascot marching around with him was young Seán Poole from Larkfield Gardens in Kimmage, where Batt and another member of the Munster team, Jackie Lyne from Killarney, were staying in digs. The landlady was

Maggie Poole, a Collins from Ardlert in Kerry by birth and married to a good-natured witty Dubliner, Paddy. I was aware of that because my sister Eileen, then a teacher in the nearby Loreto Convent, and Máirín Dunleavy, a friend from the Blasket Islands, were living across the road with a friendly Church of Ireland lady called Mrs Lowry. Of course they knew all about the football house, where the door was never locked and there was no need to knock.

Other Kerrymen had to travel for the game, and among them was Paddy Bawn Brosnan from Dingle, who was ranked as number-one favourite footballer by followers from Dunquin in his native Kerry to the Bloody Foreland of Donegal. He was a fisherman by profession, who came ashore to play football anywhere along the western seaboard where the drifting shoals of mackerel or herring might attract him.

Tom 'Gega' O'Connor was another Dingle man on that Munster team – one of Kerry's greatest from 1937 onwards and winner of five All-Ireland medals. It turned out to be his last appearance on a football field outside of Kerry, as he emigrated to New York shortly afterwards. The young Tom Ashe from Dingle was also there.

As usual there were quite a few Cork men on the Munster team: Moll Driscoll in goal, Con McGrath at midfield and big Nellie Duggan on the forty. The burly Mick Cahill from Mullinahone in Tipperary was also in the blue of the South, as was a Clare man with a reputation in football, Noel Crowley. There were notable names on the Leinster team as well: Seán Boyle of Louth, the Boyler White of Kildare, Paddy O'Brien of Meath at midfield and a young man on the way up – 21-year-old Kevin Heffernan from Dublin.

Of course I was nervous about the whole operation, but my being only eighteen years of age must have been some help: I felt no sense of responsibility or anything of the nature. I remember feeling part of all the drama from throw-in onwards, and it was a joy to be watching the best players in the land before a crowd of 40,000-plus. I thought it was a fine game, and the teams finished on level terms at 2–7 a side. I enjoyed myself immensely, and to crown it all I received a cheque for six pounds through the post a few days later – an enormous amount of money to a student at the time. I bought a pair of brown shoes in Standard Shoes of Henry Street that very evening and had enough left over for a bet or two in Shelbourne Park on Saturday night.

I had found the experience tremendously exciting, but I wasn't sure how well I'd done, and a Coláiste Íosagáin education almost guaranteed against taking oneself too seriously. My uncle Joe called to Pat's on Friday evening to congratulate me. He had stayed at home to listen, as much in fear of me 'making a show of myself' as anything else, he admitted.

He gave me a fiver before he left.

The following letter, dated 20 Márta, appeared in the *Irish Press* six days later.

A Chara,

The watchdogs of English who guard the microphones of Radio Éireann slumbered.

Irish broke out from the pens of Children's Hour, the outworn news bulletins and the romanticism and sentimentality of the Seanchaidhe's corner and donned the twenty century new look [*sic*].

On Saint Patrick's Day we got a lively, vigorous and thrilling account of the match from Croke Park which was far superior to its English counterpart.

The watchdogs have since awakened and Irish is again safely penned in.

Today, the commentary on the replay of the same match was in English.

Our station is, indeed, jealous of its self-imposed task of anglicisation.

Seán Sanndair

The signature was that of a man better known as Reics Carlo, or Cathal Ó Sandair, an author of several thrilling books of intrigue and mystery in the Irish language. I was familiar with the books: Uncle Joe never came to Kerry during my young days without bringing the latest. I felt greatly honoured on learning that a man of his standing had taken the trouble of writing to the paper about me; however, his great love of Irish was never in doubt, and he may have permitted himself the freedom to exaggerate in order to make a point about the language.

Cathal Ó Sandair was born in England, but learned Irish with enthusiasm when he came to live here. I got to know him years later and felt privileged when his son John Saunders asked me on behalf of the family to say a few words at Cathal's funeral mass.

There was another interesting sequel to the broadcast. My brother Padraig was staying in digs in Anglesey Road, Ballsbridge, at the time, and in the company of other friends often went to the local on Saturday night. I had a habit of calling, especially if I happened to be at the dogs in nearby Shelbourne Park and in the need of a few bob from the working brother.

I dropped in on the Saturday night of that week – I must have had late leave – and the company was sporting and good.

Before we left, a member of the company bought a drink for all, then proceeded to embarrass me by proposing a toast to the man from Kerry who had broadcast a match on St Patrick's Day. He was a fellow Kerryman, Jerry O'Callaghan from Currow, Castleisland, a loyal civil servant, great friend of my late brother, and father of Miriam O'Callaghan of RTE.

Finally, I appreciated a telegram I received from Coláiste Íosagáin – the message was in Irish and the names appended included Padraig and Seán Ua Murchadha, Seán Ó hAiniféin, Labhrás Durras Ó Domhnaill and Paidí Mac Giolla Comhaill (Coyle).

Ba dheas uatha é.

As the letter above states, I was not engaged to broadcast the replay fixed for the following Sunday – Micheál O'Hehir returned to do so. That neither worried nor surprised me, and that was to be the way over the next thirty-six years when we both worked in sport on radio. As far as I was concerned he was the people's choice and when available ought be the commentator on duty. It was a sad day for sport when a stroke silenced his broadcasting voice on 6 August 1985.

To get back to the replay, a combination of events conspired to make it a memorable and strange sporting encounter. It began with a decision by the Munster Council to keep the team in Dublin between the matches. I'm sure that accommodation was available in Barry's Hotel, but the gregarious and generous Maggie Poole had other ideas. All were invited to Larkfield Gardens, food and drink was provided and some bedrooms cleared to make way for dancing. A hilarious extended weekend began on the Thursday night, and there was little variation in the agenda between then and Sunday except to honour invitations to visit places such as the zoo and the Garda Club, where a no-thirst policy also prevailed.

It was not surprising, then, when a crew more akin to Slattery's Mounted Foot than a football team convened in Barry's Hotel a few hours before the starting time of the replay on Sunday. Some required 'steadying' before starting out on foot up the road to Croke Park. The fresh air was a welcome change, but they had to face the Leinster men, all of whom had returned to their homes on Thursday; there was a rumour that they might even have trained.

The result of that particular replay defies all logic and remains a deep mystery to this very day: Munster 4–9, Leinster 1–4. It was a rout of gigantic proportions and Munster's biggest ever win in inter-provincial football. I often think about it and wonder about the value of current training techniques. Is it time for some scholar to engage in scientific research to establish the best methods of preparing the mind rather than the body for competition?

I think it is time to give philosophers a say in the preparation of teams for major engagements.

Life returned to normal in Pat's pretty soon after my broadcasting debut, and there was an early break for the summer holidays. I went home and worked on the farm for the duration, something I always looked forward to – saving the hay and corn; carrying the milk to the creamery with a lively horse and enjoying the craic in a queue of men, women, horses, ponies and donkeys. And then there were dances in Dingle three miles west, or Lispole five to the east by road or two by sea if the tides answered, or fifteen miles away over Garraí na dTor to Anascaul. The latter journey would generally be undertaken on occasions such as carnivals, patterns or fairs, and involved a fifteen-mile cycle before the hall was reached.

Jimmy Rohan supplied the music at the all-night dances in Anascaul; 'all-night' meant 'Amhrán na bhFiann' at 3 a.m., or sometimes later if it was raining heavily outside. There would be the usual delays then, as some people might wander to 'see a man about a dog' or another chore before the peloton would assemble for the journey home with the dawn. Even after such late nights I would still expect an early call to go to catch the horse before putting the appropriate tackle on him for the daily creamery run.

The boat trips to the Lispole dances were best of all. The Farrells had an old rowing boat known as the 'Tar Pot' on account of the smearing of tar that made it as black as the ten of spades. Another unusual feature of this craft was that a portion of its stern was held together with concrete. This was our mode of transport when we crossed the Short Strand to Lispole.

The tide needed to be in because the lagoon dried out with the ebb, so the return home was dictated by the pull of the moon on the returning tide. It was great fun rowing the Pot, mooring close to the Tobar Road and walking the remainder of the journey to the Lispole Hall.

If the tide was 'early' there could be a few hands of cards in Thomasheen Kane's or in the home of Willie and Roseanne Moriarty before the five or six hours of dancing would begin with whatever music was available. The tide would then be in again, and the walk to the boat would begin, maybe in the company of the Tobar and Kinard lads and lasses. It was a great sight to witness the expanse of the Trá Beag glisten under the summer moonlight as we rowed the Pot to the south-west towards anchorage in Poll A' Chúille close to the third fairway of the golf links.

'Cruising down the River' was a pop hit of the time and a favourite of Mike Kennedy's, the best oarsman of all; however, Donnchadh Quinn was the best singer. We were of the opinion that not even John McCormack could sing 'Noreen Bán' as well, or 'Lonely I Wandered through Scenes of My Childhood'.

The same Donnchadh did wander to England on the beet, then went sheep-shearing to Australia before enlisting for the mammoth Snowy Mountains Hydroelectric Scheme. He is now a millionaire in Melbourne thanks to his adherence to the ethic of honesty and hard work. He had left school early, but he returned for further education in Australia when he came down from the Snowy Mountains. He has never lost his love of horses and greyhounds, and has had winners in both pursuits.

The Tar Pot's main function was for use in 'hauling' – fishing that begins close to the end of the waves by rowing outwards to sea paying out a net and returning in a semicircle in the hope of surrounding some salmon. Another boat was often used in this exercise; she didn't have a name, but was owned by an adventure-seeking Listowel solicitor, Paddy Fitzgibbon, who was based in Dingle. She was a lighter craft than the Pot and was permanently berthed in Dún Síon and available to us at all times.

The hauling had to be done after nightfall for the want of a licence, and there could be anything up to a score people working the operation. There would be two good men on the oars, an expert on the net payout, and sometimes a man at the bow directing matters. A few more would be holding the rope on dry land and others waiting for the arc to be completed before getting a grip at the other end. Then the laborious work of hauling the net ashore would begin, with an eye on the enclosed area on the lookout for the harvest.

The king of all fish, *an bradán*, was the desired catch, but the nets often surrendered limp on the sand without a single one. But an array of flat fish would be left on dry ground – plaice, sole, turbot, an odd dogfish and plenty of what we called Johnny Molloys. We did of course net salmon sometimes, and there would be great excitement on suspecting a hit when an inordinate amount of splashing would indicate gill-cuffed kings strenuously objecting to an unscheduled landing.

I don't think it was dangerous, though Seán Kelliher, a neighbour from nearby Imleach, disappeared from the bow one night and went under the Pot before quickly surfacing like a cork on the other side. He was hauled back aboard, and the rowing then continued. You need luck everywhere, but my father used always to say, 'Is gaire cabhair Dé ná an doras' – the help of God is nearer than the door, and a door need not always mean a door.

There was a night, too, when Fitzie the solicitor got a generous dousing from a breaking wave that the Pot failed to mount. I was sent to his bungalow, an Irish mile away close to the Mail Road, to fetch dry clothing. I rooted around in the dark and came on the necessary items, but the shirt turned out to be a pyjama top that glowed in the moonlight when the boat set out on the last haul of the night for the fifth time.

A mysterious drama took place on the strand on a Sunday summer evening sometime in the late 1940s.

The weather was fine, and Dan Griffin went for a stroll to wet his feet. He then noticed an absolute miracle being enacted before his eyes; the waves were no more than riplets that died on caressing the shore, but left great numbers of fish behind on the sodden sand. He alerted the elders of the village, who came to Poll A' Chúille with the intention of launching. They didn't know that a group of us had left for Lispole in the Pot. Finding no boat and cursing the crazy youth, they hoisted the hauling net on their shoulders and moved quickly towards the new Klondyke.

On our return the observant Mike Kennedy spotted that the net was missing. Stealing was unknown, and it remained a mystery until the following morning when the 'senior team' of the village detailed their exploits. They collected buckets of fish along the sand, but surmised that there were many more in the shallows. Short of a boat they managed to encircle them with the net by wading knee-deep in the water before dropping the net and bringing more fish ashore than the twelve Apostles and Our Lord that night long ago on the Sea of Galilee.

There were many explanations as to why the fish landed voluntarily; the most convincing stated that it was in pursuit of a species of sprat that had invaded the beach area.

★

Summer 1949 sped by, and, by the time the call came to return to Pat's for my second and final year, the harvest was home, with the oats cut, bound, stooked and stacked in readiness for the greatest day of all: 'thrashing' day.

All farmers in dairying areas invariably set a few acres under oats as feed for cows and horses, with a bit of barley thrown in and wheat during emergencies. Sowing wheat was compulsory during the war unless one could plead a good case, but generally it was accepted in the spirit of the times. It was illegal to mill white flour, as the removal of the brown element from the grain would reduce the bulk.

We and all the neighbours grew our quota of wheat, and it was a noble crop to work with. When the year turned out to be reasonably fine the harvest was good and there was plenty of brown flour available. And some people even managed to convert portions of it into home-made white flour.

I first saw the operation in action while drinking a cup of tea in a house in Garfinny one St Stephen's Day. We were given a demonstration by the young lady of the house, who was the proud owner of a pair of nylon or silk stockings. They were hard to get at the time, but the odd pair arrived in parcels from America. The inventor never meant them for milling purposes, but for our friend in Garfinny they were too valuable to wear because she used them in making white flour. It was easy: pour in the brown stuff and shake to your heart's content while watching the white powder drop into a dish and the browns being held by the mesh of the stockings. The process was a marvel of engineering on a par with the wonderful works of a wheelbarrow in its day.

By the way, it was Máire Quinn who brought the first pair of nylons to Dún Síon. She and Ellen Farrell were the trendsetters in fashion, and Máire's nylons, which she actually wore, were a topic of conversation. The idea caught on when supplies became available after the Emergency ended.

Kenny Kelliher from the village of Balinvounig and his neighbour Mikey Nelligan were the owners of a threshing machine and tractor that toured in the season of opportunity. Kenny's mother was a lady from London known as Alice, and on appropriate occasions the Union Jack was flown from the roof of the home. Nobody minded – the Kellihers were sound and generous people. The Nelligans had a reputation for brains and two of them, Willie and May, served in the British Army during the war.

I always looked forward to the annual visit of the thresher (which we pronounced 'thrasher'). The owners of the plant set the scene by rigging the outfit with its belts and bags, and a large can of emergency petrol on stand-by. The *meitheal* – a team drawn from the neighbouring houses in the village and further afield – would have assembled by then. One man would climb to the top of a stack of corn, usually oats, at the side of the tractor carrying a two-pronged pike or fork for pitching sheaves two at a time to the top of the thrasher, where another pair would be kneeling and holding two sharp knives. Their job would be to cut the binds on the sheaves and feed them in unison into the bowels of the gurgling thrasher as the next pair of sheaves landed softly at their knees. Another pair of men would be stationed near the bags in readiness for the emission of the bounteous grain, and yet another two to sweep away the straw being belched forth. They in turn would land great heaps of light straw on to a spot where others, often children, would pack it into a reek that rose towards the heavens as work proceeded. Other children would assume the task of watching for mice and the odd rat that would leap from the shrinking stack, often destined to be caught in midair by a good dog with the fielding agility of Mick O'Connell. Finally, two of the strongest men available would be warmed up for the heavy-duty work of hoisting bags filled with grain on to their backs and away to a barn loft.

On a signal the entire *meitheal* would swing into action amid banter and jokes about good men, great men, mighty men and slackers, all in the spirit of fun. There would be breaks for dinner and tea, with cigarettes and a few bottles of stout doing the rounds, and when the last sheaf had been segregated into grain, straw and some chaff for the finches there would be more repetitions of 'The Lord spare you the health' than one would hear at a meeting of the

Vatican Council. And then the circus would move on to the next haggard, another *meitheal*, another day and more fun and camaraderie.

I think that work as a farmer would have appealed to me. For as long as I can remember I had a love of the open air, and maybe that is why I prefer work at a playing pitch to a studio, no matter how comfortable. I would advocate a day at the thrashing as a possible cure for the mental ills that afflict some unfortunate people.

The thrashing was an autumnal event, the culmination of a cycle that started with the spring ploughing – a wonderful time of year. Who couldn't but envy the poet Raftaire, with his wise words of moons ago: 'Anois teacht an earraigh' – Spring has come, and it is time to be on the move . . .

Observance of farm work gave meaning to the poems and other things we learned at school; for instance, that depiction of seasonal work by Seosamh Mac Cathmhaoil:

> I will go with my father aploughing
> To the green field by the sea
> And the rooks and the crows and the seagulls
> Will come flocking after me.
> I will sing to the patient horses
> With the lark in the white of the air
> And my father will sing the plough-song
> That blesses the cleaving share.

I would have marvelled at all of that, from watching my father direct a pair of horses along an imaginary straight line up the centre of a green field turning the first *scríob* and continuing until the entire field was turned to red and inspected for worms by the birds of the air in convention. From then on it was the sowing of the seeds, the sprouting, and the changing colours through to the eventual golden brown of the harvest.

Turf-cutting day was another of my favourites. A *meitheal* would gather in the village before setting out in horse carts to a location that would be at least twelve miles away. In our case it was usually in a place called Com A' Lochaigh, close to where the philosopher John Moriarty's father came from. The team would leave base very early on a May morning. A few of us younger folk would follow with Tim Kevane's donkey and cart, laden with enough food supplies and utensils for ten to twelve adults. Com A' Lochaigh was a peaceful and beautiful spot on a fine day, nestling low at the angle made by Mount Brandon and Coum Mouish.

On arrival the men would set to work in a row, with *sleáns* for cutting and pikes for moving heavy, wet sods along the line to firmer ground, where they would be left to dry. At some stage one worker would be released from duty, usually the man whose *meitheal* it was on the day, and his immediate chore would be to fetch a bucket of spring water for the tea and the midday meal. There was no shortage of wells spouting the pure water. It was a simple job to light a fire, and it never took long to get the kettle singing and the tea made. Home-made bread with plenty of butter, jam and eggs made up the menu, and the meal would be followed by a smoke and the lively talk that always accompanied *meitheals*.

It would be back to work once more then, until the afternoon break for more sustenance. The day was long and the work hard, but the camaraderie more than made up for it. The journey home was usually broken by a visit to one of the pubs in Dingle town. Horses have a great homing instinct, but many of them had picked up enough wisdom as they grew older to stop without being asked at the appropriate public house.

Chapter Five

The hurling final had already been played by the time I got back to St Pat's in September 1949, but I paid my way into Hill 16 to see Cavan attempt to win its third consecutive All-Ireland football final. Meath provided the opposition, and I had a leaning towards them for four reasons: they had never won an All-Ireland; they wore the Kerry colours of green and gold; Frankie Byrne, a past pupil of Coláiste Íosagáin, was among the forwards; and four of them – goalkeeper Kevin Smyth, the converted fullback Paddy 'Hands' O'Brien, full forward Bill Halpenny and the man in the cap, Peter McDermott – had played for Leinster on the day of my first broadcast six months earlier.

They put on a show of resolute football that rocked the champions in most departments. The fullback line of Micheál O'Brien, Paddy O'Brien and Kevin McConnell was on its way to immortality; Paddy Dixon was outstanding further out; Jim Kearney, who had come out of retirement to play at midfield, was sensational; and the forwards worked as a unit, with Halpenny scoring the goal and McDermott conspicuous and busy inside the fourteen-yard line. And there was no mistaking the tidy Frankie Byrne, with his classic sidestep, who was the free-taker.

McDermott is an extraordinary man with an exceptional CV. He was born in Cork in 1918 and first played at senior grade for Meath in 1940. He won five Leinster titles and two All-Irelands before retiring in 1954 at the age of thirty-six, after captaining Meath to beat Kerry in the All-Ireland final. Current-day players and followers are bemused to hear that he had refereed the 1953 All-Ireland final between Kerry and Armagh while still an active inter-county player. Such was not deemed strange in those days, and there is an even better example of the perceived integrity of players of that era. Simon Deignan of Cavan, an officer of the Irish

Army stationed in Tralee, refereed the most important Munster final of all time – that of 1947, with a trip to New York for the All-Ireland finalists that year. It was played in the old Cork Athletic Grounds, with the winners ranked as favourites to qualify for the All-Ireland final. Cavan had already qualified for the All-Ireland semi-final, and here was the bould Simon a week later with a say in deciding possible opponents of his in an All-Ireland final later. What's more, three colleagues on his Tralee club team, John Mitchel's, were in the Kerry lineout against Cork. Yet not a murmur of complaint was heard from any source before or after the game.

The Oireachtas Tournament in hurling had a high profile in the 1940s. The four leading teams of the year would be drawn for semi-final pairings, with the All-Ireland finalists seeded. The final was always staged in Croke Park during the October Oireachtas Festival.

Tipperary had beaten Laois rather easily in the All-Ireland final on the first Sunday of September, and the pair qualified to meet again in the Oireachtas final in late October. The finals had been broadcast in Irish in the past, and I was delighted to be invited to commentate this time round.

Pat's was still my abode, and shanks' mare the logical transport to Croke Park. I was lucky once more because there was not a thing on earth about the Laois players that my uncle in Portlaoise did not know. Polish-born Paddy Rustchitzko was captain.

Laois played much better than in the All-Ireland final six weeks earlier and held Tipp to a winning margin of five points. My abiding memory of the game is the wrist work of Tommy Doyle, the Tipperary left halfback, and if anyone has a recording of the broadcast I am willing to bet that at some stage I said, 'Tá an camán ag iomrothlú thart ar rìghe a láimhe' – the hurley is revolving about his wrist. It appeared to me as if the stick was the spoke of a wheel, and the wrist acting as the hub. I have not seen Doyle's wrist work bettered since. Doyle won his first All-Ireland medal in Killarney in 1937, and his fifth in 1951.

★

My second year at St Pat's was more academically intense than the first. I continued to broadcast *as Gaeilge*, commenting on the 1950 Railway Cup final, and before the end of June I had qualified as a national teacher. I did not make any effort to secure full-time paid work, but rather headed for Kerry for the summer and took up the familiar pattern of former years. Schools reopened in September, but I was oblivious to the fact and continued working on the farm to my heart's content into October.

It must have been a wet autumn because I well remember an emergency that developed when spring water began to seep towards the surface of the potato field. This necessitated getting the crop out of the ground as speedily as possible, and I am credited with setting a record by unearthing more than twenty sackloads of produce in one afternoon with a trusted spade.

Then one day a telegram arrived with an invitation from Leon Ó Dubhghaill to act as substitute teacher for him in St Finbarr's School in Cabra West in Dublin for the duration of the Oireachtas. He was the hardworking secretary of the organization and normally took a fortnight's break from his teaching post to oversee the many cultural events of the festival. Nothing for me then but straighten out for Dublin once more: no need to change at Mallow.

I was heartily welcomed to Finbarr's by the principal, Mr McCarthy, a large man from Cork. I found teaching a very pleasant experience. It was a coincidence that two of Radio Éireann's newsreaders in Irish, Liam Budhlaeir from the Kerry Gaeltacht and Séamus Mac Cnáimhsí from Donegal, were on the staff at the time, as well as that quintessential Dublin Gaeilgeoir, Paddy Bán Ó Broin. Budhlaeir went full-time at RTE shortly afterwards, and finished his broadcasting career as head of the Irish Department in the news-room. He possessed the finest radio speaking voice I have heard.

At lunch time most of the pupils went home, and the teachers got a ninety-minute break. I remember the teachers dashing off to a house that had a radio to hear a fifteen-minute sponsored slot that nearly always featured songs by Connie Foley of Tralee. He was a great favourite at the time and made 'The Wild Colonial Boy' popular countrywide.

My grand-uncle Tim
Moriarty, flanked by his
nieces Ellie and May, 1904

My father Thady, mother Katie,
uncle Joe holding brother Paddy,
and grand-aunt Della, 1927

Wearing my *geansaí*,
aged about three

Coláiste Íosagáin football team, *c.* 1948; I am at the extreme right of the
back row. Seán Murphy, winner of All–Ireland medals with Kerry at minor,
junior and senior levels and member of GAA football teams of the
century and millennium, is at the extreme right of the front row

Saving hay: I'm second from left, with brother Dónal, sister Eileen (holding dog),
father and aunt May, early 1950s

Graduation from
University College
Dublin, 1952

With my young pupils on confirmation day at St Laurence O'Toole's, 1953

A portrait with five of my siblings in Dublin, *c.* 1953: myself, Náis, Pádraig, Dónal, Máire, Eileen

In Ballybunion, 1950s, with the late Paddy Desmond, left, and Joe Coakley

With Helena on our wedding day, 1970

With Helena in Ballybunion, early 1970s

Golf *as Gaeilge* at Ceann Sibéal, Ballyferriter, late 1980s: myself, brother Paddy and former Kerry footballer Micheál Ó Sé

With Mick O'Dwyer, Jack O'Shea and Mick O'Connell

At Lansdowne Road for a soccer match with Kerry legends Jack O'Shea, Moss Keane, Mick O'Connell and John B. Keane

With greyhound, *camán* and helicopter, 1998

On Dún Síon beach,
c. 2001

Broadcasting in
Croke Park

There was a wild colonial boy
Jack Duggan was his name
He was born and raised in Ireland
In a place called Castlemaine

The ballad went on to relate Jack's fondness for roaming, robbing the rich to pay the poor, and eventually dying an outlaw's death somewhere in Australia's Outback. The same Jack was certainly a favourite in St Finbarr's during the second half of October 1950.

Strangely, I was not making any enquiries about work after Leon's Oireachtas break, but fortunately for me a Dingle teacher friend, Séamus (James) Kavanagh, or JK for short, called to me on the Thursday of my second week in Cabra. He was a brother to the aforementioned Patrick Kavanagh, or PK. He brought news that a job of some sort might be available shortly in St Laurence O'Toole's Christian Brothers School in Seville Place, close to the Dublin docks: he told me that he had arranged an interview with Brother Loughnane on the following night.

That put paid to the dogs at Harold's Cross.

Brother Loughnane was from Feakle in Co. Clare. After he explained that the job would not become officially available until the Department of Education inspector called to check matters such as enrolment and classroom capacity, the interview took the form of a discussion on sport. He must have been a cousin of Dr Bill Loughnane, who won hurling All-Irelands with Dublin, and of the illustrious Ger, who was yet to burst on the scene.

He offered me the job beginning on Monday, and prior to official ratification, with the warning that I would have to be rushed to obscurity as soon as the inspector darkened the door of the school. That happened a few days into the first week, and on cue I made my way to the flat, parapeted roof of the school while the inspection of numbers and space went on below.

The post was ratified shortly afterwards, and I became a temporary supernumerary teacher in Larriers – as St Laurence O'Toole's was familiarly known – with the friendly Brother Loughnane as boss. The students, who came from the vicinity of Seville Place and Sheriff Street, and from further down the docks and East Wall, were lovely kids. Although many of them were poor, they were decked out like the royal family for their confirmation day. Some say it was extravagant, but it was the parents' way of showing pride in their children, and that was good.

I remember the young Luke Kelly from those days – he was small for his age even then, and always smiling and full of harmless mischief. He was mad about football and fairly good at it also. And did anybody on earth ever sing 'Raglan Road' in later life like that very fine soul from Larriers?

From as far back as I can remember curiosity has directed me towards finding out as much as I can about people and places that are different. Even though I have had a very close connection with Irish culture over a long number of years, I have always wanted to see 'the other side', or *an taobh eile*, as we say in Irish. This may have been fostered by boarding-school life, where the students were drawn from diverse areas. It came naturally to us to compare dialects and customs, and this led to an appreciation of difference which I find particularly helpful to this day.

In Coláiste Íosagáin we had a fad for reciting poetry at random, especially those works of fiction that recounted the deeds of the great warriors – Fionn Mac Cumhail, Goll Mac Morna, Conán Maol Mallachtach Mac Morna (the bald, swearing Conán), Caol An Iarainn et al. But my favourite was a poem of a different type – 'Comhairle na Bard Scolóige Dá Mhac', the advice of a bard to his son. Two lines in particular encapsulate a wonderful philosophy:

> Na tabhair do bhreith ar an gcéad scéal
> Go mbeiridh an taobh eile ort.

The advice is never to pass judgement on a story until you have heard the other side. I have always tried to follow that piece of bardic *comhairle*.

It didn't take a long time to come to the conclusion that a much wider array of differences existed in Dublin than in Dún Síon, and that was interesting. Few people spoke Irish regularly, not everyone played Gaelic or even supported it and of course there were religious differences. It would have been easy for me to cocoon myself within a life that devoted itself to Irish culture alone, but such never had an attraction for me.

The GAA operated a ban against the sports of soccer, rugby and cricket until 1971, and it was forbidden to members even to attend foreign dances. But I still went along to Lansdowne Road to see a few rugby internationals, and there was hardly a dance hall in the city and beyond that I and my friends did not frequent.

And we were members of the GAA.

It is quite a while ago since I watched the famous French giants Moga and Soro play in Lansdowne. And I saw the great Jack Kyle, and Karl Mullen, and many more of the home-grown players. Several well-known Gaelic players attended rugby and soccer matches in attire that they would not normally wear, thus making it more difficult for members of the GAA's official vigilante committees to spot them. It was plain sailing for GAA *gardaí* – they went to the matches on duty, and that was okay!

Some counties had their own vigilante committees, but nobody knew the personnel; it has been said that in some cases well-known players with a habit of going to 'forbidden games' were in fact appointed as vigilantes in order to avoid possible subsequent suspension.

It was a good day for the GAA when the ban was abolished in 1971. I often wondered why the ban lasted so long, but it did have its advocates, and many of those would have been people who had served the Irish cause well during the critical opening twenty years of the twentieth century. They were respected for that, and it was felt in many quarters that it would be wrong to oppose them on matters such as the ban. But Gaelic games have been strong enough to stand on their own for a long time now and need not fear competition if the organization at local and national levels is good.

None of my siblings was forced to emigrate, and this was a change from previous generations. But most of us left Dún Síon: by the mid 1950s Padraig, Dónal, Eileen, Máire, Kathleen and I were all in Dublin, leaving Náis and Siobhán at home.

Siobhán suffered from poor health from the age of nine or ten onwards, and died in 1960 at the age of twenty-five.

Some of the older generation of Moriartys were gifted with longevity, but others died young. My father's sister Ellie caught the Great Flu of 1918 in New York and died of it in the year in which she was due to get married. His brother John, a member of the New York police, died young also after catching pneumonia; I have a distant memory of his policeman's heavy raincoat hanging at the back of the kitchen door at home. Náis and I often took it to the fields on wet days, and it was always handy as cover in the horse trap on the way to mass on a bad morning. It must have been a custom with the New York police to return the uniforms of deceased members to the family.

Another brother, Con, who stayed at home, was a victim of tuberculosis and died young, but the remainder of my father's generation – himself, my Auntie May and brothers Michael, Dan and Joe – averaged ninety years and enjoyed life as much as possible to the end.

Aunty May died in 1974 at the age of ninety-three, and my father rather unexpectedly on a July day in 1977 in his eighty-eighth year.

That day was a free Sunday for me, and I had journeyed down to Carlow with Seán Óg Ó Ceallacháin to see Dublin and Wexford play a Leinster football championship game. It was a fine day, and I had found a grand sunny spot close to the TV scaffold, all set to watch the match without a care in the world. Before long, though, a message arrived from the studio asking me to ring home. I did, and it was then I learned of my father's death.

Seán Óg gave me his car to drive back to Dublin to collect my wife, Helena, before driving to Kerry for the wake and funeral.

My father was always a great judge of horses, so it was fitting that the hearse at his funeral was drawn by two good horses and a few people travelled on horseback.

Earlier that year I had bought him a nice walking stick. On examination he decided not to use it, but instructed me to place it in his coffin before he was buried. 'It will be useful when I go on walks around the place at night,' he said.

The old people had a great belief in the afterlife.

As for my generation, Padraig was the leader of the clan in Dublin and an inspiration to all. He was never afraid of hard work or study, and acquired many professional qualifications; he spent all his working life with the ESB. I have no trouble in remembering when he got married to Esther: it was 29 September 1953, two days after Esther's brother Gerald O'Sullivan won an All-Ireland medal with Kerry by defeating Armagh in the final.

One of Padraig's ESB colleagues was Kevin Heffernan, the famous and popular Dublin footballer; they got on well, though they were divided on football matters for spells of some years. Padraig – known as Paddy outside the family – became Chief Executive of the ESB in due course and Chairman of the Board after retirement. He also served as Chairman of the RTE Authority for a term, but resigned on his appointment as Chief Executive of the ESB. Despite spending his working life in business he maintained in close contact at all times with the Irish language and allied cultural matters, such as the development of Ionad An Bhlascaoid, the literary heritage centre on the Dunquin mainland, overlooking the Blasket Islands.

He died in 1997 at the age of seventy-one. He was a patient in St Vincent's Hospital at the time, but there seemed to be no danger to his life. I was in London on the Saturday night of that week doing a broadcast on the English Greyhound Derby and as usual caught the earliest flight home on Sunday morning in order to catch one of the GAA matches of the day. Helena was waiting at the airport, and we set off for Clones for a broadcast of an Ulster championship game in the afternoon. I arrived with plenty of time to spare and was amazed that producer Ian Corr had already called. When I rang back he told me I was to ring my sister Eileen; she had the sad news that Padraig had taken a bad turn. Luckily, the former Antrim footballer and BBC commentator Paddy O'Hara was present, and he took charge of my RTE duties for the afternoon.

Sadly, I didn't make it to Vincent's before Padraig died.

He was buried in Dún Chaoin graveyard, where he has a terrific view of the Blasket Islands that meant a good deal to him on account of the literary works that emanated from islanders such as Tomás Ó Criomhthain, Peig Sayers and Muiris Ó Súilleabháin.

Three other members of the family also became teachers: my sisters Eileen and Máire – the most scholarly member of the family, who was familiar with all the works of Shakespeare at sixteen – and my brother Dónal. Eileen married Mick Devane from the Páidí Ó Sé area of Ventry; Máire married John Davis, a Dubliner; and Dónal, who taught in Ballyfermot for most of his career, married Eileen O'Shea from Anascaul. Kathleen brought a taste of hurling into the family when she married Bill Barry, who played in goal for the Kilkenny minors in the All-Ireland finals of 1956 and 1957.

That was a New York wedding, where they lived for a few years, and I went over to give the 'baby' of the family away.

The home place always had a great pull on all of us. Náis is long settled there and married to Bridie Griffin from Lisdargan. Being on the home sod he would be regarded as our Taoiseach, and there is always a great welcome awaiting us whenever we call.

My favourite time of the year around Dingle is Christmas. It has been that way ever, and memories of early Christmases are vivid. The preparations would begin early with provision of holly and ivy from the many fences and ditches where it grew copiously. 'Bringing home Christmas' was our phrase for the shopping outing to Dingle a few days before the big feast. That was a job for parents, and Dingle town would be as busy as Broadway in the days leading up to Christmas. My father and mother would leave early in the day with the horse and cart, and while they would be 'gone for Christmas' the rest of us would be busy decorating the house and doing other chores, with the girls in full charge.

We would be on the lookout for the return from three o'clock onwards. Emptying the cart was an exciting job. There would be at least six candles of varied colours, each at least two feet in length; decorating paper for the windowsills and candle holders; a few feet of solid salted ling fish for the fasting days ahead; fresh meat from the butcher; big, round currant loaves and a few of my favourite butter loaves; jams of all description in big brown earthenware jars; and the *Irish Press* and *Kerryman*.

Before the candles could be lit it was necessary to procure something that would hold them firm in position on the sills. Sometimes it was an empty jam jar filled with fine, glistening sand from the beach, but more often than not a turnip minus the head and tail did the needful. It was easy to make a hole in the centre for the base of the candle, and a strip of decorating paper attached gave it a festive look.

The local custom was to have a lighted candle at each window to the front of the house; it made for a wonderful spectacle of light, with Conor Hill and Strickeen in the background and thousands of stars overhead competing with hundreds of flickering candles in the windows of the villages that stretched from Baile An tSagairt on the left along the foot of the hills to Gabhlán to the north of Lispole.

First mass was at half-seven on Christmas morning in Dingle church, three miles away. It meant an early rising for everyone and a feed of grain for the horse before we tackled him under the cart for the journey. Everybody would be fasting, and not even a drink of water was allowed from midnight on, but I can never recall that being a problem for anyone. At about half-six the carts would begin to roll noisily from every house in the village on the way to Dingle, with a lantern hanging by the heel of the front left shaft. We could see our neighbours in Imleach setting forth at the same time, young and old together – the Kellihers, the Rohans and the Connors moving in unison with the lanterns along a road that ran parallel to ours. Once we had travelled a mile and a half, the byroad from Beenbane would join ours, and more horse carts and donkeys would emerge to join the parade. Before long we would reach the cross leading on to the Mail Road into Dingle, where we met yet more carts coming from the east like the three wise men. The steel wheels and shod hooves created plenty of noise on the tarred road, and a keen ear might even be able to identify particular horses from the sound of their hooves. The Mail Road was one of five that converged on the town, which lay low at the seafront, but rose steeply to where the candlelit hospital glowed brightly on Cnoc A' Chairn. We would tie our horse to a pole outside Barrys forge or to a pillar post in some adjacent yard.

My memory tells of a packed chapel and lights that seemed brilliantly bright; however, a three-mile spin in the dark could easily have exaggerated the effect.

To me at that time no place on earth could hold the magic of the Dingle church for first mass on a Christmas morning. I had heard of John McCormack and other famous singers, but could any of them compare with Garret Fox as his powerful voice wafted the 'Adeste', 'Silent Night' and other hymns into every nook of the church without the aid of amplification? The mass was in Latin, and that added to the mystique; we assumed that the bevy of nuns behind glass close to the crib on the right and the line of Christian Brothers at the front understood every word, and the rest of us would be forgiven.

I have heard mass bells in many places all over the world, but I have yet to hear a sound as haunting as the one that resonates from the Dingle altar bell once it gets even the gentlest of taps on its mushroom-like flank. It seems as if it never dies, but escapes instead towards the heavens. I return to Dingle for Christmas frequently, and the family, though born in Dublin and now grown up, looks forward to the visits.

The remainder of Christmas Day during my childhood would be much the same as elsewhere – the dinner, with a home-reared turkey playing a big part in it, then preparations for the 'wran' on the following day. I don't think we ever referred to it as Stephen's Day; it was always the Wran's Day. The custom of traversing the countryside dressed in home-made costumes and wearing a false face is rooted deep in tradition.

We often made up a bunch of twelve to fifteen, boys and girls of school-going age, with Johnny Quinn playing music, his brother

Donnchadh singing, my brother Padraig dancing steps and the rest ready to dance a set as soon as we entered the kitchen of every house. We were very proud of our outfits one year in particular, when the fun-loving Máire Quinn made long slacks from the material of white flour bags before dying them in a colour of deep red. We dressed in Quinn's that wran morning and set off for Beenbane, the nearest village, with the first glimmer of dawn, to the sound of Johnny's melodeon. Collecting money for a ball night and the craic of the outing were always the objectives, and our wran like all others was made feel welcome in every village. It was well after dark when we returned that particular day to call and perform in the eight houses of Dún Síon, the final lap of a day well in excess of twelve hours spent walking, dancing, talking and eating over an extensive area.

The ball night always took place during the twelve days of Christmas, and the venue for Dún Síon's was the clubhouse on the golf links. It had a solid, corrugated-iron roof, a wooden floor ideal for dancing and a semi-open reception area where food was available during a night that usually lasted until morning. The preparations were done by the personnel of the wran, and these consisted of tidying the golf house, providing the necessary furniture and ordering food and a few barrels of porter in Dingle. Everybody in the neighbourhood would be invited, plus a few guests from outside; occasionally a few uninvited strawboys would turn up.

The straws were uninvited people who would come along in disguise, using straw to cover their clothing and face. Straws often appeared at weddings also; at certain times they would be given a drink in honour of the occasion and allowed to have a straw dance on their own.

Dancing a dozen sets or more in the course of the night meant that little work was ever done on the following day. Ball nights as such have died out, but the wrans are bigger and better than ever, especially in Dingle town, where the rivalry between the Green and Gold and the Goat Street combinations is keen. They provide excellent entertainment as they parade in a pageant of colour and music, collecting for some worthy cause.

The Goat Street wran has one advantage over all others: it includes a fife-and-drum band with an Ulster Orange flavour to the music. It is said that soldiers coming home from the Boer War in South Africa introduced this music to Dingle, where it still flourishes. As well as ringing in the New Year and partaking in other events, the band maintains a lovely custom of parading through the town at sunrise on St Patrick's morning – surely the earliest parade of the national festival.

By way of acquainting my own family with the old custom of the wran, we organized our own outing a few years ago. We brought acceptable rigs with us from Dublin, and complete with our own music, dancers and false faces we took off to travel the countryside as in days of yore. It was decided that I would remain silent in case my voice would be recognized, as guessing who the visitors might be is part of the ritual in each house. Some of the guesses were amusing, like the one that came from an old man whose memory obviously went back a long way – 'He has the stand of a constable, whoever he is' was his comment on the silent figure who had often been in the same house before. The fun was as good as ever, and we finished up in Dingle that evening and gave what money we had collected to Tom Greaney for the local old folks' home.

We might repeat the exercise some time in the near future, seeing that the family's connections have broadened to embrace the English, Greek and Chinese cultures. I might even dress up as a big Chinese constable this time.

Chapter Six

Shortly after settling in at my teaching job by the docks I decided to register for a Bachelor of Arts degree through evening classes at University College Dublin. The degree would take two years – one less than normal because of my teacher's qualification from St Pat's. The search for *an taobh eile* was one reason for pursuing the BA, but there was another – a monetary reward from the Department of Education for those with extra qualifications.

UCD was still housed in Earlsfort Terrace in central Dublin. My subjects were Irish, Economics and Archaeology, and as at Coláiste Íosagáin there was no pressure attached to the exercise – no job depended on the result. Neither did lectures and study interfere with social life, which revolved around football, hurling, greyhound racing, card playing, 'going to pictures', theatres and dances. The lectures in Irish from Professor Cormac Ó Cadhlaigh and Tomás de Bhaldraithe were memorable, and it was stimulating to listen to the legendary Professor of Economics George O'Brien. For an example of a man with an inordinate amount of common sense, there was no equal to Seán P. Ó Ríordáin, Professor of Archaeology. Meeting and studying with people from different walks of life was the best education of all.

I remember once at the start of an Archaeology class suggesting that we ought to adjourn to Harold's Cross greyhound track to see the final of the Callanan Cup. I failed to get support once the Professor interjected by saying that to him it seemed that examining or talking about some artefact thousands of years old but still extant was far more exciting than watching live animals in a futile chase of an electric hare.

It was the definitive example of *an taobh eile*.

As far as I can remember, the fees for the course amounted to about £30 per annum; fortunately some assistance was available in the form of a Reid Scholarship. A man of that name, a servant of the Empire, had left money in trust to assist the education of students from Kerry. I and others benefited to the extent of £10 a year while in Pat's, and I was no sooner enrolled in UCD than Séamus Kavanagh, who had seen to it earlier that I applied for the job in Seville Place, brought me an application form. That was generous, because JK himself was an applicant, and the number of such scholarships was limited. As it turned out we both were lucky, and it eased the burden of the fees.

Graduation, in July 1952, was pleasant – hiring and wearing a gown, marching up the middle of the Aula Maxima, shaking hands with the President and receiving the Latin-inscribed parchment – but it was no great deal. I didn't bother telling any members of the family about it, and it was the same with scores of other graduates. Times were certainly simpler then.

The ceremony took place midweek; the following Sunday was the date of the Munster football final between Kerry and Cork. As was often the case, a group of us finished up in the Crystal Ballroom in South Anne Street off Grafton Street in Dublin on the Saturday night. It was a regular haunt of ours – free admission if the manager, legendary Kerry footballer Paddy Kennedy, was about.

We would 'case' the place before approaching: that was easy, as the entrance had an abundance of glistening mirrors, and a perfect view of the situation was attainable from the door of Keogh's pub some distance down and across the street. It was our custom to approach when the great gentleman of Anascaul was in evidence.

Naturally there was a long discussion on football the night before a Munster final, but hardly a thought given to a possible win for Cork. After all, the Rebels had scored only two victories over the Kingdom since 1907. Little dancing was done as the Kerry caucus grew in numbers, and before long PK and I were offered a lift by car to Cork in the morning. The final message from the Good Samaritan, a man from near Farranfore, was to be at Kelly's Corner on the South Circular Road at 10.15 a.m.

It was time for the last dance then, a 'Paul Jones' and 'Amhrán na bhFiann'.

We were at Kelly's Corner before the appointed time, but it passed by, as did 10.30, with neither sighting nor sounding of the expected transport. By eleven it was time to abandon corner; the train had departed by then, and hitching became the sole hope of reaching Cork in time. We took a bus to the outskirts of Inchicore and had reasonable luck until we reached Abbeyleix with match time still on target. But we remained stranded outside that town for a long time. We were joined by a man from Cork called Ted Hogan, a cricket journalist from the Phoenix Club and an interesting man; he soon despaired of seeing a ball being kicked in Cork, crossed the road and waved us goodbye as he secured a drive back towards Dublin.

Eventually in bits and pieces we made it to Cork around six o'clock, unaware of the day's drama: cars of the 1950s did not have radios. But the news that Cork had demolished Kerry was easily found in Patrick's Street, where we disembarked. It is one of my greatest regrets that I missed that game as it was the last played by Dingle's greatest legend, Paddy Bawn Brosnan, who almost single-handedly fought off an intensive sixty-minute Cork onslaught. The final score of Cork 0–11, Kerry 0–2 tells its own story.

Paddy was a favourite throughout the land. He had stayed on at school for a long time with his own purpose in mind, as related many a time by his teacher of Latin, Seán Gillen. Seán arrived in Dingle as a young teacher and could not help but notice the line of sturdy students manning the back row during his first Latin class. Addressing one of them, the Bawn as it so happens, he asked for the possessive case of the noun *agricola*. The answer, delivered in the tone used to communicate with full forwards in later life, was: 'We're only here for the football.'

He played fullback on the Kerry team beaten by Galway in the replayed All-Ireland final of 1938; he was on the Dingle team that made the breakthrough in winning the county title for the first time the same year and added five more before he retired; he won three All-Ireland medals, one as a wing forward; he played in the Polo Grounds final of 1947; he was a regular on Munster Railway

Cup teams, winning two medals and starring on the team of 1949, thereby giving this first-time broadcaster the privilege of talking about a football god. He did all of that without ever owning a pair of football boots in his life.

He told me that his good friend Paddy Donoghue from Dykegate Lane always had some to spare and never saw the star short. It had to be an honour for the tall O'Donoghue to see his boots play in All-Ireland finals.

Cork was a lively place on that July night of 1952, and we stayed until the morning. We were as free as the seagulls that glide and dive in all directions off the Dún Mór at home, and we wondered about our next stop.

The morning newspaper contained a report of the film *Moby Dick* being shot in Youghal, a mere twenty miles from Cork. We made straight for Youghal and arrived early enough in the day, entertaining a feeling that it would be great to be offered jobs as extras. Although we spent a few days at the seaside resort, we failed dismally to get work before returning to Dingle with film ambitions shattered.

The Munster football final of the following year, 1953, was the occasion of another transportation mix-up. I travelled from Dingle to Killarney, where the match was played, in Stevie Kelliher's Volkswagen van. There must have been a misunderstanding about the return time because when I reached the departure point late at night there was no sign of man or van. I was in a right pucker, as the *seanchaí* Éamonn Kelly might say, because I had spent all my money in the course of a good night after a Kerry win. But my old luck held good: a friend, Jerry Byrne, who had played for Kerry and was now a fellow member of the Geraldine Club in Dublin, came up the street. I explained my predicament, and he had an immediate solution: 'Follow me. I can open the window of the bar in the Glebe Hotel – there will be people there, but be gone before Mrs Cooper appears in the morning.' He loaned me a ten-shilling note, more than enough to take me to Dingle on the morrow.

As Jerry had predicted, there were people in the bar, drinking past closing time, and it did not take long before I joined in the match analysis; it was not Mrs Cooper that disturbed the peace, but an unexpected visit from the gardaí.

Before their entry to the bar itself one of the 'found-ons' feigned a weakness and was lying on the floor with the rest of us in attendance. He was a Kerryman who worked for the *Irish Independent* at the time, and naturally the gardaí were a little alarmed. It was then that another genius informed the gardaí that the situation would right itself, as he personally could vouch for the fact that the 'patient's' people were always good to recover.

It may have helped that I was wearing a Pioneer pin and that a man who had played for Kerry about twelve hours earlier was present as well.

The gardaí left confident that 'our man' was in safe hands, and we were all gone before Mrs Cooper rose in the morning.

I have rarely been without a greyhound over the past fifty years, and sometimes a leg of a horse. My first dog, owned in partnership with PK, was called Reenadoon. It would have been outlandish to believe that we would both be millionaires by Christmas of that year, but there was nothing wrong in hoping as we watched the dog grow and develop. Our plan was to pull off a coup in the dog's first race. It was to be at the Newbridge track in Kildare, close enough to Dunlavin in Wicklow, where my friend was principal teacher. We took our flying machine to Newbridge for the obligatory trial that entitled him to race. Being unfit, his trial time was only moderate.

The serious work then began. Reenadoon was placed in training in Dunlavin, with a card-playing friend Chris Lawlor, the local chemist, as operations manager. I journeyed down frequently to see him and arranged a series of trials in Chapelizod in Dublin as part of the preparations. He was on the best food menu available and making terrific progress.

We informed the Newbridge track manager that we wished to enter our dog for a race and were duly given a date for a particular

Wednesday meeting. The Chapelizod boss advised us that a run under lights on Sunday night would be the ideal final phase of preparations. The Lizard, as the Chapelizod track was known, was not a registered one, and ran a meeting on Sunday nights when there was no opposition from official tracks. Of course 'official dogs' were not supposed to race in such places, but there was a way round that problem: we renamed our white hope as 'Brown Bramble' and entered him for a race carrying a very minor prize. We placed a bet on him also because we knew his potential, but we didn't go heavy as the Sunday Lizard bookies were a cautious lot and easily frightened.

To our amazement, he failed to win – despite definite assistance from a friendly hare-driver. It was infinitely worse when we learned that the winner's time was slower than any of the trials run by our hero on the same surface. The verdict of the experts present was that the dog was a dishonest one and failed on the test of determination to win. That is bad news for an owner, and we decided there and then to get rid of him by offering him for sale at public auction in Shelbourne Park as soon as possible.

Meanwhile he was due to race in Newbridge on the coming Wednesday, and we decided to let him take his chance. There was no question of backing a 'jady' dog, and so we kept our hands in our pockets. He opened as favourite, then drifted in stages to 5/1 as they went to traps without a shilling of our money on him. That should have been the moment for faith, but we held firm.

The *Wicklow People* of the following week carried the sad story: 'Bookies' fortune continued in the third race when Wicklow tracker Reenadoon won readily at 5/1.'

The cutting from the *People* has browned with age in my wallet.

He was sold for the sum of 80 guineas at the Shelbourne Park sales, and the last reference to him was an insert in the *Sporting Press* a month later showing that he had won a good race at the King's Heath in Birmingham before being disqualified in his next race for displaying 'propensities to fighting'.

The Lizard experts had real foresight after all.

But the dog had given us fantastic excitement, even if mixed with some exasperation. And isn't that the way with racing in all parts of the globe, whether it's horses, dogs or camels?

During my early years in Dublin I played football for the Geraldine Club. My outstanding memory comes from a league game – it could have been against St Mary's of Saggart – in which I played full forward and scored three goals. As I turned round following the third I could hear my old friend from Baile Bhúirne days, John Long from Ventry, shouting loudly from his centre-back berth: 'Mo cheol thú, a Mhichíl, caith baothléim.' As ever he was smiling and prancing about in delight – a football field was truly his paradise.

Naturally I was delighted with myself, but I was brought down to earth early the following week. Máirín Dunleavy from the Blasket Islands, a friend of my sister Eileen, apparently met Declan Horgan from Killarney at some Dublin function on the Monday night. She mentioned that she had heard of my starring role on Sunday and asked Horgan, another Geraldine's man, about it. He confirmed the facts, but added:

'Isn't it very sad about the goalkeeper?'

'What's wrong with him?'

'I was walking along O'Connell Street this evening, and I saw him making baskets in a window.'

Whatever association catered for the needs of the blind in the 1950s operated such a window between the Carlton cinema and where the Royal Dublin Hotel stands today. I often stopped and watched the skilled craftsmen at work, but never identified the goalkeeper I had sent the wrong way three times in the one match.

Chapter Seven

My conversion to hurling was brought about by the Wexford team of the 1950s, and to this day they remain my favourite hurling team of all time. The country had heard of Nick Rackard throughout the 1940s as a lone campaigner for a place for Wexford in the hurling world. I had seen him play both hurling and football, and the same drive was evident no matter what the game was. His position was full forward, and in football his style was that of a rugby forward: head down and go for the line.

Hurling was his true love, and as early as 1943 he became the first player from his county to play in a Railway Cup final. That was progress as the men from the south-east had not won a Leinster title in hurling since 1918. He went to St Kieran's College in Kilkenny in 1938, proclaiming his roots by having purple-and-gold trimmings on his hurleys. He won everyone over when starring regularly on the college teams. He was a Wexford senior before he left Kieran's, and the county's cause was his for ever more. The breakthrough came with the winning of the Leinster title of 1951.

I remember the obvious pride of the players as they marched round before the game with four Rackards in the parade: goalkeeper Jimmy, defenders Bobby and Billy, and Nicky at full forward. They beat League champions Galway in the All-Ireland semi-final, but did not really stand up to the experienced Tipperary in the final. Yet, they had that quality that made spectators take notice of them even in defeat. They were big men and played a manly sporting game, catching the sliotar more often than was customary at the time. I looked forward to seeing them in action every chance I got, and the story that the Rackard home was once that of the patriot noted in song and story as 'Kelly, the boy from Killanne' added to the sense of history in the making.

Tell me who is the lad with the bright curling hair
He who rides at the head of the band
Seven feet is his height with some inches to spare
And he looks like a king in command.

That was Nick Rackard to me, and I got the opportunity to talk about his exploits when broadcasting several Oireachtas finals; the Slaneysiders won in 1951, 1953, 1955 and 1956 with a fair bit of style. They attracted a huge following for every match, and it was no surprise when their All-Ireland final meeting with Cork in 1954 drew a crowd of 84,856, still a record for a hurling match. Rackard had scored 7–7 against Antrim in the semi-final, and there was a feeling that their great moment was not far away.

I watched the final from Hill 16 in the company of Seán Murphy, the Kerry footballer then getting ready for his final against Meath a fortnight later. I can still feel the tension that gripped the ground during the parade. (I actually like pre-match parades.)

Christy Ring was going for his record eighth All-Ireland medal and was the centre of most people's attention. There was never much between the teams, and Wexford could easily have established a good lead before Johnny Creedon got a goal for Cork that provided the winning margin.

Television had not yet come, but some film footage of Ring playing in that match came to light quite recently. A Cork priest, home from the missions, attended the final carrying an ordinary cine-camera with which he was recording scenes from Ireland for friends. A shot of players kissing the bishop's ring was on the priority list, and he captured Ring in this role as Cork captain.

Fortunately he let the camera run now and then during the match and recorded some of the maestro's action for posterity. Film-maker Joe McCarthy got hold of the footage in time for inclusion in a documentary about Ring that was broadcast in March 2004, the twenty-fifth anniversary of his death.

The crowds continued to follow Wexford as they won their way to the Oireachtas final with Clare in October. I remember almost every puck of two fantastic games between the sides before Clare took the Tomás Ághas Cup in the end. I thoroughly enjoyed broadcasting both games *as Gaeilge* and was delighted to see a St Pat's colleague, Mick Hayes, play a starring role in goal for Clare. I often think that Jimmy Smyth scored the best goal of all time in the drawn match.

It all happened for the Yellow Bellies in 1955 – another Leinster title at the expense of Kilkenny, a win over Limerick in the All-Ireland semi-final, and a win at last in an All-Ireland final when they comprehensively beat Galway for the county's second All-Ireland, and the first since 1910.

A truly fine team had arrived on the scene, and their greatness was magnified by their subsequent performances. There was no question of sitting back and enjoying the spoils of victory. Instead they felt they had a duty to the game, and to their followers – by no means confined to Wexford – to continue to hurl like champions.

The Oireachtas was next up, and Kilkenny were beaten in the October final before a good crowd.

The National League had an autumn start back then; by May Wexford had won a place in the final against Tipperary. In between, Leinster won the Railway Cup by beating the stars of Munster in the St Patrick's Day final, before a crowd in excess of 46,000. This was a different Leinster team to the one of 1943 when Nick Rackard was the first and only hurler from the county to play in a final. This time there were ten purple-and-gold men on the winning team – the three Rackards, Art Foley, Nick O'Donnell, Jim English, Jim Morrissey, Ned Wheeler, Tim Flood and Séamus Hearne.

I will never forget the League final played in Croke Park on 6 May.

There had been whisperings that perhaps Wexford had got a 'handy All-Ireland' in September, considering that they had not met either Cork or Tipperary en route. Sunday would tell.

I watched the match from the centre of the large standing area then under the Cusack Stand – the perfect spot with the wind blowing from Canal to Railway. Wexford captain Jim English won the toss and decided that his men would face the breeze in the first half. Tipp did all the hurling and led by fifteen points at half-time.

It was beginning to look as if the whisperings were true.

But what a second-half performance – the greatest and most thorough recovery I have ever seen on a field of play, ending in a four-point victory for Wexford. The whisperings died a death that afternoon.

When the 1956 All-Ireland final came along, Wexford were matched against Cork, the team that had denied them victory two years earlier. The attendance was immense – the second-highest on record at 83,096 – and the atmosphere extraordinary. Hurling has thrown up many exciting and memorable finals, but that 1956 one stands comparison with the best whether you assess it on quality, atmosphere, drama, sportsmanship, impressive individual performances, continuity of play or all six wrapped up together.

Wexford led at half-time, but it looked ominous for them when Cork forged two points ahead early in the second half. The champions recovered to lead by two points close to the end.

The real drama was yet to come, and Christy Ring and Wexford goalkeeper Art Foley were the key actors.

There are at least two versions of what happened as Ring drove hard towards the Wexford goal. One states that he fired a powerful shot that was on target for a goal until Foley blocked, held and cleared to safety. It continues with Ring shaking Foley's hand and congratulating him on the excellence of the save.

I recorded the other version from Foley for an RTE series in conjunction with the GAA centenary celebrations in 1984 – admittedly nearly thirty years after the event. What was Art's recollection?

I paraphrase: 'Ring was approaching. He was slightly off balance – a fellow Corkman may have caused it. His shot was rising – it might even have gone over the bar; I stuck out my hurley, the ball glanced off it and Mick Morrissey cleared it away.'

In other words, he never caught the sliotar in his hand, as millions believe he did. By the way, Micheál O'Hehir's commentary, which is available, has him blocking but not catching.

And did Ring dash to the goal line to congratulate his adversary?

According to Art he did advance, and words were exchanged.

It was the defining moment of that wonderful All-Ireland final, and before long Wexford tore down the field for Nick Rackard to blast home another goal.

It secured the county's greatest ever triumph.

I saw it all and it was pure magic; however, the immediate aftermath must be unparalleled in world sport. Rather than race towards team-mates in the ecstatic moment of victory, Bobby Rackard and Nick O'Donnell approached Christy Ring and raised him high on their shoulders in acknowledgement of possibly the greatest hurler that ever lived. To them there would be plenty of time for celebration, but right at the death of that All-Ireland final there was an opportunity to acclaim Ringey's contribution to hurling and the gallantry of his attempt at winning a ninth All-Ireland medal.

Why shouldn't they be my favourite team of all time? I am far from being alone among non-Wexford people. Even a team chosen and trained in heaven would be unlikely to dislodge them.

The 1950s was a memorable decade in football. The Sam Maguire Cup was taken in triumph to seven different counties; only the incredible 1990s, when Sam went to eight counties, bettered that spread. The 1950s tour began in Mayo, and before the decade was out it had visited Cavan, Meath, Kerry, Galway, Louth and Dublin.

Those times also marked the arrival on the scene of a player who was to become an icon of Gaelic football – Mick O'Connell from Valentia Island in Kerry. And one can never dismiss the first appearance of a new-style Dublin team – in a way the most significant development in football of the past fifty years.

A game needs to be vibrant and have strong support in areas of large population, and the Dublin team of the 1950s ensured that it would be so in the capital for evermore. Hitherto many players from other counties domiciled in Dublin were selected for the county team, according to the practice of the time. It is easy to understand why that was so: they were good players for a start, and unable to play for their home clubs due, among other things, to problems of transport during the war.

The Dublin team that won the All-Ireland of 1942 had two players from the Dingle area at midfield: Joe Fitzgerald from the Gaeltacht, who captained the side, and Mick Falvey from the town of Dingle. It was stranger still to see a third man from the same stretch of country opposing them in the All-Ireland final that year, when Dan Kavanagh of Dún Chaoin was one of Galway's midfielders. That must be a record in Gaelic games – three players from Corca Dhuibhne in West Kerry at midfield in an All-Ireland final when Kerry was not involved!

By the way, Dan Kavanagh has two more claims to fame. He played later with Kerry and won an All-Ireland medal in 1946, and he is credited with introducing Brylcreem to West Kerry. Being a student of engineering at University College Galway, he was well versed in the rages of the time, one of which was the use of hair oil. He became a disciple, and so the new religion found its way into the Kerry Gaeltacht. It was an immediate hit, and it must have been good for the hair, as to this day you will not find that many bald men around Dunquin. Dan himself is now in his eighties, living in Killarney, and the hairline still reaches well down his forehead. If players were allowed to endorse products then as now, it is possible that some imaginative promotional agent could have made a millionaire of the young footballer.

In addition to the midfielders, other non-natives featured on that 1942 Dublin team. Caleb Crone of Cork was at corner back and won an All-Ireland medal with his native county in 1945. Paddy Henry from Mayo was at halfback, and another Kerryman, Jimmy Joy, was on the forty. They and others like them gave great service to Dublin football, but the scene changed towards the end of the 1940s. A rule was introduced confining eligibility to play football for Dublin to natives and those who had played at under-age level in the county. The change may have been inspired by the rise to prominence of the St Vincent's Club and success for the minors in inter-county competition. It has been extremely good for Dublin football and the GAA at large.

The new Dublin caused the first real ripple of excitement when winning the National League title of 1953. They attracted a colourful and vocal following that did not need programmes to identify 'their own'. The team had an extraordinary make-up – fourteen St Vincent's players and a goalkeeper called Pascal O'Grady from the Air Corps club.

Dublin's opposition in the League final happened to be All-Ireland champions Cavan, but they were brushed aside by the fast-moving football of youthful Dublin. There were many commendable features to their play, such as the long kicking of Mick Moylan at corner back, the dashing play of Norman Allen, Jim Crowley and Cathal O'Leary further out, and the dynamism of Ollie Freaney and Kevin Heffernan up front. But the most lasting impression on me was the utter enthusiasm surrounding the team, which was almost contagious. I think John D. Hickey put everything in proper focus when describing the game in Monday's *Independent*: he finished his paragraph of praise with the observation that 'even their misses were good'.

The importance of that League success has never been adequately acknowledged. Incidentally, I missed the opening quarter of that final because Radio Éireann had asked me to do a live ten-minute preview of the final in Irish from the GPO studio in Henry Street, after which I made the mad dash on my bicycle to Croke Park and my usual berth underneath the Cusack Stand.

Times were certainly different then – there was no problem about leaving an unlocked bike leaning against the Railway wall and finding it still there after the game.

An All-Ireland title was always a target for the Blues, and disappointments along the hard road were put to positive use. The first came in the championship of that year shortly after the League success. I remember the dejection that descended on Dublin followers in Navan that day when beaten by Meath.

Hopes were naturally high, and I once heard the late Noel Drumgoole talk about the entry to Páirc Tailteann on that occasion.

A Dublin fruit dealer outside the gate recognized Kevin Heffernan, and like thousands of other enlightened followers she had her own piece of advice for Heffo: 'Go in there and dismantle them fellows.'

It did not happen for them, but who would be surprised by a Meath win; the nucleus of the great champion side of 1949 was there and proud of the burgeoning status of football in the Royal County.

Dublin experienced a further dose of disappointment in 1954.

But by the time summer 1955 came along there was hope on a scale never experienced in Dublin, before signalling a light at the end of a tunnel reaching into the depths of September. The cause of it all was the brilliant football being played by Dublin on the way to another League title culminating in a win over Meath.

The Dubs' winning margin was a staggering twelve points over the defending All-Ireland champions, and once again the team was predominantly Vincent's – eleven from the club started the game and another, Mossy Whelan, came on as a substitute. When the teams met again in the Leinster final the margin was even greater: Dublin 5–12, Meath 0–7.

Football hype was now at a record height, and if television existed at the time it would have zoned in on Gaelic football for most of the time. The talk was primarily about Dublin, though they were not universally popular. There was a perception that the Dubs felt that their brand of football was superior to the old-fashioned catch-and-kick for which Kerry and others were famous.

After two drawn All-Ireland semi-finals, the replays in Croke Park produced the ideal All-Ireland final pairing of Kerry v Dublin. It was billed as the clash of the new versus the old, east versus west, urban versus rural, Dublin versus the rest and everything short of heaven versus hell. Dublin were strong favourites, and in all the hype not enough significance was attached to a few Dublin injuries. The great battler Norman Allen was ruled out with an injury, the scare about a late injury in training to midfielder Jim McGuinness turned out to be factual, and captain Denis Mahony was on alert with a threatened appendicitis.

Such a backdrop suited Kerry and their shrewd trainer Dr Éamonn O'Sullivan.

When the big day eventually came, 87,102 spectators jammed Croke Park. The teams provided a great exhibition of Gaelic football, with Kerry always a shade the better side, inspired by the lordly captain John Dowling at midfield. It had been said that it would be a test between the old football and the new, and if old meant catching and kicking, then it must be said that catching was a major factor in Kerry's win. I recall a few great high fetches by Jerome O'Shea in the Kerry goal mouth towards the end of the game, with no Dub around to challenge him seriously. It was the same at centrefield, where Denny O'Shea was able to lend good support to Dowling in the aerial tussles.

Kerry had good fielders also in the halfback line, where all good teams must show strength. Seán Murphy, John Cronin and Tom Moriarty were confident from the opening seconds, and an injury to Moriarty early in the game did not affect the team's pattern of play in the slightest.

It would be wrong to attribute Kerry's win to old-time football; it was a blend of both styles that gave them victory. That 1955 All-Ireland victory ranks as one the Kingdom's most satisfying performances ever, and in hindsight it was cruel on Dublin that most of the country celebrated with Kerry.

The powerful and popular Dowling was the Kerry hero. I remember being on Hill 16 another day when Kerry and Dublin were again in action, but Kerry were slow in coming out on to the field. There was speculation among some Dublin followers as to the cause of the delay, and one of them offered the view that they were possibly trying to get the chains off Dowling in the Kerry dressing room. The Strand Road man had that type of effect on people who did not know him.

The disappointment of Dublin followers after the defeat of 1955 was immense. I have never witnessed such utter deflation among followers to this day, but in fairness to them they did not seek an angle for complaint.

I still cannot figure out why the Dublin tactics dictated that full forward Kevin Heffernan should stay close to goal rather than wander like the will-o'-the-wisp he had been when destroying the Meath defence in the Leinster final. I knew what was going on in the Kerry camp prior to the game, and it was almost taken for granted that Heffo would roam. The possibility was brewing great fear in the south-west because fullback Ned Roche had never been tested for mobility outfield. His forte was close play round the goal area; that, surprisingly, is what he had to contend with in that much-talked-about All-Ireland final.

Once the game had settled into history, there were positive aspects for Dublin to dwell on. They never really gave up and were going strong at the finish. I have no trouble in calling to mind the superconfident Ollie Freaney scoring a goal from a close-in free late in the game. He wouldn't be the type of man who would attribute any great element of luck to the result, and it was that belief that brought a worthy team the just reward of an All-Ireland title three years down the hard road.

A win over Derry in the 1958 final brought an end to sixteen years of drought. Ten Vincent's players started in the final and, as happened in 1955, the sturdy, silent Whelan came on as a sub. Kevin Heffernan was captain, and I remember being in the dressing room when he returned with the Sam Maguire Cup. I went along to congratulate Kevin, who was a colleague of my brother Paddy in the ESB. He seemed drained of all energy as he sat down in the dressing room under the Cusack Stand. Like all first-time winners he was thinking of the heartbreaks and other setbacks that now magnified the satisfaction of victory.

Both Dublin and Kerry could then look back on the decade with fond memories. In 1955 they had laid the foundation stone of the greatest rivalry in Gaelic football. Several chapters were with the gods for release at future dates.

A Football Team of the Century was selected as part of the GAA's centenary celebrations in 1984, and a Team of the Millennium sixteen years later. Mick O'Connell was chosen at midfield on each occasion.

The teams were the work of appointed selectors, but public opinion would have come to the same conclusion in O'Connell's case. He was the sort of player whose brilliance and style in the arts of football ensured that his name will remain legendary as long as Gaelic football is played. Top midfield players of the present day are always compared to Mick, and that is the greatest tribute of all.

I heard tell of the Valentia wonder long before he pulled on a Kerry jersey. My uncle Joe married a Valentia woman by the name of Enda Mawe, who happened to be godmother to the youngest son of Jeremiah O'Connell. Enda is now in her nineties, and when I met her recently she spoke again about the day that Mick was brought to the church to be christened: 'We travelled in a sidecar, and I was holding the baby and in terror of my life that I would drop him – the island road was not the best, and the horse was moving well at right angles to our position facing the hedge. Jeremiah shouted at me every now and then not to drop that child, but I held on and we got to the church on time.'

I wouldn't be too surprised if the catching ability associated with the name of O'Connell in his football life wasn't nurtured along the Valentia road on his first day out of home – he might have been the one doing the catching.

Joe, Enda and their children were regular visitors to Dingle, and whenever I met Joe he was always raving about the skills of this amazing young godson of Enda's. Joe had won a Munster Junior championship medal as a fullback with Kerry in 1927 and was a good judge. He was the first from Dún Síon to wear a Kerry jersey and the only one until my nephew Micheál, a son of Náis and Bridie, captained the senior team in a League game against Down after winning a Kerry county championship with West Kerry in 1990.

Joe always predicted that Mick would put Valentia firmly on the football map, and he certainly lived up to the promise. He played minor for the county in 1955 and was a member of a team beaten by Tipperary. He made an impression with his high fielding and accurate kicking, and was picked for the seniors the following year. It was an achievement for a nineteen-year-old to be selected on a senior championship team defending an All-Ireland title won with class against Dublin less than a year earlier.

I was there to see him and the promising twenty-year-old Tom Long line out against Cork in the old Athletic Grounds by the Lee. Kerry were lucky to earn a draw, but the new lads were classed a success and picked for the replay in Killarney.

I was there also, but this time as commentator – my first time outside of Croke Park and my first commentary in English. Phil Greene, then Head of Sport in Radio Éireann, had contacted me during the week with the news that the station was planning to broadcast more than one game on certain Sundays, and he wanted me to be part of it. I was glad to oblige and arrived in Fitzgerald Stadium in plenty of time.

I was used to getting glimpses of the Hill of Howth from Micheál O'Hehir's box in Croke Park, but it could not compare with the majestic sweep of the McGillicuddy Reeks visible from the Killarney box. For that reason it remains my favourite venue for a sporting contest.

I remember Mick playing on the wing at first, alongside Mick Gould of Macroom, and later at midfield. In my commentary I used my classified information on Mick, and the knowledge I had about Seán Murphy from our days in Baile Bhúirne and from sharing accommodation with him in Dublin for a few years. And wasn't that Niall Fitzgerald playing for Cork who used to travel from Macroom to Baile Bhúirne to play football, and who was the first person I ever saw pole-vaulting in our field in the Coláiste? It was Fitzie himself who scored the winning point for Cork – over the bar on the mountain end of the field as the last seconds ticked away. In a strange way I, a Kerryman, was glad for him. Though he was a Macrompian and not a student in Coláiste Íosagáin, we regarded him as one of us.

I enjoyed that broadcast, and there was no hurry out of the town once proceedings ended. The big news of the day for the observant was that a new Gaelic star was launched in defeat – the islander Mick O'Connell.

Over the next sixteen years, omitting a two-year break due to premature retirement, he thrilled thousands all over Ireland and beyond with countless displays of Gaelic football at its best. Counting a replay in 1972, he played in ten All-Ireland finals, winning four and captaining the champion team in 1959. By disposition he was a quiet man and not overfond of some of the trappings that go with the game. That might explain how the Sam Maguire was left in the Croke Park dressing room in the aftermath of the 1959 final while Mick headed for the next train out of Dublin to the island life he always loved. The rest of the players were celebrating in a Bray hotel as Mick completed the last leg of the homeward journey by rowing across to Dairbhre. Undoubtedly they were of the opinion that the captain had taken the famous trophy. But those who really knew him would understand that he would be uneasy with such a gigantic ornament on the train and would prefer the anonymity of a quiet corner.

Cleaners found the Sam Maguire Cup in the dressing room sometime on Monday.

I have often been asked what qualities made Mick O'Connell unique. I could have a shot at explaining and still be wide of the true mark because he had the mind of a true sporting genius. He believed in the purity of the skills of Gaelic football, and his passion was to try to perfect them and display them in an atmosphere of a fair contest.

I would say that D. J. Carey in hurling plays with the same attitude.

For Mick the real joy was in the execution of the art in contest without resorting to fouling or other unfair means. Through practice and maintaining a high level of fitness he was a master of the skills of the game. He was an athlete for a start, with sound limbs, great strength, a strong frame and weight that belied his supple appearance. He was good at timing his jump and going very high for the catch. The late Séamus Murphy, his midfield partner for Kerry for a season or two, once told me: 'I was waiting under a dropping ball with Phil Stuart of Derry in the All-Ireland semi-final of 1958 when I caught a glimpse of a pair of knees above my shoulder level and hands gripping the ball. It was O'Connell.'

As soon as the ball was elsewhere, Séamus told Mick that from then on the 'high ones' were his and that he himself would 'stay down'. O'Connell was equally good with both feet at kicking, whether from ground or hand.

At his best he was unequalled, and that is why the memory of him will endure. There were days when his best was not manifested, and that is more clearly understood from a story told to me in two parts by another former Kerry great, Tom 'Gega' O'Connor.

Gega won five All-Irelands with Kerry between 1937 and 1946, when Paddy Kennedy was the leading midfielder of the era. O'Connor emigrated to New York in 1949 and thus went several years without seeing Kerry in action at home. One day he picked up a magazine that contained an article on football in which Mick O'Connell was compared to Paddy Kennedy. Gega felt it was imperative for him to see the reincarnation of the player he regarded as the greatest of all time.

He visited Ireland with that in mind, and when I met him a few days later he told me his story. Alas, there was no comparison, he said: Kennedy was easily the king.

A year or two later Tom was home from New York again, and we crossed the street in Dingle to meet. 'Do you remember,' says he after a while, 'the time we were talking about Kennedy and O'Connell.'

'I do well,' says I.

'Well, I saw him play in a League final in New York since, and I must admit that my friend Kennedy could never play football like that man did.'

I suppose the moral is that comparisons, especially about different eras, should never be based on a single match or even season.

I never saw Paddy Kennedy play, but from what I have heard of him I accept that he, too, was special and, like O'Connell, very stylish. I knew him in Dublin later, and he was a quiet, unassuming man who was always quick to dwell on the virtues rather than the failings of players under discussion.

That reminds me of words spoken by his son Brian shortly after the Team of the Millennium was announced. Paddy hadn't made it, and the midfielders were Mick O'Connell and Tommy Murphy of Laois, who was known as the 'Boy Wonder' in his youth.

Brian Kennedy made no attempt to argue the case for the inclusion of his late father. 'If my father was alive he would have been absolutely delighted that Tommy Murphy was picked on the Team of the Millennium – he often said to me that the Boy Wonder was the best footballer he had ever seen or played against.'

Enough said.

Chapter Eight

I did my Higher Diploma in Education in University College Dublin in 1953, and was offered a permanent job in O'Connell's Christian Brothers School in North Richmond Street, in the shadow of Croke Park, in September of that year. I hadn't applied, as I was quite happy in Seville Place, but the advice was that it was time to be thinking of permanency because at Larriers I was still a temporary supernumerary after three years of service.

Thus I moved to O'Connell's, while my brother Dónal, who was a qualified teacher by then, took my place in Larriers.

O'Connell's CBS is one of the most famous schools in Ireland. The foundation stone was laid by Daniel O'Connell in 1828, when the Liberator was at the height of his fame. The school had a nationwide reputation for producing excellent students, many of whom went on to third-level education or entered the civil service. Listed among the past pupils you will find names such as Seán Lemass and John A. Costello, who served as Taoisigh, and Seán T. O'Kelly, who succeeded Douglas Hyde as President of Ireland in 1945, having spent years as a TD and Cabinet Minister.

From the sporting world there was the Olympic athlete Ronnie Delaney, Irish soccer international player and manager Eoin Hand, and plenty of Gaelic players of note, including Ollie Freaney and John McCarthy, who won All-Ireland medals with Dublin, and the fantastic golfer Joe Carr, who won three British Amateur Championships.

And then there was Micheál O'Hehir, the undisputed king of the sporting airwaves.

Pupils came from far and near to attend the school. Preparing for confirmation one year, I recall discovering that twenty-seven parishes were represented in the class. Not all were in Dublin, either; counties Meath and Kildare were always represented in the school.

Lunch break lasted one and a half hours, and in those traffic-free days it was not unusual for pupils to journey by bus to places as far away as Howth, Terenure and Drimnagh for lunch. It was never a problem to make it back in time.

O'Connell's had a good name as a school, and I often wondered why certain institutions carried such a reputation and it escaped others. I concluded that it depended more on the level of parents' interest and support for their children's education than on any other element.

I was to spend more than twenty-five years at the school, divided between the primary and secondary sections. At the beginning, the staff was composed predominantly of brothers; now the school is administered by lay teachers. I do not necessarily see that as a negative development, and said so in a foreword to a publication on the occasion of the school's 150th anniversary celebrations in 1979. I looked at the development as a sign that the original mission of the brothers – the creation of an educated laity – had been accomplished.

There were few if any problem pupils or parents in O'Connell's when I started teaching there in the mid 1950s. There was a slight departure from general school routine on Thursdays, when students from the nearby Clonliffe College came for an hour's practice of preaching and teaching religion in front of an audience of young scholars. Clonliffe student Joe Drumgoole was once assigned to me, and we struck up a typical Kerry–Dublin relationship from the first week on.

He was a Vincent's man and brother of the late Noel, who played hurling and football for Dublin and captained Leinster to the Railway Cup hurling title on St Patrick's Day 1962. It was a historic day for Dublin because there were eight Dublin players on the team.

Joe Drumgoole, later a well-known and modern-thinking parish priest in the diocese, was always involved in sport and passionately interested in it; however, in those pre–Vatican II times, newspapers were not allowed in places such as Clonliffe College. So our arrangement – not submitted to any council for ratification – was a means to further the education of the weekly visitor: I kept the sports pages from all papers over the preceding week, and Joe read them avidly during the practice hour while I preached the word of God.

During the mid 1960s I transferred to the secondary department of O'Connell's on the invitation of the superior, Brother Purcell. I enjoyed teaching older students, particularly in the subjects of Economics and Accountancy. I had studied for a B. Comm. degree and DPA in University College Dublin, and the commercial element of the syllabus at OCS was being expanded at the time.

It was during those courses at UCD that I saw Garret FitzGerald for the first time. There was no way I would opt for a greyhound or horse race in preference to listening to Garret's rapid output of words when he enthused about the economics of transport, on which he was expert. I was also impressed by the stately pose of Professor Paddy Lynch, as he expounded on the intricacies of political economy.

While Garret was good for the political life of the country when he took that road, he was a huge loss to the university life of Ireland. I once heard him say that he had a Kerry connection. When his parents returned from London, where they had met in the Gaelic League, their first Irish home was the coastguard station in Ventry. If they had stayed, Garret might well have won All-Irelands with Kerry; he could also have been Páidí Ó Sé's manager in later years.

And Páidí might even have joined Fine Gael.

For me as for many secondary teachers, supervising the state exam-inations of the Intermediate and Leaving Certificate was part of the year's work. It was never the practice of the Department of Education to appoint people to perform the function in the school where they taught, and thus I did the needful in various institutions round Dublin.

The most unusual posting was to Mountjoy Prison. My exam

centre was located in the area known as St Patrick's. On the first morning, having given out the papers, I informed the students of the amount of time allowed for answering. One of the students informed me immediately that I should not mention time. 'The only time that matters in here is the one you are given when you come in,' he said, by way of explanation.

Another thing I learned on that first day was that the Mountjoy students were very suspicious of authority in general. The warder on duty outside the door brought me in a pot of tea and some biscuits at eleven, as is the custom in normal schools. I had spoken to him in the morning, and he came across as a genuine person with a great interest in sport. As the class was small that day I asked him to bring in a few extra cups for the lads and he duly obliged, but I was surprised when they refused and advised me that it could be unwise to drink tea made by him.

I drank it anyway, and I found it to be as good as I ever got elsewhere. I arranged that I brought in the tea the following day, and this time it was acceptable to the students – perhaps they thought it had been made by me.

A student who was keen on Irish complained to me one day that there was a bias against the language in the prison, and that he was not allowed to listen to Radio na Gaeltachta. I agreed to check the problem and discovered that the ban in fact was against transistors that carried a VHF band, which could be a security risk.

A general-election campaign was in progress during the examinations, and I had an ideal opportunity, if I'd wished to avail of it, to give a good catch phrase to the opposition parties. A particular student was given leave from the prison in order to attend his sister's wedding, and seeing that he was being prepared for release he was given an extra day. But to everybody's surprise he clocked in well ahead of schedule.

He had a very good explanation when I sought a reason for the premature return: 'The prices out there are gone mad – I couldn't believe how much they wanted for a portion of chips. I could not afford to stay out any longer.'

★

With the passing years I got to know the geography of Dublin, from the sea to the western suburbs, as well as any taxi driver. There are no better teachers than shanks' mare and a bicycle, and both were very popular in Dublin up to the mid 1960s at least. It helped also that as a single person I lived for spells in digs and flats in various parts of the city, and that was an education in itself.

In the mid 1950s my brother Dónal, sister Máire and I bought a house in Dundrum and lived there for a few years. Máire and I moved again when Dónal got married. I stayed for a few years in a rather large establishment in Brighton Square, Rathgar, where an interesting collection of individuals resided. They included a teacher or two, an archaeologist, a dentist, a butcher, a solicitor, a tradesman and a part-time barman. All shades of religion (including atheism) and political opinion were represented, and lively discussion was the order of the day and night. That house was the scene for many hectic card sessions, nearly always following a preamble in one of the local pubs. Though I was a non-drinker, I will admit that some of the best debates I ever witnessed or took part in were conducted in taverns.

There is no shortage in this world of people who promulgate their views in a manner that is most unaccommodating to themselves. One of the residents of the Brighton Square house, a communist called Séamus, had a girlfriend who was totally against drink and refused to go into a pub at any time. But she was loyal to Séamus and dutifully stood at the door regardless of weather, waiting until the entourage emerged refreshed for the next item on the entertainment agenda.

Usually it was poker or '25'.

I remember a problem arose later when Séamus and the girlfriend decided to get married, and it was made clear to the likeable communist that going to confession was part of the ritual. Of course, this was against his principles, but the good lady had principles also, and she won out. We brought Séamus to Whitefriar Street Church, where there was a priest known as 'Flash' Haughey on account of the brevity of the usual confession ceremony conducted by him.

Everything worked out wonderfully, and it makes a good case for the relaxation of principles at appropriate times.

The strangest memory I have of Brighton Square relates to an unusual sequence of events that happened after I had left the place. I am certain that it was May 1965 because Kerry were involved in a National Football League final with Galway in Croke Park on the Sunday of the week in question. I was giving a few of the Kerry players a final run round in Bushy Park, Terenure, on the previous Thursday evening, when I injured my knee. Donie O'Sullivan, one of Kerry's stalwarts of the time, was there, along with UCD student and county fullback Páid O'Donoghue and a few others hoping to make the team in due course. I assured them that the knee would be all right – it was a recurring weakness, and we left it at that. I then repaired to Brighton Square knowing that a card game was possible. My instinct proved to be correct.

The knee soon swelled considerably, and, while it did not impede my card-playing ability in the slightest, I eventually rang Seán Murphy, the former Kerry player with whom I had stayed for a couple of years, and now a doctor in the Mater Hospital. He was on night duty, but was due an hour off at 1 a.m. and promised to call as soon as possible.

There was an adjournment while the *glúin* was examined. Seán recommended that I check in at the accident bay in the Mater immediately. Most of the members of the card school decided that they would accompany me, and we were in the Mater in jig time.

While the knee, never as famous as Pat Spillane's, was undergoing further examination, I became aware of a bit of commotion outside in the waiting area. One of my friends had fallen asleep on a chair and rolled off, triggering fears of an attack of one sort or the other. He recovered quickly, and normality reigned again. The end result was that I was detained and the rest of the school dismissed.

It had been quite a day: teaching until four in the evening . . . a bit of golf in Grange . . . some training in Bushy Park . . . a poker session . . . and finally a bed in a ward of the Mater Hospital for a few hours before a new dawn.

There was no talk of trolleys in corridors back in the 1960s.

The knee was so swollen that not much could be done in the short term. As Friday and Saturday passed along I made plans for a friend of mine to call close to match time on Sunday to get me to Croke Park for the clash of Kerry and Galway. It was seen as a crucial test for both teams, especially Kerry. They had been beaten by Galway in the All-Ireland semi-final of 1963 and in the final of 1964, and another defeat would not do the morale of the Kingdom any good.

I made one drastic mistake in the planning for Sunday afternoon: I confided in a Galway nurse. She saw to it that my clothes had been moved from the wardrobe by 2.45 p.m., leaving me with no option but comply with medical advice and rest the knee until the swelling went down. It was exasperating to listen to the match in a bed that was less than a mile from the Hogan Stand. Kerry were leading by a point, 0–8 to 0–7, with the egg timer almost empty. The ball landed in the Kerry goal mouth . . . Mattie McDonagh got possession . . . the ghosting Séamus Leydon was close by . . . and the green flag was soon waving.

Galway had won again, but the goal was controversial. Did McDonagh pick the ball off the ground? Now the Ballygar man is a good friend of mine, and he has assured me many a time that there was a perceptible bounce before he took possession. He is a very honourable man and, after all, he was the closest to the action at that crucial moment. He also had a sharp eye that enabled him to be rated as one of the best poker players west of the Shannon. I am willing to accept his version in spite of equally sharp-eyed Kerrymen holding a different view.

Don't all good games leave a talking point or two?

Chapter Nine

It was in the mid 1960s that I made a move that brought my nomadic meanderings through the city to an end.

On my return from holidays I happened to be talking to Gerry O'Donohue, a colleague in school. In the course of the conversation he enquired about my current place of abode. Never being a person who devoted too much time to organization of matters, I said I had not yet decided. He told me the following day that his aunt had a vacant apartment in her house in Rathgar and that he would check it for me if I wished.

A few days later I moved in to Templemore Avenue. It was within walking distance of Harold's Cross and not too far from Shelbourne Park, two of my favourite venues. It was no more than two miles from Grange Gold Club, where I was to be found pretty often, and crossing the city to O'Connell's was no great discomfort.

The owner of the house, Mrs McDowell, was a Dublin woman and proud of her Athlone roots. She had married Eddie McDowell, a member of a large family born in Moville in Donegal, and he had died rather suddenly in the late 1950s. Mrs McDowell herself was a wonderful character who managed to combine hard work, an adherence to principles and a great sense of adventure and humour. She had four daughters – Mary, Helena, Finola and Moya – whom I once jokingly described as delinquents; however, that description would fit most young people at some stage in their development.

Although I have always been an outdoor person, I did spend enough time about the place to get to know one of the 'delinquents' quite well. Helena was the most petite of the lot, an auburn-haired student nurse at the Mater Hospital. Some four years after my arrival in the house we were engaged and planning to marry by early summer 1970.

The news that I was settling down at last came as a surprise to my family. My father remarked that the decision would hardly interfere with my growth.

The first journey that Helena and I undertook as an engaged couple turned out to be a thrilling one. She was on duty in the Mater Hospital and due to finish at 7.30, which looked dead on time for a Saturday-night visit to Shelbourne Park. Matters became slightly more complicated when I got a call from Greyhound trainer Jack Murphy at about four in the afternoon. Jack, based in Kilmessan, County Meath, was trainer to whatever dogs I owned at the time, but they were not his immediate problem on that particular Saturday.

He had two runners in Dundalk that night, and he fancied both strongly, but as he was not feeling too well he wanted me to do a 'little business' for him at the track. The first was due to run at approximately quarter past nine and the second in the following race. I had a lovely single man's sports car at the time, a white Fiat, and in normal circumstances it would not have been difficult to make Dundalk on time if Helena and I left the North Circular Road a little after 7.30. But circumstances were not normal: snow greeted us out along the Ashbourne road.

A bad skid before Slane was halted by a good shoulder from an earthen ditch that miraculously straightened the car out on to the road again, leaving it racing like a good dog that takes a wallop at a bend. There was obviously some wing damage, but it was not the hour for inspection as I explained to Helena that a promise to Jack Murphy was almost sacred.

When we reached Slane the weather was so bad that I decided to phone the track in case racing was called off. The telephone in the kiosk at the corner did not work, and not wishing to waste precious time in calling the exchange I dashed in to Donegan's pub and got through from there.

The news was positive: 'The weather is bad here, but we always race in Dundalk, hail, rain or snow.'

It was a question then of confidence in my driving, as it was snowing more heavily than ever by now. I had a full licence dating back to the 1950s, but it had been acquired in a manner that fortunately no longer appertains: call in to the registration office, fill in a form, pay a pound and depart with a full licence. Four of us then decided one day to hire a car and learn how to drive – *mé féin*, Seán Ó hAiniféin, Patrick Kavanagh and Padraig Murphy. We went along to Murray's Car Hire close to Baggot Street Bridge, filled in another form, paid the fee and were handed the keys of a Ford Prefect.

There was no alarm when I asked that somebody from the garage drive the car out on to the street and face it down the slight incline. The idea was to get out to Wicklow as quickly as possible, and Padraig drove for the initial few miles. But we all felt there was nothing to it – in my case I was accustomed to dealing with flighty horses and capable of driving the old bike steadily with another passenger on the crossbar.

I was next to try the car. Soon my confidence was so high that I decided to light up a cigarette to prove my composure – I had seen cool people driving cars in films in that manner. We travelled back and forth through the roads of Wicklow that day, and by the time we returned to Murray's with the Prefect still to the good we believed we were all fit for the Monte Carlo Rally.

There are times when ignorance can be a boon.

The same confidence was there as Helena and I faced the rising ground out of Slane and on to Collon. The car quivered a little at the next bend, before a worse skid brought more contact with an earthen ditch, but miraculously once more the car righted itself and was on solid ground ready to sail yet again.

It was then that a concerned motorist, crawling in the opposite direction, got out of his car, ready to come to my assistance. One could not expect him to be aware of the gravity of my situation, and with the engine running all the time in my wounded white Fiat all I did was open the window and wave as we took off towards Dundalk for the fourth time. We duly reached the track only to see Hop It Billy, one of Jack's fancied runners, rounding the last bend as we got inside the gate: he was well clear of the field and went on to win at 3/1. Jack's money and my own was still in the pocket.

My ultimate decision was one that any sort of a gambler would make: place the lot on the second dog and hope for the best. The Lord looks after his own, and the second came up at the better odds of 7/2. It ended up a good night, and Jack did not mind when I deducted a little from a good bundle of pounds for repairs to a car wing-damaged in the call of duty.

The same Jack Murphy was one of the many fine characters that one meets in racing. He was a gifted horesman in his youth and bought and sold horses for clients in England, but training greyhounds was his real profession.

Luck plays its part all the time, and Jack was the recipient of an extraordinary touch of it once. He was at the Navan track one day when Larry Clancy from Kells arrived with a string of dogs for trials. He casually asked Jack to hold a few while he sorted trial details in the office. On his return there was the usual conversation about breeding, which led to Jack making an offer for one of the dogs on the basis that its sire was the same as that of one of his winners in Harold's Cross the night before. The deal was for £300, not a bad amount for an untried young dog in those days.

Jack told me about his acquisition when I met him at the track that night, but his expectations were no greater than would apply to any other unraced greyhound. The story had changed dramatically by the time I met him a week later: 'I gave that dog a trial, and he is so fast that I am afraid to race him.'

He was a good businessman and wisely decided not to race the 'machine' until he had sold him. He acted as an agent at the time for a Scotsman called Cyril Young, who went by Cyril Scotland as a greyhound owner. Jack's instructions were to be on the lookout for fast young dogs with a premium on early pace. He thought that his latest one, named Lively Band, fitted the bill admirably; Cyril was sent the details and a deal was quickly done.

He was a man of means, being a large shareholder in the Bank of Scotland, and he paid £3,000 for the unraced animal. Jack would train the dog, receive 10 per cent of its winnings, and a bonus of £1,000 if the Band should win a Derby.

It was the beginning of a fairy tale. The Band was unbeaten

when the Derby final came around in Shelbourne Park in September 1974. He was in his preferred trap one, with a favourite's chance of claiming the £11,000 first prize. We both had a long-odds interest on him, and Michael O'Carroll of RTE television had asked me to be on stand-by to interview a winning connection as soon as the race was over.

He even asked me did I know Jack Murphy!

In my opinion there was going to be only one winner, and I was with Jack in the centre of the track for the duration of the race. I am convinced there was telepathic communication between man and dog on that memorable occasion. As the hare sped along towards the traps, the Band was informed to steady up and be ready for a slick start; he did so and raced clear as Jack kept him posted on what was happening behind: 'Ger McKenna's dog [Wind Jammer] is only two lengths behind . . . I would be happier if you increased the lead . . . That's it, my boy!' And then as he rounded the last bend in total command came the greeting: 'Go on and come home alone as I always knew you would!'

The race had lasted only 29.11 seconds, but aficionados of the sport would have viewed it as a long, intense, operatic drama.

Jack would never race a dog that had even a minor injury. We had a setback when the Band was disqualified from taking his place in the final of the English Derby in White City the following year for showing propensities of fighting in the semi-final. Jack always maintained that his dog was innocent of the charge, and felt vindicated when he won the St Leger Classic in Limerick on his return.

Jack had an unfortunate ending to his life after developing motor neurone disease. He informed me of his plight one night in Shelbourne Park. I had come in a little late and was told by another friend that Jack's dog had won the first race by five lengths at the attractive price of 5/1. It was when I congratulated him later that he imparted the bad news he had got that very day.

It made the winning of Derbies and bets against the odds so insignificant in an instant, but in keeping with the nature of gambling he was amazingly philosophical about everything: 'They told me I have little chance of living for another year, but who knows . . . we must organize a big night for the Motor Neurone Disease Society in the Navan track shortly and do everything to help them.'

He did that in style and attended on the night, even though his condition was deteriorating rapidly with each passing day.

He also cooperated in the writing of a book on his life – growing up around Drumcollogher in Limerick, the football, his stint riding horses, the dogs, acting on the amateur circuit, playing inter-county football for Waterford, etc. The proceeds from sales of the book went to the Motor Neurone Society.

He was a loss to racing and a much greater loss to members of his family and a large circle of friends.

In those days, buying a house was part of the preparations for marriage. I must hold the record for the amount of time spent on the chore.

It happened thus.

Donie O'Sullivan, the Kerry football captain of that year, 1970, called to see me and mentioned that he had just bought a new house in Blanchardstown, where he was teaching at the time. His description appealed to me: it was a fairly big house, the walls were solid, it was in a secluded small estate to the back of the Greyhound Bar, plenty of open space, the builder was an honest man . . .

I asked Donie to enquire if any of the batch of twelve new houses in the estate was still available and if so to offer the builder whatever Donie himself had paid. He rang me the next day telling me that I had bought a house. I was unconcerned about not having viewed it or tested it for flaws that I would know nothing about anyway. On my visit to Grange that Wednesday afternoon I won a golf competition and a voucher that got me a kitchen table and six chairs that have survived to this day.

On our wedding day, Helena and I clocked the best time ever coming down the aisle of the Church of the Three Patrons in Rathgar: my late brother Paddy said it was 29.30 seconds from the sacristy to the church yard.

Helena and I have been blessed with eight children. She has always been the steadying influence on the team.

All our children are university graduates, and I believe that this qualification is of more value to them than if all my bets had won and given them a million euro each. We are very proud of all of them.

Helena's mother spent a considerable amount of time with us. I believe that the children learned as much from her as they did at school or university. Her fantastic spirit and zest for life lasted into the fine age of eighty-seven years.

She was never in robust health for a good number of years, but was willing to travel anywhere at short notice. Once, when she was well in her eighties, her daughter Finola wanted to bring her on a trip to South Africa, but doctor's advice was not in favour. In the end she wanted me to decide. Knowing the answer she was hoping for, I said: 'Why not?' She phoned the doctor and told him to be expecting a postcard from South Africa. She enjoyed the trip immensely and returned with the spirit of a teenager.

We hardly ever went on a holiday to Kerry without bringing her, and I doubt if the children would have travelled without her.

It was in our house that she died in 2001.

Only Doireann, the youngest of our children and now a postgraduate student, lives at home. She acts as my assistant at every match on which I commentate nowadays, as did each member of the family as they were growing up.

The eldest, Éamonn, has his own physiotherapy clinic in Maynooth and is married to Alison Kelly. They have three children: Caoimhe, Béibhinn and Tadhg.

Niamh currently works with Oki and is about to set up her own business in Germany. She and her husband, George, who is Greek, have a son whose name could yet cause some commentator a huge headache: Leonidas Ó Muircheartaigh Kalaitzidis.

Aonghus divides his time between Munich and Kansas working with General Electric.

Cormac is a consultant sports physician with the Singapore Sports

Council. He is engaged to Maybelle, who comes from that part of the world and was a classmate of his in UCD.

Neasa, also a doctor, works in the Mater Hospital in Dublin and is married to a former rugby player from Luton who bears a name that originated in the Glens of Antrim, Dominic Wilkinson.

Nuala is a barrister and divides her time between Geneva and New York, working on United Nations legal and human rights projects.

That leaves Éadaoin, who is currently doing postgraduate work in University College Galway. *Aoibhinn beatha an scoláire.*

Beatha dhuine a thoil has always been my motto – let each follow their own wishes. It is not a worry to us that some of our children live abroad, though I would be of a different opinion if it had been a case of forced emigration. They could have got employment in Ireland, and some may yet return. I understand the point the late Brian Lenihan was trying to make when he once said that emigration need not always be viewed as a bad feature of Irish life. There are thousands of people who were born in Ireland but live abroad at the moment, and they are avid followers of what is happening at home. Radio and Internet links have special significance for them, and it is for that reason that I greet them on air from time to time.

Chapter Ten

There was no radio in the Dún Síon of my young days. The nearest wireless set was a mile away in Sheehy's of Baile an tSagairt, and anyone anxious to come and listen was welcome at any time. I recall being there during an All-Ireland football final between Kerry and Galway; no theatre ever experienced a full house like Sheehy's kitchen and its immediate environs for that great drama. If the sound weakened or wobbled now and then it was left to Mikey, the youngest of the fourteen grown Sheehy offspring, to restore the equilibrium.

The year was either 1938 or 1939; if the former, it would have been the first of ninety-nine All-Ireland finals broadcast by Micheál O'Hehir. The notion of an All-Ireland final coming out of a box in the corner of a kitchen was far too complex to comprehend at my age, but it seemed to me that the *bosca* was made for excitement.

There was another radio a half-mile further afield in Kelliher's of Ballinvounig, and a third in the lighthouse that guards the entrance to Dingle Harbour. The town had a few as well, and the most popular location for people from our side of the parish was the *garda* barracks.

There was not a single radio station operating in Ireland when the first Dáil convened in 1918. The War of Independence and the Civil War had come and gone by the time a government with executive and administrative functions began doing what it was elected to do: improve the lot of citizens. There was general agreement that the new state should strive towards having its own radio service, as the more developed ones had. Judged in the context of the era it was an ambitious objective, but on 1 January 1926 Ireland's infant radio station, 2RN, commenced broadcasting.

The first words spoken on 2RN were in Irish, delivered by Douglas Hyde, later to become the first President of Ireland. It was entirely correct that the opening words were in the native language, and I would be equally adamant in upholding that principle for all nations. Thus an English person promoting cricket and the language that fostered it is a kindred spirit with anyone in this country working towards preservation of hurling, the Irish language or other aspects of native culture.

I use the word 'working' deliberately because we could easily have too many people in favour of this and that, with too few active in pursuit of the objective.

In August 1926 an Ó hÉigeartaigh from Cork is reputed to have presented himself in Croke Park in an excited state. He explained that 2RN was willing to carry a running commentary on the forthcoming All-Ireland hurling semi-final between Kilkenny and Galway. It was a revolutionary suggestion for the time: some two minutes from an athletics meeting in the United States was the total to date of live broadcasting of sport.

The GAA ran with the idea, and history was made on 29 August 1926 when that hurling semi-final went out live on air from start to finish. The scoreline of 6–2 to Kilkenny, 5–1 to Galway suggests that the game was a lively one and suitable for an exciting commentary. Sports broadcasting is now enormous business, and I think we should pride ourselves in the fact that the fledgling 2RN set it all in motion.

The commentator for that first broadcast, a Cork man called P. D. Mehigan, was a respected journalist with the *Irish Times*, cousin of Dr Scully in Dingle, a noted athlete in his day, well known as a red-coated judge on horseback at coursing meetings and, above all, a hurler of repute. He played for London against Cork in the All-Ireland final of 1902 and for Cork in the refixed final of 1905 against Kilkenny when the Cats were victorious in Dungarvan. Cork had won the original game, but as was common enough in those days an objection was lodged. It had been alleged that a member of the Crown Forces had been aboard Rebel Cork's team.

At any rate, more than a score years later Paddy Mehigan was back in the hurling limelight – this time as the pioneer of commentators. He continued to broadcast into the 1930s, and stories abound about the West Cork man. He is credited with enlisting a blind fiddler one day to continue his fiddling at the microphone until he himself returned after attending to a call of nature. There is even a story that his broadcasting career ended when he forgot to come back for the second half of an exciting match. Believe it if you have no better to do, but he was the first Irish sports commentator, and he set the scene for all of us privileged to follow. There should be a room to honour his memory in Croke Park.

Another early GAA commentator was Éamonn de Barra, whose career truly had an abrupt ending according to legend. He was working away one day in the mid 1930s when he found himself surrounded by republicans carrying guns and demanding that he hand over the microphone. He had little option, and the nation was given an unexpected message not related at all to sporting matters. The story is that de Barra never broadcast again.

And then there is the strange case of Father Michael Hamilton, later a respected Monsignor, who commentated on the 1937 football final between Kerry and Cavan, and gave Cavan as the winners when in fact the game had ended in a draw. It was a chaotic day in Croke Park, with restricted entry due to development works on the Cusack Stand and an inevitable breaking open of gates. The mistake was not the Monsignor's fault: the white flag had been waved to register what was apparently the winning score, which was duly recorded on the board by an unofficial enthusiast who had usurped the position of the scoreboard keeper. What the Monsignor did not know was that the referee had disallowed the score on the grounds that it had been a throw.

Chaos followed throughout Cavan when it became clear later that all the turf, coal and wood burned in bonfires had been a total waste. As for the Monsignor, he did not pursue a radio career any further.

A man I knew, Dave Hanly, broadcast the hurling final of 1938 three weeks after O'Hehir's first-ever commentary; the fact that his native Waterford was in opposition to Dublin may have been a factor in the choice. The day marked the last of Dublin's six

All-Ireland titles and was unique for the fact that Jim Byrne of the Eoghan Rua Club became the first and only Dublin native to win an All-Ireland hurling medal.

It was O'Hehir from then on, and he has the distinction of having broadcast a total of ninety-nine All-Ireland finals between hurling and football.

From the days of 2RN in the 1920s until the arrival of television in 1962, the radio had a monopoly of the airwaves. The coming of Radio Teilifís Éireann in 1962 was big news at the time; I missed the opening ceremony in Dublin, as I was enjoying the Christmas break in Kerry and television sets were as scarce in Dingle on that historic night as wirelesses were in 1926. I knew that my colleague Micheál O'Hehir was playing a role in the opening night's programmes and that he was to be Head of Sport for RTE.

I had seen a little television prior to that, courtesy of a teacher in O'Connell's, John Galligan. He lived in Malahide, where there was good reception for the staple diet of the time – the BBC in black and white. I admit that it was exciting, especially the current affairs programme *Panorama*. But it could not compare at all to RTE once I got back to Dublin, where sets were selling with the rapidity of mobile phones today. All programmes were popular. My favourite item of the day's schedule was the national anthem, an orchestral version that went out at the end of the day's broadcasting accompanied by images of Ireland at work. It was the ending that particularly appealed to me: an Aer Lingus plane ascending, and caressing the soft clouds before disappearing into the vastness of the sky. For me it symbolized the magnificent progress brought about by the people of Ireland in four decades of independence and signalled Ireland's readiness to open up and meet the world.

Television had great possibilities for promoting sport, but it was looked upon with suspicion in many quarters. The big fear was that live broadcasts could lead to a drastic reduction in the numbers that would attend matches. The GAA discussed the problem, and the arrangement arrived at gave RTE permission to televise the Railway Cup finals and All-Ireland semi-finals and finals live, provided that 50 per cent of the commentary was in the Irish language. Other sporting associations were not as enthusiastic at the outset, and I would say that the presence of Micheál O'Hehir on RTE's negotiating team was a factor in the GAA's decision to take a gamble.

The semi-finals of the All-Ireland football championships of 1962 were first on the live TV agenda. I had gone in July on a motorbike holiday to France and Spain with my friend of Baile Bhúirne days, John Hanafin, or Seán Ó hAiniféin as we knew him then. Unbeknownst to me, there were plans to involve me in the television broadcast. Even upon my return from holiday I was not easy to locate, as one who changed address frequently in those unmarried days. Eventually, while on a visit to the dogs I got a message to ring Una Gormley in RTE urgently. I did so and was told that Seán Óg Ó Ceallachain and I were to share the broadcast, alternating between Gaeilge from me and English from Seán. And that is how the closing stages of the championships of 1962 were relayed.

I don't think that the system of co-commentators worked that well, with its rigid adherence to changing from Irish to English on cue. It led to a critical review in one of the daily papers, which, by coincidence or otherwise, I did not read. I was therefore perplexed on receiving a note from Micheál O'Hehir telling me not to be worried: he never mentioned what the cause of the worry might be. When I met him on the following Sunday for the second semi-final he made another vague reference to it. At this stage I found out about the article, and got an idea also about how I had missed it in the paper in the first place. I recalled going into the paper shop in Dingle one day only to be told by Josie O'Connor that all copies had been sold. This could have been true, as it was in the middle of the tourist season, but my reading of it was that Josie had read the particular article and hadn't the heart to charge me for something containing criticism. She was that sort of person.

I have never heard anybody say that they enjoy receiving criticism, but I was never a great worrier, and anyway the point being made was that co-commentating did not work. Some genius hit upon a solution for the following year: why not relay the minor games on telly as well and have an exclusively Irish commentary, thereby fulfilling the requirement of 50 per cent Gaeilge in the overall package? This definitely was an Irish solution to an Irish problem, and I believe it worked very well.

Over the following twenty-three years or thereabouts I had the honour of commentating in Irish on all minor semi-finals and finals in both hurling and football, as well as one of the St Patrick's Day Railway Cup finals. I found the job extremely stimulating, getting to know the young stars of the year and through them promoting the Irish language. It was satisfying to hear from members of the public who had only 'a little Irish' that they enjoyed the challenge, and I am glad to see that the 'minor experiment' is still ongoing. I know that one or two producers in RTE favoured a phasing out of the practice a few years ago, but fair play to the GAA for resisting an effort at what some saw as modernization. It would be a sad day for the national broadcaster if it were to turn its back on a language that was to the forefront in restoring national pride over the closing years of the nineteenth century and thereafter. Nowadays TG4 broadcasts GAA, soccer and rugby games *as Gaeilge*, to the great delight of a public ever more interested in involving the language in as many aspects of Irish life as possible.

One of my biggest broadcasting bloopers concerned something off the field of play during one of those televised minor matches. The year was 1968, and Sligo won its one and only Connacht minor title, which set up an All-Ireland semi-final meeting with Armagh. The star of the side was Aidan Richardson: big and strong, redheaded and a cousin of the Dunleavys of Salthill in Galway.

Everything was moving along nicely until a message from the producer in the broadcasting van reached me via headphones that he had 'somebody on camera three . . . he's wearing a chain . . . he must be the Lord Mayor . . . he will be on the screen as soon as the ball goes dead . . . identify.'

My mind went into overdrive, trying to recall who had been appointed Lord Mayor of Dublin a few weeks ealier. I congratulated myself as the name of Frank Cluskey flashed into my mind just as the image of the chained figure appeared on screen.

Now the bearded Frank had a distinctive appearance, but I admit I would not have known him at the time if he had walked into the box. I passed a comment acknowledging Frank's presence, and before long I was describing the football once more. Soon the producer was telling me and all others on call that we had made a dreadful mistake: 'They're ringing in to the studio in Donnybrook from all over Sligo . . . it's the Mayor of Sligo and RTE does not seem to know him.'

My immediate fear then was that the image would reappear and that I would be asked to re-identify: I had no clue who the Mayor of Sligo was. Fortunately it was close to half-time, and when the whistle blew there was an immediate break for a commercial or something of the sort. I took my chance and dashed to the press box nearby, sought out the correspondent from the *Sligo Champion* and got the information as quickly as possible. I was then in a position to tell the producer to put the man with the chain on again and give him a good spread. In due course he reappeared, and after an apology I informed the public that the Mayor of Sligo was John Fallon, a fine sportsman himself and father of Seán, the famous soccer player with Glasgow Celtic.

By the way, Sligo won the match, but lost the All-Ireland final by a single point to a strong Cork team.

Apart from my work on the televised All-Ireland minor semi-finals and finals, I remained in radio rather than switch to television. I have often been asked why. I was invited to switch and gave the matter some consideration before deciding that the radio would remain my number-one interest. There were a few angles to it, and loyalty to the radio was certainly one of them. Work on the radio was generally live, and there is a level of excitement and anticipation in a live programme that a recorded one can never capture. Also, until recently television's live output in Gaelic games was confined to All-Ireland semi-finals and finals. The introduction of the programme *Sunday Sport* by Maurice Quinn in the early 1970s was another of my reasons for opting to stay with the radio. The programme was lively and varied, and it was good to work with producers such as Ian P. Corr, Dermot Kelly, Pat O'Donovan and

Noel Coughlan. At the present time RTE Radio Sport still leads the way, under the guidance of Roy Willoughby and Paddy Glackin. There is, though, one aspect of RTE's radio coverage with which I disagree: the overemphasis on English soccer to the detriment of the home sport. I have no problem with the major events in England being covered, as there is a good level of interest in such here. But it is annoying to a huge number of people to get very frequent coverage of minor cross-channel events ahead of and at the expense of home news on all sports. In my travels abroad I tend to note how foreign sports are covered elsewhere, and I have not come across any country that devotes so much attention to the sport of another as we do.

Chapter Eleven

Mick Finucane, a colleague in the Commercial Department in my time, is now the principal of O'Connell's CBS, and I have often wondered whether I would have been offered the vice-principal post if I had remained a teacher rather than go into broadcasting full-time. I was loath to leave the profession, but decided to take the leap at the end of 1981, when Raidió na Gaeltachta was expanding its range of programmes. I was offered a job as a Clár Reachtaire based in RTE in Donnybrook, covering current affairs and sport, from early January 1982. Naturally I was very proud of the progress made by Raidió na Gaeltachta during its ten years of existence and glad to be now taking an active part in further development.

Most Irish people are interested in politics, and that is particularly true of Gaeltacht people. Raidió na Gaeltachta always covered politics extensively, and one of my briefs was to be in Leinster House for certain sittings of Dáil Éireann.

I knew a number of Ministers, TDs and Senators from their various connections with the GAA and racing, and I'm afraid many of our conversations were about sport when we met along what some people call the 'corridors of power' or in places such as the canteen or bar. I have a high regard for most members of that profession in spite of the bad publicity often attached to their cause. My view is that a very high percentage of them are honest and hardworking, with a more difficult and less pleasant job than most of us.

I have never aligned myself to any political party, though I admit having attended a Fianna Fáil meeting on invitation a long number of years ago. Dún Síon was predominantly but not exclusively Fianna Fáil, and my father had been in the IRB in his youth. His gun lay across rafters for years until the wooden part disintegrated and the barrel rusted. Náis and I took it down more than once just to have a look at it.

My father showed me a site one time where arms were buried, the spot being marked as so many steps from the end of the white straw at the beach in a line between two well-known landmarks. I would say they are well decommissioned by now.

People test me now and then in search of clues about possible allegiance to one party or another. I remember being at the Ploughing Championships once when the Fine Gael party had an exhibition and information stand close to where I was on duty as a guest of the *Farmers' Journal*. A few of our Fine Gael 'neighbours' dropped in, and we chatted nonchalantly about the GAA among other matters. As they were about to leave, one of the Fine Gael men threw out the casual remark: 'You wouldn't be one of us at all, I'd be thinking.' I was curious as to how he had arrived at such a conclusion and said so. He responded: 'You're a bit close to the Irish.'

I felt that I had to spring to the defence of his party immediately because from my observations all parties had good Gaelic speakers and advocates, as well as large numbers who had little interest. I then started to list all the FG *gaeilgeoirí*, going back to Dick Mulcahy at the time of its founding and throwing in the likes of Alan Dukes, Jim Doogue, Peter Barry, Michael Noonan, Enda Kenny, Jim Higgins, Dinny McGinley . . .

I was not too long on Dáil duty when sensational news radiated from there and shocked the public at large. It was January 1982, and the Minister for Finance, John Bruton, delivered his budget speech on behalf of a coalition government that had Garret FitzGerald as Taoiseach.

One feature of the budget was the proposed introduction of VAT on children's shoes. I was in the press gallery as the spokespersons of opposition parties responded to the speech before the vote on the financial provisions of the budget. The Independent TD Jim Kemmy had supported the government since its formation the previous June, giving it a razor-thin majority in the Dáil. It might have been my instinct for backing dogs on a hunch that caused me to leave the gallery as the vote was being taken by the Ceann Comhairle, with deputies moving towards the Tá and Níl lobbies.

I went straight to Raidió na Gaeltachta's improvised studio and ventured to say that the government was about to fall – a scoop for RNG. Jim Kemmy had joined the Níls, and the days of that government were over.

The ensuing general-election campaign promised to be an exciting one, and I arranged with RNG that I would follow the Taoiseach on the opening day. Wexford was the destination, and there was plenty of hurling speculation as the day wound on with experienced electioneers presenting Garret and other members of his team to the public here and there. There was no shortage of colour material for a detailed report on a day with the Taoiseach which I was preparing for an evening RNG programme. Sadly, though, proceedings drew to a sudden halt as the members of the entourage were disembarking from the bus in Enniscorthy. Dedicated *Irish Independent* photographer Joe Shakespeare seemed to be all set to photograph the Taoiseach as he alighted, but at that precise moment Joe collapsed and died.

The schedule for the remainder of the day was cancelled as a mark of respect to Joe, one of the true professionals in the business he loved.

Ireland has had eleven heads of government since independence. Without introducing politics in the usual sense, I would say that Jack Lynch was different from the rest.

For a start it is said that he was loath to enter politics in the first place and that he would have been elected to the Dáil in Cork regardless of what party he represented. His sporting accomplishments, as the only player in the history of the GAA to have won six senior All-Ireland medals in a row, gave him a huge profile that set him apart.

He won four hurling medals in succession from 1941 to 1944, and kept up the sequence by winning with the footballers in 1945 when the hurlers failed. He completed the record a year later when the hurlers had an exciting win over Kilkenny in a great All-Ireland final.

On account of my involvement with sport I had occasion to meet Jack several times, and he was always good company. I felt he was conscious of the part that hurling had played in his fame, and I heard him say once that he could go into known strongholds of other parties at election times and be sure of a hearty welcome. 'They might not vote for my party, but they would be glad that I came and they would let me know, and the hurling talk would begin then.'

I recall the aftermath of a hurling All-Ireland in the 1980s when Kilkenny had beaten Cork. RTE had a temporary studio at the back of the Hogan Stand, and I was on the lookout for likely interviewees. I spotted Jack and invited him to come to the studio; he graciously agreed, even though it was a dark moment for Cork. In the course of the interview I mentioned the great performance given in goal by Kilkenny's Noel Skehan – an excellent custodian in general, I might add. Lynch agreed with me, but added: 'Why wouldn't he with the half-door he was carrying.' It was the time when the *bos* on goalkeepers' hurleys were on growth-promoting steriods.

But of course not in Cork.

In the spring general election of 1973, Lynch's Fianna Fáil government had been rejected by the people, and another gentleman, Liam Cosgrave, became Taoiseach. Shortly afterwards I was in Thurles for a hurling match and had occasion to visit the toilet area during the half-time break. I judged from the accents that those on either side of me were Tipperary men, and before we left one posed the following question to his neighbour of the moment.

'What do you think of the new Taoiseach?'

The response captured Lynch's magnetism for the ordinary person.

'I don't know, but somehow I could never imagine him in here with us now, firing against the wall, like Jack would.'

The tone of the speaker suggested goodwill towards Liam

Cosgrave, but yet the point had to be made that there was only one Lynch.

I travelled with him once in a state car from Ennis to Dublin – a journey that was much too short. He spoke freely of Christy Ring, Willie John Daly, Tommy Doyle, Jim Langton, John Keane and the lot, and he looked forward to meeting them at every opportunity, regardless of county loyalties or politics. 'We were all players, and even though we fought hard on the field there was a bond between us that is impossible to break.'

He seemed to have a mischievous sense of humour at times, and this came to the fore when I mentioned the GAA centenary hurling final of 1984, which was played in Semple Stadium, Thurles, as a gesture to the cradle town of the GAA. I recalled the pre-match presentation of all living All-Ireland-winning captains, from Eudie Coughlan of Cork in 1931 to Kilkenny's Liam Fennelly of 1983. Each received a warm reception, but when Jack Lynch's name was called as Cork captain of 1942 there was a spontaneous explosion of appreciative applause.

Lynch asked me had I heard what Charlie Haughey said at the time. I hadn't, and said so. Lynch said: 'He asked the person next to him, *"Was Lynch that good?"'* Maybe Charlie's own sense of humour was sharp that day as well.

Jack Lynch never had the same profile as a footballer, but he had a great *grá* for his contemporaries in Cavan and Kerry, particularly Kerry's legendary fullback Joe Keohane. Joe played both minor and senior championship football for Kerry in 1936, and over the next dozen years won five All-Ireland medals. He was an extraordinary character of many qualities and was selected as fullback on the GAA Team of the Millennium. There were many times when he himself might agree that he could have been the best ever in the position, but it would be purely out of roguery or for the sake of keeping a good debate alive.

One would need to have known the late Joe to fully appreciate the following story told to me by Jack Lynch himself. Apparently he and Joe were in the same company one night when the talk about famous footballing fullbacks got a great airing. Neither Joe nor Jack said much, but at the end the consensus was that Tralee's Joe really was the best of all time. The opportunity was too great for a Corkman to resist, and as the debate seemed almost over he asked Joe did he remember the Munster Colleges Football team of 1935. Joe pleaded loss of memory of the selection, only to be told by Jack that he had come across an old match programme of the time containing the line-out.

JL: Who was the Number 2 on the team, Joe?

JK: I don't know, Jack.

JL: The programme says J. Keohane, Tralee, CBS. And who was the Number 3 on the team, Joe?

JK: I couldn't tell you, Jack.

JL: The programme says J. Lynch, North Monastery, Cork.

Of course the addendum gave rise to great hilarity and extended the length of the gathering by several hours.

I often think that former sportsmen value the comradeship of field friends and foes alike more than the clashes and medals that made them famous. They look forward to opportunities to meet again, unlike many professional sportspeople to whom sport is a mere business.

Perhaps Shakespeare was thinking of amateur sportspeople when he penned the simple lines:

What friends thou hast and acquaintances tried
grapple to thy heart with hoops of steel.

Chapter Twelve

My connection with Kerry footballers resident in Dublin went back to the immediate post-Pat's days of the 1950s. In comparison to the present time, very little training was done by the footballers and hurlers of those days. The old guard maintains that the spartan lifestyle of the time was a fitness programme on its own. The bicycle was the common mode of conveyance to work, and if the last bus had left at night before the dances ended there was no custom of taking a taxi home. Country people in particular thought nothing of walking four or five miles back to their flats or digs.

Once there was a good stretch in the day, the popular mode of tuning up for the season was a bit of kicking and a few laps of the pitch. I remember moving into new digs one time in the early 1950s and meeting another resident of the house coming down the stairs as Kerry footballer Seán Murphy and I were entering. This stranger was carrying a football and a pair of boots, and asked us would we come with him for a few kicks. We agreed and soon we were on the field in Pat's, kicking away now aware of the fact that the man we were trying to get fit was Mickey Furlong from Offaly: he had told us so on the way. Word had come from Offaly that he had been picked to play on Sunday, hence his anxiety about fitness.

It was obvious that he did not recognize Seán, and we did not make him any the wiser as we kicked away. He did say to me at one stage that 'yer man isn't bad', before it eventually dawned on Furlong that he was in the presence of a Kerry footballer of repute. We had a great laugh about it.

Mickey played football and hurling for the county, as well as hurling with Faugh's and football with Seán McDermott's in Dublin. He was a classy player who enjoyed a good social life to the detriment of his fitness in days when the Faithful County was winning little in either code. Mickey had a habit of addressing friends from a distance with 'Sarsfield, how are you!' and it was great to hear the greeting at any time.

Offaly lost a good player when he emigrated to the United States.

I got to know the other Furlongs later, and it was good to see the fortunes of the county rise because to a man they loved the game of football. Tom was a class player and a 'county man' before joining Mickey in New York, where he won a National League medal when New York beat Galway in the final of 1967. Martin was the most successful of the lot; my first sighting of him was as goalkeeper on the Offaly minor team of 1964. He was 'Máirtín' Furlong to me then because I was commentating in Irish on the All-Ireland semi-finals and final.

The Number 1 was one of the stars in Offaly's first-ever All-Ireland success in any grade of football. That minor team I saw in 1964 was the basis of the county's rise to prominence in the senior grade during the remainder of the 1960s and the early 1970s. When they brought the Sam Maguire to the Midlands in 1971 and again the following year, eight of the minors who played in 1964 took part.

Paddy McCormack, the Ironman from Rhode, was the only survivor from the 1961 side that had lost the All-Ireland final to Down: he was fullback on that all-conquering 1971–72 team. I remember Paddy calling to see me shortly after Cork's unexpected victory in the Munster final of 1971. He was known as a man who played football hard, and information on Cork was the reason for his visit. In order to get him going I ventured to suggest that he might experience great difficulty with the Cork forwards in the All-Ireland semi-final. I stressed the huge height of full forward Ray Cummins in particular, but the Ironman was not impressed.

'You never know,' he said, 'his head could be as low as my own before the game is over.'

As it turned out there was far more to the astute Cummins's play than height advantage, but Offaly won the day.

When Offaly won a third All-Ireland in 1982 with the most famous final goal of all time by Séamus Darby, the incredible Martin

Furlong was still minding the goal and did so for another few years as well.

There was an interesting sequel for me as I walked along the North Circular Road on my way home some two hours after the final whistle. Suddenly I heard loud hooting from an Offaly car as it screeched to a halt a few yards ahead of me. A door opened and out jumped a very happy-looking man yelling for all he was worth, 'Sarsfield, how are you!' There he was – the same Mickey Furlong that I had first met thirty years down the back road. It was great to meet him once more. In a way, meeting people is as important to GAA folk as the games that supply the topics and the heroes.

When Martin Furlong eventually retired from football, he, too, crossed the big pond to New York. The old family home was knocked down, and the site became part of the Tullamore Court Hotel – the bar part in fact, and no marks for guessing that it is now named the Furlong Bar. I had the honour a few years ago of officially opening it on a night of wonderful reminiscence.

I know for certain that it went on for a long time because I had occasion to ring sometime after midday on the morrow enquiring about a coat I had left behind. I could hear the sound of festivities in the background and asked the reason for such – a wedding, perhaps? I was then told by the receptionist, 'Last night hasn't ended yet.'

I remember being out in Portobello Barracks in Rathmines, Dublin, in 1954 when Tim O'Donnell, a member of Kerry's four-in-a-row team of 1929–32, was overseeing the training of a few Kerry players in preparation for an All-Ireland final with Meath. Collective training was outlawed by the GAA Congress of that year, which meant that there was no way the Dublin contingent could go to Kerry for the customary two weeks together with the celebrated trainer Dr Éamonn O'Sullivan.

Over the following years players such as Seán Murphy, Kevin Coffey, Donie O'Sullivan, Páid O'Donoghue, Mick Gleeson, Liam Higgins and others would have been around for training in Dublin, and I would not be too far away once the championship air was in circulation. I remember training in St Pat's field for the All-Ireland final of 1972 against Offaly. Goalkeeper Éamonn Fitzgerald was there along with Donie O'Sullivan, Mick Gleeson, John O'Keeffe and a very young Ger Power, who had joined the civil service. Power may have been an unofficial sub at the tail end of the panel, but even then he was showing signs of the confidence he displayed many a time later. He was very anxious to get a chance sometime, and asked me after training one night did I know when some of 'them fellows' would retire. I knew what he meant because it was easy to read the mind of a nineteen-year-old who was absolutely mad about playing football.

He had played for the Kerry minors in the final of 1970 but lost to Galway, and lost the under-21 final of 1972 to the same opposition. His father, the late Jackie Power of Limerick hurling fame, would have taken him to many of Kerry's games since he was knee-high; he would have seen Mick O'Dwyer, Mick O'Connell and others playing for fifteen years and setting many records. They were still playing in 1972, and the young man was simply wondering when he would get his chance.

As things worked out, in 1972 Offaly won after a replay, and that marked the last Championship appearance in Croke Park for twelve of the Kerry players that lined out that day. Many of them, especially O'Dwyer and O'Connell, had given fantastic service to the county. The three survivors were John O'Keeffe and the brothers Brendan and Paudie Lynch, who had a bit to contribute still.

Losing an All-Ireland final is difficult for players, and it takes some time to get over the utter disappointment the loss imposes. I will never forget a meeting with Brendan Lynch on the night of that 1972 replay. The Kerry 'wake' was held in the International Hotel in Bray, and at some hour I went down the stairs to the toilet area. Brendan Lynch was there washing his hands – killing time as much as anything else. He looked dejected, and I tried to cheer him up by reminding him that he was only twenty-four years of age and already the holder of two senior All-Ireland medals. His reply acknowledged my reading of the situation, but he was quick to add: 'It's not myself at all, but poor Paudie . . . he has nothing . . . there seems to be some *mí-ádh* on him, and he might never win anything.'

He then outlined Paudie's history for me, and to be honest it was discouraging. He lost to Wicklow in the All-Ireland junior home final of 1969. He lost to Galway (in a replay) in the All-Ireland minor final of 1970. He lost to Galway in the All-Ireland under-21 final of 1972. He lost to Bellaghy of Derry in the All-Ireland club final of 1972 when playing with University College Cork. And on this day he had lost to Offaly in the replay of the All-Ireland senior final.

I could then understand Brendan's dejection, but the younger brother's perseverance was to bring him several honours, beginning with an under-21 All-Ireland medal when Kerry beat Mayo in Ennis in 1973. I was broadcasting that game, and Kerry's winning goal was scored by Martin Ferris, now Sinn Féin TD representing North Kerry. It is possible that Martin would have won senior All-Irelands with the Kingdom over the following years, but his republican associations meant that he was seldom available for training while the glory run was in progress.

The 1973 side was an extraordinary under-21 team, containing nine members of the senior team that carved more glory for themselves, their county and Gaelic football in the years ahead.

And by the way Paudie Lynch proved that perseverance pays by collecting five senior All-Ireland medals.

The great saga had begun with the appointment of Mick O'Dwyer as manager in late spring of 1975. He had won four All-Ireland medals during a playing career that started as a minor in 1954 and ended twenty years later. The Waterville man had a passion for football, a great sense of the importance of fitness, a little quota of roguery and the memory of an elephant. He believed he never got fair play as a minor and reminds himself from time to time that he scored 1–5 against Waterford in the semi-final of 1954, but found himself as third sub for the Munster final, which Kerry won, and did not get the medal to which he was entitled. He was then relegated to fifth sub for the All-Ireland semi-final and to the ranks of the unofficial subs for the final. Dublin won the final by a point. There was no use in a young lad from South Kerry complaining: Waterville was not a noted nursery of footballers, but he believed that patience would eventually bring recognition if he was good enough.

He trained assiduously and was selected for Kerry's opening Championship game of 1957, against Waterford in Dungarvan. Defeat for Kerry was the startling sports news of that day, but by the end of September 1959 O'Dwyer had won his first All-Ireland medal as a solid methodical left halfback. He won a second in 1962, but the emerging superb Galway three-in-a-row team of the 1960s proved to be Kerry's masters, beating them in the All-Ireland semi-final of 1963 and in the finals of 1964 and 1965.

It seemed the end of another era for the Kingdom, and, whether prompted by County Board personnel or not, a number of players retired, including O'Dwyer, Mick O'Connell, Johnny Cullotty and Séamus Murphy. Two lean years followed, and morale was low in the county when O'Dwyer organized a challenge game for charity in the spring of 1968 between the Kerry team of the day and a 'selection from the past'. O'Dwyer, O'Connell and Cullotty played with the 'past', and following good displays the door was then open for a comeback – an honoured facet of the culture of Gaelic games. Séamus Murphy joined them in the second coming.

It would not be charitable to say that this was in the mind of Micko when he arranged that particular charity game.

The four returning stars helped Kerry to three more All-Ireland finals, with victories in 1969 and 1970.

Shortly after the appointment of O'Dwyer as Kerry manager in 1975, Gerald McKenna, Chairman of the Kerry County Board, got on to me saying that he wanted a man 'in Havana' as well. He asked me if I would 'look after' the lads in Dublin, and who could resist such a request? The Chairman had a wonderful facility with words and the capacity to combine serious business with light-heartedness. He explained that training would need to be serious, considering the standards set by Kevin Heffernan when guiding Dublin to All-Ireland success the year before.

I knew I was not qualified to train top footballers, but I had my own theories and never lacked the urge to gamble and try. I had noted many times in my wanderings that freshness as much as fitness was a characteristic of winning horses and greyhounds, and for evermore freshness was high on my system of training.

My pupils were very keen and natural athletes: regulars John O'Keeffe, Ger Power and Pat McCarthy, a few fringe players such as Ray Prendeville and 'immigrants' from other counties to make up numbers.

O'Keeffe was in many ways the ideal Gaelic footballer: tall and athletic, skilful in the arts of the game, pacey and a martyr for fitness and training.

Power was different – extremely fast, always on his toes like a good greyhound, requiring less training than most and, above all, confident of his own ability.

McCarthy was as strong as any man I ever knew, as exemplified once in an encounter with a bull in Ardfert. I didn't witness it, but I'm told the bull wisely backed off after a few shoulders from McCarthy, even though the midfielder ended up in a hedge.

We were not long in training that summer before I got another phone call from Kerry. *Fear Gaeltachta a bhí ann* – Séamus Mac Gearailt, former footballer and winner of All-Ireland medals at all levels. He was trainer of the Kerry minor team, and one of the lads had gone to Dublin on a Fás course *agus d'iarr sé orm súil a choimeád air*. The minor in question was Jack O'Shea; Mac Gearailt thought a lot of him, and before long he, too, was training with the 'men'.

The year 1975 was a memorable one in football. A strong Derry team was back in business in Ulster, and the new Kerry team of 'fifteen bachelors' ousted Cork in Munster. Dublin powered through Leinster, roared on by the ever increasing numbers of Heffo's Army. Many of them were originally soccer followers that got sucked into the Gaelic by the mania that developed during Dublin's miraculous surge to the top in 1974. They fell in without knowing where it had all started or even where it might end. 'Are we in Europe now?' was one of the questions directed at Heffo by lingering foot soldiers as he left Croke Park after that All-Ireland final of 1974.

Three cheers for the man who converted them; he certainly deserved the honour bestowed on him recently when Dublin Corporation declared him a freeman of the city.

Sligo beat Mayo to win the Connacht title of 1975 – the second to come to the county and the first since 1928. I was lucky: I was in Castlebar that day, with that great Dub Jack Keating working as technician in the box with me.

Surveying the scene in the immediate aftermath of the final whistle who did I see on the terrace down below me but an old friend, Eddie Masterson, the colossus from Tubbercurry. Eddie was a football fanatic and brother of the ubiquitous Joe Masterson, who had played for Sligo and Connacht. Eddie qualified as a solicitor, and before starting work in Dublin he decided to stay a night in Barry's Hotel out of respect for the most recognizable GAA hotel in the country.

For years teams playing in the All-Ireland final had stayed in Barry's on the Saturday night, and as a landmark it was better known in those days than Nelson's Pillar in the middle of O'Connell Street. Eddie moved in, but was so captivated with the atmosphere that he never moved out, and it was there he died thirty years later.

He was far more interested in showbands and football and the writing of ballads than in the profundity of the law. He was the composer of 'The Ironman from Rhode', a song about the aforementioned Paddy McCormack, a man whose forceful brand of football gave rise to the title.

Once when the role of umpires was being debated, Eddie made the observation that they expend unnecessary energy in the execution of their task. He suggested that it could be simplified thus: a nod upwards and inwards should imply a point to anyone with a modicum of intelligence; similarly the same but downwards should be capable of interpretation as a goal; a simple nod towards the corner flag should be OK for a wide; and a state of total inertia with eyes directed at midfield should do for a fifty or seventy.

Only a genius could advance a theory like it, and there are many scholars who were awarded PhDs from Harvard for less.

And here he was in Castlebar on Sligo's greatest day with pen and paper in hand, looking up at us in the box, ready to compose yet another ballad – this time about Sligo and the great Mickey Kearins, an ornament to Gaelic football over an extended career with club, county and province.

Of course Eddie and thousands more from Sligo were in Croke Park in August when Sligo lined out against Kerry in the All-Ireland semi-final, but alas they failed to recapture Connacht form and the Munster men won handily.

Two weeks later Dublin beat Derry, and the stage was set for another Kerry–Dublin final. As champions Dublin were clear favourites and seen as better than a year earlier. This was the first seventy-minute All-Ireland final after a five-year experiment with eighty minutes.

There was talk of Dublin experience against the youth of Kerry, Heffo against Micko and the trappings of 1955 all over. I was busy with the training for this eagerly awaited clash and with Jacko for the minor final, which, by the way, I would be broadcasting on television.

One might wonder whether I had the necessary impartiality, but I must say that I never found it a problem. I never hesitated to be critical of someone I had trained if it was merited, and thankfully nobody ever accused me of bias in broadcasting. My guiding principle and advice to beginners is to talk about what is actually happening rather than what you would wish was happening, then you will wrong nobody.

One can never be sure of a result in advance, but from time to time a premonition presents itself, as it did to me ten days before that final of 1975. After a lively training session I knew my trio were in perfect shape, fresh and eager like the good greyhound before a race. I regarded freshness as one of the key elements going to battle, and I could sense they had it. But it was an outburst of confidence from the normally reserved John O'Keeffe that really convinced me that Kerry would win on Sunday week.

He was a converted fullback since the start of the Championship and had settled in perfectly. I was flabbergasted as I listened to him telling me that he could give yards in a sprint to any of the Dublin forwards, that he was younger than most and that he felt good about all aspects of his game. I was never a person for writing letters, but that night I wrote to the late Andy Molneaux, Secretary of the Kerry County Board, giving him my prediction and the logic behind it.

The fourth Sunday in September soon came, and Kerry won the double. My man Jacko played well for the minors and scored the only goal of the game, and Micko's senior team had a surprise seven-point win over Dublin.

There were many stars for Kerry that day, and I was happy that my three were as good as any. Essentially it was a classic team performance, and for goalkeeper Paudie O'Mahony it was especially satisfactory: he did not concede a single goal in the Championship. Inspiring captain Mickey Ned O'Sullivan finished up in the Mater Hospital suffering from concussion, and it was quiet man John Egan who steadied the ship early on with a tasty goal.

O'Dwyer was over the moon with the result and performance: less than six months as manager and an All-Ireland under his belt with the youngest team ever to win the Championship. He let the players go their own ways for a few hours before the banquet in the Grand Hotel in Malahide and came out with me to my house for a chat. He spoke mostly to himself: 'Aren't they great lads . . . they're mighty . . . I knew they were good, but I did not think they could be that good . . . Jaykus, wasn't that a great goal by Egan . . . what do you think, Micheál? . . .'

But I was hardly given a chance to answer.

The craic was good that night in Malahide, and on the following evening I was in Heuston Station to see the champions off on their way to the traditional hearty welcome home to the Kingdom.

Chapter Thirteen

I would venture to say that the train had hardly reached Kerry before Kevin Heffernan was giving some thought to 1976 and how he might recover the pride that had dissipated with the unexpected defeat. I got the first inkling of that on the Tuesday after the final when I went along to Clontarf Golf Club for a game with another Kerryman, Fr John O'Connell. On entering the lounge I was more than surprised to see the Dublin players all seated around Heffo. It was obvious that the disappointment had not yet worn off, and it is a safe assumption that they had not an appetite for golf either. I exchanged a few words with Kevin, but it was not the time for a big conversation. The padre and I went about our golfing business quickly, not too worried about pars or birdies.

I wasn't aware of it at the time, but I have subsequently become convinced that the great resurrection that Heffo orchestrated the following year had its origin in Clontarf Golf Club that day. He had been more than thirty years on the inter-county circuit by then and had been part of some spectacular wins for Dublin. But there was one item on the wish list of all true Dub followers that had yet to be ticked off: a win over Kerry within living memory.

The last was recorded in 1934, when Dublin travelled to Tralee for an All-Ireland semi-final replay with Kerry and truly gave a team of legends their final curtain. In the meantime the Green and Gold had victories over their great rivals in the semi-finals of 1941, 1959, 1962 and 1965 and in the finals of 1955 and 1975. A sports psychologist might have recommended that these dates should have been in large print on the walls of the Dublin dressing room, but Heffo needed no reminding.

He had learned a good deal playing against Kerry, in the minor All-Ireland final of 1946, the senior final of 1955 and the senior semi-final of 1962; the experience of 1975 was also put to good use. If the ambition of finally beating Kerry was to be attained, Heffo needed players with total commitment. He had plenty from the team of 1974 – Brian Mullins, Tony Hanahoe, David Hickey, John McCarthy, Robbie Kelleher, Jimmy Keaveney and others – but he needed a few more.

Speed was one of the elements in Kerry's winning formula, and Heffo needed an antidote. A strong and fast halfback line was the answer, and that is where the rebuilding began in the spring of 1976. I have rarely seen as rapid a transition to senior level as the solidly built Tommy Drumm underwent once given his chance at right halfback. Pat O'Neill, who was known for his power, drive and commitment, was ideal for the left. There was a vacancy, however, still to be filled in the centre.

One day in early February a Dublin selection to play Kerry in a challenge game in Tralee appeared in the morning papers listing one K. Moran. I and thousands of others had never seen the name before, and I was curious.

Ian Corr and Dermot Kelly produced an Irish-language sports programme on Radio 1 at the time, which the late Liam Campbell and I presented. I thought it would be nice if I could locate this mystery man and record a piece with him, provided of course he spoke a bit of Gaeilge.

Nobody seemed to know anything about K. Moran. Eventually I discovered that he was a student in UCD. That evening I landed myself where the UCD team was training and asked a bystander which of the lads was K. Moran. I was told there was no such person, and when I said that he had been selected for Dublin my informant said it must have been a misprint. In the end a college source gave me an address in Drimnagh, and I can still see the place in my mind's eye: a shop with the word 'Kokonut' written in large letters above the door.

It was there I met Kevin Moran for the first time and recorded his first interview *as Gaeilge*. He was quiet but friendly, and quick to point out that he did not play Gaelic for UCD; he played soccer with Pegasus instead. He was, however, a member of the Good Counsel Gaelic Club in Drimnagh and played with them. I would not describe him as a fluent Irish-speaker, but we strung a few minutes together, and I wished him luck in Tralee.

He turned out to be the discovery of the year, and a win over Derry in the League final was a clear indication that Dublin were far from a spent force.

The public at large wanted a Kerry–Dublin All-Ireland final in September, and it materialized. Kerry were extremely fortunate to get out of Munster that year; put another way, misfortune as never seen before rained on Cork in a replay of the Munster final. Cork were leading by seven points with the game in its final quarter when the first of a series of bizarre incidents took place. It was desperation time for Kerry, and rather than kick a point from a close free Mikey Sheehy kicked sideways to Seán Walsh, who blasted a shot towards the Cork goal. Brian Murphy seemed to block the ball on the goal line, but to the consternation of Cork people in heaven, hell and on earth a Kerry goal was flagged, and there was no court of appeal.

Was Brian Murphy behind the line when he blocked the ball? I was not present, but TV pictures do not give that impression.

Cork responded like good teams ought and sallied down the field in a swift move that ended with Declan Barron fisting to the Kerry net. Red flags waved freely – but not for long because Barron's effort was deemed to have been a 'square ball', a decision that caused even some Kerry followers to blush.

After these two strokes of good fortune, it was little wonder that Kerry tacked on the four points needed for a draw.

Believe it or not, there was one remaining quirk of fate left before the end of normal time. Ace sniper Mikey Sheehy won possession and took a shot for the winning point that was dead on target. But, miracle of miracles, the effuxion of time before the ball actually passed over the Cork crossbar forced referee John Maloney to blow for full time. Extra time was then played, and Kerry retained the provincial title on a day of wonders.

I hold that Cork would have stood a great chance of winning the All-Ireland title that year if they had survived the onslaught of misfortune that day. The memory of the 1974 semi-final defeat by

Dublin would have helped their cause, and only the sight of Kerry would have motivated Dublin to the level they attained in the All-Ireland final of that year. As it was they had only two points to spare over Meath in the Leinster final and three over Galway in the All-Ireland semi-final.

These facts and Kerry's massive sixteen-point win over Derry in their penultimate match meant that the reigning champions were very strongly fancied to win the final.

That is the way Kevin Heffernan wanted it, and when his greatest hour arrived the team was ready. I will never forget the explosive start to the match, with the pacey Kevin Moran sweeping upfield from his centre-back position, exchanging passes with a team-mate and taking an electrifying, awesome drop kick that rocketed just inches wide of the Kerry goal. The record books might call it a wide, but Moran's stylish move laid a marker for Dublin's comfortable win on the day, by 3–8 to 0–10.

It was a momentous result for Dublin football, but it was no more than the efforts of the players and selectors Kevin Heffernan, Lorcan Redmond and Donal Colfer over three gruelling years deserved. The result wounded Kerry pride grievously, and as 'trainer of the exiles' I was very much aware of that, but isn't that the way of serious sport ever?

I remember the Kerry celebrations in Malahide that night and in particular the approach of the host for the night, Fr Michael Heffernan, President of the Kerry Association in Dublin. It was his task to address an audience that was somewhat subdued, and he began his homily, if I can call it such, by stating that he, too, was subdued when he left the presbytery in High Street earlier in the evening. He continued by telling us that before long he witnessed a sight that would lighten the heart of any Kerry person: 'There in front of me on an open patch of ground I saw for the first time ever Dublin children kicking a football and jumping to catch it in the air – now is that not a miracle brought about by Dublin's win over us today? Maybe it is for the good of the game.'

Fr Heffernan's homily reminds me of one of Seán Ó Síocháin's favourite true stories. It concerns Tipperary man Paddy Leahy, one-time famous hurler and ever a passionate supporter of the Blue and Gold. It hurt him deeply whenever Tipp lost an important match, but he always summoned the courage to shake the hand of the winners and say with some feeling, 'Whatever is best for the game; whatever is best for the Association.' Seán recalls being with him at the All-Ireland final of 1967 when Kilkenny beat Tipperary in a final for the first time since 1922. They were on the Hogan Stand, and the atmosphere could not have been to the liking of any Tipperary person as the McCarthy Cup was being presented to the Kilkenny captain. When that was over and done with Paddy suggested to Seán that perhaps he should go to the Tipperary dressing room in their hour of disappointment.

The room was on the other side of the field, and as they were setting forth the Bishop of Kilkenny appeared on the scene, full of the joys of September. Leahy shook the bishop's hand while uttering his well-rehearsed words: 'Whatever is best for the game; whatever is best for the Association.'

When they had parted from the bishop, Paddy turned to his *compánach* and said with feeling: 'Good Jesus, Seán, it's very hard to say it today.'

There was consternation and surprise when, in the aftermath of the 1976 All-Ireland final, Kevin Heffernan announced his retirement from managership of the Dublin team. The suave Tony Hanahoe became player-manager.

Football followers at large wanted to see a return engagement of Dublin and Kerry in 1977, and the big two duly qualified for the National League final. It was a good game won narrowly by Kerry. Anticipation of another Championship meeting was rampant long before the destinations of the provincial titles were decided, but the public's prayers were answered when Dublin and Kerry qualified to meet in the All-Ireland semi-final.

I have watched the build-up to various sporting events over the years – All-Ireland finals, World Cups, Triple Crowns, Olympics, Grand Nationals, Cheltenham, and so on – but was there any single one that could measure up to that 1977 encounter between Kerry and Dublin? It was a semi-final in name only. The atmosphere was well beyond anything experienced before.

In hindsight some experts have found fault with some minutiae of play, but it must be judged in the currency of its enactment. It was magnificent, with nods of favour from the gods switching from side to side, before a driving finish brought Dublin goals from David Hickey and Bernard Brogan to create the greatest level of excitement ever on Hill 16. The Dublin team reached its peak that day and won the final in September by defeating Armagh.

Dublin had now won three All-Ireland titles in four years, and the goal of making it three in a row looked attainable with the Kerry nemesis well and truly interred.

This Dublin team had already done a lot for the GAA and asked little in return.

There were murmurings against O'Dwyer in Kerry, but he does not think it reached the level where caucus meetings took place. He kept his thoughts to himself, offering no excuses for defeats in successive years.

He knew just as well as Heffernan did two years earlier that his team needed some fresh talent. He had four young players, midfielder Jack O'Shea, forward Seán Walsh, defender Mick Spillane and goalkeeper Charlie Nelligan – each of whom already held an All-Ireland minor medal, three under-21 medals and a National League.

The final ingredient being welded into the Kerry team during the League campaign of 1977–78 was Eoin Liston, the bearded twenty-year-old from Ballybunion. He might easily have been born in Dublin, as it was there his parents settled on marrying. His brother Padraig was born in the capital.

But the Limerick father and Kerry mother moved to Kerry, and it was in Ballybunion that big Eoin first saw the light of day. O'Dwyer saw his strength and football acumen as ideally suited for the full-forward berth, but the trouble was that Liston was not too keen on the rigours of training. The manager would have heard him mutter complaints, but he knew that the bearded white hope would put up with anything rather than serve in the family bar at home.

'I knew I had him from then on' was how Micko put it.

All five of Kerry's youngsters were still under-21 players, and each went on to collect seven All-Irelands between 1978 and 1986. I regard it as one of my greatest honours to have been associated with these men, and the memories of those days, good and bad, will stay with me for ever.

I resumed my training duties for 1978 on the first day of spring. By then my panel included Jack O'Shea, Mick Spillane, Charlie Nelligan, Paudie O'Mahony, Barry Walsh, Pat McCarthy and the usual quota of other 'displaced' county players.

Our base was in Belfield, thanks to the authorities of UCD, and as ever the emphasis was on enjoyment and comradeship.

The current Director of Sport in UCD is Brian Mullins, the great midfield rival of Jacko in those years. I reminded him of that one day recently while out in Belfield, and he retorted by saying that we might not have trained there if he had been Director at the time. I put the remark down to his sense of humour: he couldn't but have a *grá* for Kerry, seeing that his uncle Billy Casey had won five All-Irelands with the Kingdom in his day.

We always planned for a year that would last until September. When it was cut short along the way there were no recriminations, just a hopeful eye towards the new year. Mick O'Dwyer had an admirable attitude towards defeat: 'No amount of complaining and regret will change the result . . . better by far to allow the victors to enjoy their success . . . look towards the next Championship because nobody has won that yet and we have a dang good chance of taking it.'

That is not to say that defeats did not hurt the man hugely.

In 1978, as in previous years, Dublin and Kerry were away in front of the pack. By May, Dublin had added another National League to their harvest. They had eleven points to spare in the Leinster final in July and the same margin as they swept Down aside in the All-Ireland semi-final in August. On the surface at least they were bang on target for their third consecutive All-Ireland – an achievement that would match that of the county in the 1897–99 period and again that of 1921–23.

But Kerry's preparations were going well. Eleven players from the Kingdom won Railway Cup medals with Munster in March, and the passage to the All-Ireland final was smooth. They beat Cork by seven points in the Munster final and Roscommon by a dozen in the All-Ireland semi-final.

Considering the results of the previous two years it was not surprising that Dublin were exceptionally strong favourites in the final, with Kerry freely available at 5/2. Although I bet on dogs and horses now and then, I had a point of never gambling on the result of a match even at times when I had strong convictions concerning the outcome. The football final of 1978 fitted into that category, and Mick O'Dwyer's confidence was one of the reasons for it. He spoke of the youth of the side and the determination to make amends for the losses of 1976 and 1977. I myself had taken particular notice of the power, pace and confidence of the twenty-year-old pair of midfielders, Jack O'Shea and Seán Walsh. Like Mick O'Connell and Séamus Murphy before them they had a perfect understanding of each other's play. It was a good sign also that each wished to be placed on Brian Mullins, the undisputed king of midfielders at the time.

It was Jacko's fourth season training with me and he had developed into a superb athlete. He had natural stamina, as he showed while at school in Cahersiveen when he ran fourth to John Treacy in the All-Ireland Colleges Cross-Country championships. He had a great sense of position and rarely if ever missed a training session.

He deserves to be ranked with the greatest midfielders of all time, and his brilliant form was consistent from match to match over a senior career that stretched from 1977 to 1992.

I was pretty sure in my own mind during the week preceding the final of 1978 that Kerry were in with a right chance – so much so that I went on a mission across the North Circular Road from O'Connell's CBS on the Wednesday to a gambling Dub who ran a timber business close by. He and I had many a fine discussion on football, horses and dogs whenever I visited his premises. Indeed I often called and spotted a familar 'Back in an Hour' notice prominent inside the window; I would know well where to find him, and it would not be in a church.

He had told me several times during the summer of 1978 that he thought Dublin were unbeatable and that he had backed them substantially to win the All-Ireland. The reason for my Wednesday call was to try to convince him that at 5/2 he ought lay off some of his money on Kerry. I wouldn't like to see anyone lose so much on a gamble, and I pleaded strongly with him to be cautious.

When he said, 'Hold on a minute,' before disappearing into the office, I thought he was relenting, but he returned with a fairly heavy wad of notes and told me that if I was so confident to 'cover' his amount. I told him that I had a principle of not backing teams, and we left it with a shake of hands and a word about a dog for that night.

Sunday came, and it turned out to be another sensational day in Croke Park. I commentated on the minor game for television as Mayo beat Dublin. I was on radio duty on the sideline for the senior game and lodged myself in the Kerry dugout. It was a wet day, but the weather did not prevent Dublin from getting into their stride quickly. I must admit that I was seriously doubting my judgement and confidence as Dublin tacked on five points and looked to be in tune.

Murt Galvin, a Kerry official, muttering to himself next to me in the dugout, seemed to be of the same opinion.

But then a quickly taken long free by Mick Spillane ended up in the hands of John Egan, and against the run of play the Sneem man produced his favourite trick of scoring an unexpected goal. In my opinion that – and not the celebrated Mikey Sheehy goal before half-time – was the turning point of the game.

However, the memory of Sheehy's audacious goal from a chip over the head of Paddy Cullen will live for ever and a day. The free that led to it originated with a dubious decision by referee Séamus Aldridge. Paddy Cullen was well out of his goal at the time. Dublin player Robbie Kelleher handed the ball to Sheehy, and it was only a pure football artist that could have manoeuvred the ball over the head of Cullen into the net from a fairly sharp angle. But

I saw no reason for a free at the time: the segment of play that preceded it was as innocent as ever occurred among humans since Adam and Eve left the Garden of Paradise. Referee Aldridge of Kildare has held his silence to this day, even after revelation of more serious matters contained in state papers of the era. My reading is that it was a retrospective free, punishing a genuine foul that had not been penalized earlier in the passage of play. In any case, Sheehy had the presence of mind and the craft to jump on the gift horse with alacrity.

The day was Kerry's from then on, with the second half belonging to Eoin Liston, who scored all three of his goals in front of his brother's county folk on Hill 16. Kerry's winning margin was seventeen points.

It was Dublin's turn again to be shattered, and a fine team that had given pride to Dublin people was now in decline. Even though Dublin and Kerry were to play again in the final of 1979, the competitive heights of the four previous years could not be reached again. Kerry went on to win six of the next eight All-Irelands, and it is not county loyalty that forges my opinion that they were the best football team of all time.

They played an enterprising brand of football that was spectacular to behold and did not depend on negative tactics to contain an opposition. Like all true champions, they had an extraordinary ability to consign past successes to history at the beginning of each season and focus on the next target. They enjoyed winning, but as a group they also gained enjoyment from the preparation and the friendships made.

O'Dwyer would never give his opinion as to which of the lot was the greatest of all, but a phrase he used casually on a few occasions hinted at Pat Spillane. Whenever he rang me about a player being injured, he was prone to add, as if speaking to himself: 'Wouldn't it be worse if it was Spillane?'

But he could have been joking also, as the roguery never left him.

That Kerry dynasty produced the only holders of eight All-Ireland medals in the history of Gaelic football: Ogie Moran, Páidí

Ó Sé, Pat Spillane, Ger Power and Mikey Sheehy, the only man to have played from start to finish of every Championship game of the county's four-in-a row sequence.

Will their equals appear again?

The logical answer is that it is unlikely, but it can be said that a footballer to match any one of the individuals of that era surfaced in Kerry in the late 1980s. He came from Cahersiveen and his name was Maurice Fitzgerald. The young Maurice was coached by his father, Ned – a former Kerry captain – and by Mick O'Connell from an early age, and quickly developed into a superb stylist in all the arts of Gaelic football.

He played Kerry minor in 1987 and was an instant success as a senior the following year, gaining rave notices on numerous occasions. Unfortunately for him Kerry were then in decline, but he continued to impress during the lean years.

He was the most perfect two-footed player I ever saw, and without his noble presence Kerry would not have won the All-Ireland titles of 1997 and 2000. I recall his classic goal against Armagh in 2000 – a solo with the right, then the left, and finally the searing rasper with the right; and what about that last-minute equalizing point from a line ball against Dublin in Thurles the following year – fifty yards out on the right, then that graceful double-bending lob that looped over the bar with plenty to spare.

Mention of Maurice brings to mind colleagues of great merit such as Séamus Moynihan and Daragh Ó Sé, but as their careers are ongoing I feel it is best to delay further comment.

Chapter Fourteen

I have always spoken Irish to anyone willing to do likewise. With the exception of my stints at university, I received my own education through the medium of Irish and feel that it was a good system. It was my intention, then, that our children be given the same opportunity of education through the medium of Irish as I had been allowed, but there was no such school in our area at the time.

In May 1975 I and a few others organized a meeting with the aim of founding an all-Irish school for the Clonsilla/Blanchardstown/Castleknock area. As I am a believer in the theory that one should never postpone until tomorrow what can be done today, I proposed that we found such a school to open on the first day of the new school year: 1 July. I received very strong support, and before the meeting ended I was the chairman of an action committee.

In order to start a school, we were required to have twenty-five pupils of school-going age and premises deemed suitable by the Department of Education. By the middle of June we had seventeen students, including our eldest, Éamonn, and the promise of ten others who would have reached the required age of four years by the autumn.

The old vocational school in the village of Blanchardstown had been vacant since the opening of the pioneering community school at nearby Coolmine. We made representations to the County Dublin VEC for a single room in the vocational school, and Chief Executive Séamus Ó Donnchadha was of immense help in providing such for one year. Our application was accepted by the Department of Education, and we were sanctioned to open as Scoil Oilibhéir on 1 July 1975.

I was appointed Chairman of the Board of Management by the archbishop – the first lay person to fill such a post – and I was waiting at the school door from the crack of dawn on the first day to admit seventeen four-year-olds. Siobhán Nic Óda, a native of Carrick-on-Suir, was our principal teacher. It was her very first day's teaching.

For me it was a moment to savour as enthusiastically as any All-Ireland. The school's success exceeded our expectations, thanks to the cooperation of parents and teachers. We needed a second room and an additional teacher the following year, and so on in succeeding years, until the building eventually became too small to accommodate growing numbers.

Before I retired from the post of Cathaoirleach nine years later, a brand-new school in the sylvan setting of the Coolmine Woods was opened, with an enrolment nearing 300 pupils.

Through my experience in helping to establish Scoil Oilibhéir, I became interested in the Gaelscoileanna movement. In 1973, when the movement was founded, there were only fourteen primary schools teaching through the medium of Irish outside the Gaeltacht areas. By 1976 I was the National President of the movement, leading a committee that was determined to get the tide running the other way for the sake of preserving something in which we all believed. There were better workers than me on the committee, but my profile as an RTE person was helpful to the cause. I was willing to travel anywhere to encourage others to set up Irish schools, and I have made innumerable friends in the process.

We decided that the recruitment of a full-time organizer would be of immense benefit, and with that in mind we approached Bord na Gaeilge for financial assistance. Chief Executive Micheál Grae received the delegation, and he assured us that he would recommend our application at the next meeting of the board. The application was accepted, and I firmly hold the view that it was the best decision ever recorded in the minutes of Bord na Gaeilge. I say so with the experience of serving on the same board subsequently for a period of nine years, with seven as Chairman.

Conal Ó Móráin was Gaelscoileanna's first full-time organizer, and I am glad to say that the movement continues to receive support from Bord na Gaeilge's successor body, Foras na Gaeilge. There are now nearly 200 all-Irish primary schools in non-Gaeltacht areas.

It helped considerably also that John Wilson was Minister for Education at a crucial period in the movement's development; he was fluent in many languages, including Irish. He put a structure in place that eased many of the burdens associated with the founding of new schools. Even though visits to government departments are meant to be confined to business, I could never let an opportunity to discuss sport pass by. Naturally John and I found a few minutes to talk again about the All-Ireland football final of 1947 in the Polo Grounds in New York, with John on the field as part of the winning Cavan team.

Winning an All-Ireland at any time is the dream of every player, but beating Kerry in the only final ever played outside of Ireland elevates the achievement to the pinnacle. Understandably, Cavan got every honour bar sainthood on their return to Breffni. No matter where John Wilson and I meet, Irish is the general medium of our conversation; however, I could never stay with the former Tánaiste if he decided to use his Greek.

Once I was at a meeting concerning Irish in Leitrim when a lady approached me in connection with the Gaelscoileanna movement. I mentioned the part played by John Wilson, and she then told me this story about John and another fine Cavan character, Joe Stafford, a team-mate of John's in the Polo Grounds.

'Following a match somewhere in Meath long ago I got a drive home in one of the Cavan cars,' the lady told me. 'I was in the back seat sitting between John Wilson and a very funny man called Joe Stafford. We were all very young and Wilson was holding my hand while we travelled a few miles of the journey. We were talking about the match when Stafford changed the subject: "Wilson," said he, "we never played a match without changing over at half-time. For the sake of fair play I think I should hold her hand for the rest of the journey."'

★

Bord na Gaeilge has been one of the important players in the promotion of the Irish language since its inception in 1978. Serving members of An Bord are government appointees, and I was surprised to get a telephone call from Leinster House one day in 1990 telling me to hold on for the Minister for the Gaeltacht, who at the time was Charles J. Haughey.

He invited me (*as Gaeilge*) to become a member of Bord na Gaeilge. I deemed it a privilege and thanked him for the honour.

Proinsias Mac Aonghusa was the Chairman at the time, and I always had great respect for him. He was deeply involved in the Irish movement and was innovative in his approach, whether in the written word or in television programmes such as *Féach* and many more. I succeeded him as Chairman when the term of the existing board expired in 1992, and was reappointed in 1996, when Michael D. Higgins was Minister for the Gaeltacht. TG4, or Teilifís na Gaeilge as it was in the beginning, is a magnificent monument to his tenure in office, and though he faced opposition on a few fronts he never flagged in his belief that the new service was needed.

'Use whatever you have of it rather than talk about it' would be a summary of my approach to the use of Irish, and I advocated that it belonged to the entire community, rather than a minority regarded as specialists. Specialists can be off-putting for learners and enthusiasts. Working on behalf of the Irish language has brought me into contact with people of other traditions, and that in itself is good because all traditions deserve recognition.

Bord na Gaeilge once sponsored an unusual event at Galgorm Castle in Ballymena, County Antrim. The background to it was that Diarmuid Ó Doibhlinn of the University of Ulster in Coleraine was editing a book of poems collected by a poet and Irish speaker from Antrim whose name was Rose Young, or Róis Ní Ógáin, as she preferred.

Róis was a relative of the Brookeborough family and was born in Galgorm Castle. She was a loyal unionist, a member of the Orange Order, etc., but also a member of the Gaelic League, and she never saw a contradiction in the mix. She kept her diaries in

Irish, and they contained references to loyalist meetings, as well as accounts of classes with the Gaelic League on the Falls Road and trips to the Gaeltacht. What a pity we have not thousands like Rois – and maybe a few Gaelic footballers and hurlers learning to play the Lambeg drums in perfect peace in a loyalist setting. When Bord na Gaeilge heard that the Brookeborough family was anxious to honour Rois's Irish interest we were glad to be part of it.

A function to commemorate Rois Ní Ógáin was organized at Galgorm Castle. The poet's niece Lady Brookeborough and I unveiled a plaque bearing a bilingual message:

Rose Young, poet, was born here.
Rugadh Rois Ní Ógáin, file, anseo.

Later I enquired of Lady Brookeborough if she had any Irish herself. She said she had none, but after a while she enquired about the meaning of '*tré na chéile*'. I said it meant all mixed up, and she then told me that her horseman often used the phrase when teaching her how to ride horses in her youth. A little later she volunteered to tell me what the Irish word *gríosach* meant, and she had it dead right as she looked towards the fireplace.

The Good Friday Agreement brought my tenure as Chairman of Bord na Gaeilge to an end at midnight on 6 December 1999. As the writ of the Bord established in 1978 did not run beyond the Irish border, a new Act was needed to reconstitute it as a cross-border body. It was necessary therefore to abolish the old Bord na Gaeilge before bringing Foras na Gaeilge into existence. The process was interesting to watch, with a programmed death giving way to a birth almost instantaneously. Foras na Gaeilge is now working satisfactorily on both sides of the border. Máiréad Uí Mháirtín is the current Cathaoirleach, and the former Galway hurling captain and later GAA President Joe McDonagh is Chief Executive. Funding is larger, and the spirit of Irish is stronger than ever. Courage for all to use it in all types of places remains a target.

I call in to the offices in Merrion Square from time to time to keep in touch with what is happening, and *bíonn fáilte mhór i gcónaí ag gach éinne romham*.

There is talk that An Foras is to be moved to Donegal as part of the government's decentralization programme. I am in agreement with the principle, but in the case of certain government institutions I believe that a Dublin headquarters is best. I would place Foras na Gaeilge in that category because it is important that the language be seen as belonging to the entire population. A Dublin HQ makes that easier to promote.

Coláiste Mhuire was an Irish secondary school run by the Christian Brothers in Dublin's Parnell Square from the early 1930s onwards. People famous in different walks of life, including Alan Dukes, Risteárd Mulcahy and Brian Mullins, received their second-level education *as Gaeilge* there.

There was an Ó Muircheartaigh presence at the school from the early 1950s, when the sons of my uncle Joe enrolled there. They were followed by the children of my brothers Padraig and Dónal and my sister Eileen. In due course my own three lads followed suit, and when the youngest, Cormac, had finished his Leaving Certificate, I was asked to become Chairman of the Board of Management for the sake of continuity of the family connection.

I worked there with wonderful people – Christian Brothers, teachers, board members, parents and friends of the school – over the following nine years. In my time we admitted girls to the Coláiste for the first time, and moved to more comfortable accommodation in the grounds of the School for the Blind in Cabra while the Department of Education contemplates the necessary refurbishment to the original premises.

It does not mean, though, that I have no further connection with the Irish-language world. My late brother Paddy had been Chairman of Cairde Choláiste Íde in Dingle for a number of years prior to his death, and I was asked to succeed him in the post. Saying no was not an option because I knew what was involved.

Coláiste Íde, located in the former home of Lord Ventry beside

Dingle Harbour, had been a boarding school for girls run by the Irish Sisters of Mercy since the 1920s. My sisters Eileen and Máire had each spent four years there. As the century was drawing to a close its future as a school was in danger when it became apparent that the nuns could no longer muster sufficent members of the community to run the place satisfactorily, and a decision was taken to oversee a phased closing down. It was then that a number of locals met with a view to keeping the place in operation and run by lay people.

Cairde Choláiste Íde, with Paddy as Chairman, came into being with that remit, and I must say that the difficult transactions were well in progress when circumstances brought me to the chair. A magnificent institution has been saved, and with a vast amount of refurbishment completed the place is running smoothly as the only all-Irish boarding school for girls in the country.

Some say that the use of Irish is being eroded in Gaeltacht areas, and it may be true. The same has happened over generations in the other parts of the country, but my hope is that the language will survive in all its vitality in the Gaeltachtaí. A major revival is taking place in the cities and big towns. More Irish is now spoken on a daily basis in Dublin, Belfast, Cork and Galway than in any Gaeltacht, and I find that encouraging. The proportion of people who speak Irish to me in all sorts of places has grown phenomenally.

The area where I grew up in Kerry was known as a 'Breac-Ghaeltacht', which meant that Irish was not the only language in everyday use. To this day I am a disciple of bilingualism. All languages are valuable assets to those who possess them, and English is especially useful. People without a knowledge of English who emigrated in the early part of the past century and before were at a disadvantage in places such as England and the United States. The ideal goal as I see it would be fluency in Irish and English for all school pupils by the end of primary education, and teaching through the medium of Irish is by far the easiest road to that goal. The more the younger generation travel, and happily they do a lot of it, the more they appreciate their Irishness; I see them as the generation that will ensure that the distinctiveness of our culture lives on in the varied worlds of language, games, singing and dancing.

I meet an inordinate number of people who are anxious to speak in Irish to me, sometimes apologizing for their lack of fluency. I think it is encouraging that they are willing to speak whatever of the language they possess. I was in Kilkenny once to speak on behalf of Bord na Gaeilge at the launch of a promotional scheme. Many public representatives were present, and one approached me at some point in the aftermath informing me that he had very little Irish, but had no difficulty in understanding me. I thanked him for the compliment, and as he was responding I got a tap on the shoulder inviting me outside for a group photograph. When I was half-turned away I said to my friend, 'Beidh mé ar ais' (I will be back), and added that I felt sure he understood the phrase.

'By God, I do. You have to go,' was his assuring reply, and we then shook hands.

There is nothing wrong with confidence in one's own ability: team managers are preaching that gospel to players all the time.

St Brigid's GAA Club, founded in 1932, was a decided benefit to the large number of people who moved into our part of west Dublin in the early 1970s and subsequently. It responded to the growth in the number of young people in the community, and before long committees devoted to promotion and development sprang up in the club. By the early 1980s I was Chairman of the club's Development Committee, and plans were drawn up to build a large complex that would be adequate to cater for an ever-increasing number of teams.

Unfortunately, I had to relinquish the post in May of 1986 after suffering a minor heart attack in unusual circumstances. It had been my intention to attend a function promoting tourism at six one evening. The attraction was that Con Houlihan, my favourite sportswriter, was to be the speaker. I left Donnybrook where I was working on Radio na Gaeltachta's *Adhmhaidin* programme in good time, but took a strange decision on reaching the Stillorgan Road: instead of going right I opted to turn left and proceed to Belfield, where I was due to start training some Kerry footballers at seven.

Only in hindsight did I see that it was unusual for me to opt out of something I had settled on.

Finding myself with a bit of time on my hands in Belfield, I went to a secluded part of the grounds carrying a nine-iron golf club and a few golf balls. I hit them for a while as addicts do until I noticed that I was getting less than a hundred yards into the shots. That was not very good, so I quit and waited for the players to turn up for training.

The Munster championship was in progress at the time, and I had a few of the Kerry lads, notably Jack O'Shea and Mick Spillane, under my care. They were going for their eighth All-Ireland win in twelve years. I remember we had Kieran Murray of Monaghan, another All-Star at the time, among others in attendance. But my reading of the session was that it was not up to scratch, and I have a distinct recollection of telling them that as footballers they were all in decline.

Again it is only in retrospect that it makes sense, as does my refusal to go for the customary meal with them at the end.

As I headed for home it dawned on me that everything I had done from six o'clock onwards had been negative. I then took an extraordinary decision: I called into Mrs McDowell's in Templemore Avenue and asked Helena's young sister Moya to call an ambulance. Before long I was in St Vincent's Hospital. An examination took place, and to my great surprise I was informed that I had suffered a heart attack.

I was in the right place with the best of attention; I made a quick recovery, and I had my Kerry men in real shape by September when they collected another All-Ireland medal.

Meanwhile the Brigid's Club continued the development that has witnessed fantastic success over the years. An emphasis was placed on underage activities and a veritable army of volunteers took charge of teams at different levels. My own three lads, Éamonn, Aonghus and Cormac, all benefited from it. Cormac played on a team that went five years without defeat in league or championship. Later he was on the senior team that won the Dublin League, and he played for Dublin at minor and under-21 level. Éamonn won a Dublin Intermediate Championship with the club. Aonghus was more into the hurling, but he did captain Scoil Oilibhéir to a Dublin Schools' football title in Croke Park with a very young Cormac as full-forward.

The club has progressed on all fronts, and it is one of my regrets that I have had very little time to spend there due to other work and voluntary commitments. The Irish movement simply devours time, and I am also a Director of the National Lottery and Chairman of Guaranteed Irish.

I have managed to see many of Brigid's championship games, but missed the big one last year when the Dublin Senior Football title was captured for the first time. At the time the match was played I was high above the Arabian desert, on the way to Australia with the Ireland Compromise Rules team. And the omens were good as I looked down: the sand was red, and seemed to be moving, just like the Brigid's players who tog out in red. I saw them go on to win the Leinster championship on my return, a victory that was the result of good underage structures and endless work by mentors ranging from those with the under-tens to Gerry McEntee and Paddy Clarke with the winning seniors of 2003.

Chapter Fifteen

In my time I have got to know sportspeople of all sorts, and I have come to the conclusion that playing golf brings about a change of personality for a duration that stretches a few hours after the round is finished. I have been in GAA dressing rooms after major games when the adrenalin is still flowing, but I have yet to hear anybody describing a kick or puck of theirs as being outstanding in its execution. But that is what the very same people are likely to do after a round of golf. They experience no embarrassment whatsoever in praising their own shots. I think that golf is the only game that allows participants to boast in this way, and therein, perhaps, lies its huge attraction. Anyway, I love it and believe it is good for body and soul.

There was an old nine-hole course near us in Dún Síon, and we often played a few holes once the day's work on the farm would be over. I played my first game in Dublin in St Anne's, Dollymount, shortly after starting teaching in Seville Place. An acquaintance I met in UCD, Bill Isdell, had an assortment of cobwebbed clubs in the family home and two light bags. We hired a tandem and cycled leisurely through the city, along by Fairview and all the way to St Anne's at the extremity of Dollymount, with the bags balanced on our shoulders. It is obvious now that we both had an exaggerated opinion of our prowess at the game because we were content starting off with one golf ball each. We had bought them when paying the green fees and took no notice when the man on duty remarked that we definitely had the appearance of two scratch players.

We were back to him rather quickly to purchase a more realistic amount of artillery.

I purchased a few clubs, and my brothers Padraig and Dónal and I got into the habit of paying green fees at clubs here, there and everywhere, with a view eventually to joining one of them. There were no waiting lists as exist almost everywhere now.

One evening in 1958 we played at Grange Golf Club, at the foot of the Dublin mountains, and retired to the bar after play. While we were there, a presentation was made to a Mr Jerry Priestman, who had won some competition. The usual speechifying took place, and ended with Jerry inviting all to join him in a celebratory drink. As we were not members we declined the barman's offer, but before long Jerry presented himself in front of us stating that he regarded all present as members of the moment. We thought it a nice gesture, enjoyed his hospitality with an orange, and decided there and then that Grange was the club to join. It seemed to offer more than mere membership, and that is how I have found it ever since.

Joe Carroll was the professional at the time, and I decided that a lesson from gentleman Joe would be of benefit, although I was of the opinion that I was fairly good. Joe certainly sorted out the opinion whatever about the game.

I had brought a favourite spoon or three wood with me, and I was invited to take a shot right away. To me it appeared a good shot meriting some praise, but none was forthcoming as I was asked to try again. My second attempt was even better, and yet not a word of encouragement from the expert, who was in fact a genuinely nice man. He had sized me up to perfection and decided that a dose of the truth would not be out of place.

'I would hit it forty yards beyond your last one with my five iron,' he exclaimed casually, gripping his club and ready for action.

I simply would not believe him, and said so while pulling an old ten-shilling note from my pocket and throwing it on the ground as a bet.

He did likewise, then produced the greatest put-down I ever heard: 'What's more, I will do it standing on one leg.'

With that he curled the right foot round the calf of the left like a strutting cockerel and proceeded to hit the ball comfortably beyond mine.

I was dumbfounded. Joe picked up the two notes, and looking straight at me said in a rather soft tone, 'Now we'll start.'

It was the greatest lesson I ever received.

Joe was a tidy golfer and had the distinction of once doing well in the qualifying section of the British Open. I remember being in his shop one day after returning from the Open and hearing him talk of a 'lunatic' he had played with while across the water: 'He is a young American, and he told me he would be a millionaire by thirty.'

Millionaires were not that plentiful in those days, but the young Yank joined them long before the target age: he was Jack Nicklaus.

I have got great value from Grange over the years, and I would say that Padraig and Dónal got even more. Both held the offices of captain and president of the club, and I had the honour of winning Dónal's captain's prize in 1978 in unusual circumstances. It was played over two rounds on successive Saturdays. I would not have entered at all except for the family connection because the first round coincided with my eldest son Éamonn's first communion. This meant I needed to play my round at an inordinately early hour in order to be back home before 9 a.m.

It was arranged that my brother Padraig and Seán Devitt would join me to tee off as soon as the light was adequate and play while most people slept. Seán's reason for the early rising was an appointment with some Mensa members at the more Christian hour of ten. I left home before 3 a.m. and had planned to hit a few shots in Bushy Park in Terenure on the way.

As I was practising I noticed two gardaí approaching and greeted them with a good morning, even though it was far from bright. It was obvious that they did not know me, as they asked what I was doing in the park at that hour. I told them exactly: 'See that tree down there? Well, I am trying to hit nine-irons over the top of it.'

With that, they looked at each other and departed, I would say, with some sympathy in their hearts.

We teed off at 3.40 a.m., before it was fully bright, and I was in the shower at 6.50 having carded a modest score of thirty-one

Stableford points. As things turned out I was seven shots behind the leader for the second round a week later and did not seem to be in with a winning chance. My fancy was scratch man David Sheahan, who was four or five ahead of me and had an absolutely amazing record. Being busy in his work as a family doctor Dave never had much time to devote to practice, yet he won the Irish Close championship three times from a limited number of attempts and was honoured with Walker Cup selection, winning both his singles matches. He also had the distinction of beating the best professionals on the European Tour when winning the Jeyes Tournament played in Royal Dublin in 1962.

Success never altered his demeanour, and he is as content playing with a long-handicap club member as he would be with Tiger Woods.

Anyway, I had a carefree attitude for the second round of Dónal's captain's prize and scored a good thirty-eight points, which pleased me. I still did not see my aggregate sixty-nine points as a winning score and headed off to Shelbourne Park long before the first-round leaders had finished. I was having a good night when, at about 9.30, an announcement on the public address requested my presence in the office to take a telephone call. The person on the phone nowadays carries the title of the Honourable Mr Justice Diarmuid O'Donovan; his summons was that I return immediately to Grange because 'it looks as if you might be the winner of the captain's prize'.

For once I abandoned the dogs, and right enough I was the winner of my brother's prize. It is the only record I hold in Grange.

Most people admit to be playing only reasonably well or worse when asked, but one time, for a bit of 'diversion', I began to tell members that I was actually playing exceptionally well, especially on other courses. Within a week or two the captain, Bill Lennox, approached me one evening in the bar and mentioned the good reports he had heard about my golf. It ended with an invitation to play on the Barton Cup team, which proves that self-promotion works. The Barton Cup is a foursomes competition, and my partner was George McNamara, a great character from Clare who had a unique approach to the game. He was also a good storyteller and the best of company on a journey.

He came to golf by an unusual route, as he once related to me while having a leisurely practice round for the Barton. He was at the races in Phoenix Park, with a few pounds on a good tip he had received, when a friend approached and told him of an unbeatable horse in the same race. It was convincing, and George returned to the Tote window and asked to change his tickets. Before granting his wish the operator asked him was he sure he was doing the right thing. 'If I do the wrong thing I will come back and you can kick me,' was the Clare man's reply.

Well, he had acted unwisely and the original nag won, causing George to return to the window later to fulfil his promise of taking a kick. The operator declined the invitation, and with that my friend declared: 'You will never again get the opportunity.'

He bought a few golf clubs the next day and wrote off the horses completely.

Our first outing was against a team from the Heath, close to Portlaoise; it was familiar territory to me because my uncle Joe was a former captain from his days as a schools' inspector in the area. We won the match, and it was the first of a run of successes, with only one defeat over a three- or four-year span. Our greatest asset was an extraordinary ability to win matches with bad golf.

A bag of golf clubs makes a good travelling companion, and with them I have taken in tons of fresh air. Ireland has more golf courses per capita of population than most countries, and I have sampled nearly all of them. Overseas I have played on courses stretching from within the Arctic Circle in Finland to equatorial Malawi in Africa, from the United States to Bejiing, Bangkok, Singapore and Australia.

I have fond memories of a trip to Scotland in 1991, when my late brother Padraig and his son John and I spent a few pleasant days playing golf beginning in the west with Western Gales and Troon, before going on to the King's and Queen's courses at Gleneagles and finally St Andrews, the Croke Park of the game.

★

I have always tried to see as many of the big sporting events in other countries as I can manage. Two years ago my son Éamonn booked tickets for the pair of us to the Ryder Cup at the Belfry in England. While I would rank nothing I have seen elsewhere with an All-Ireland final, the week at the Belfry was most enjoyable. We were there at daybreak for even the practice days, right up to Saturday evening when I returned home for a match on Sunday. It was superbly organized, the weather was beautiful and we saw the best golfers in the world at close range. Darren Clarke, Paul McGinley and Padraig Harrington made up a quarter of the winning European team, a fair achievement for a small country.

Incidentally, both McGinley and Harrington were fair Gaelic footballers in their school days.

We met an amazing number of spectators I knew from sport back home, confirming for me an opinion I have held for some time: there is a terrific following for sport in general in the Ireland of today, and people simply flock to events where they expect to get value. It could be hurling today and soccer, rugby, golf or horses next time out. I think that is a healthy state of affairs.

I managed to get to the hallowed grounds of Augusta National in Georgia for the 2003 Masters championship. Tickets are hard to come by, but it was a help that Paddy Harrington, the former Cork footballer and father of Padraig, was aware of my ambition to go to the Masters sometime. Father and son combined to supply me with a pair, and this time my son Aonghus was the minder. The decorum and general organization of the tournament were exemplary. Nobody runs at Augusta, nobody drops litter, and one is expected to behave according to the spirit of the royal and ancient game. A simple sheet with names and starting times serves as the programme. It was brilliant to see Padraig Harrington and Darren Clarke compete there with the elite of world golf; Harrington is a particular favourite of the Augusta crowds. He is a gifted performer, and my forecast is that he will win at least one of the game's majors before his career ends.

I often played cards in his parents' home before he was born and occasionally mention to Paddy a remark he made at the end of a card school one night. We had congratulated him on the birth of Fergal, and he casually said that Breda would like a daughter. He also stated that he had told her that he was willing to try again. Padraig, now one of the world's greatest golfers, was the result of the trial.

Chapter Sixteen

I was extremely young when I saw a greyhound for the first time. He was kennelled at home and must have had some fame because people came to see him regularly. He looked huge and powerful, and through deduction I have concluded that more likely than not he was a dog called Monocotyledon owned by my uncle Joe. I have often heard that he had won a Trial Stake and qualified for the Derby, but was unable to take his place due to sickness. He was rated better than his litter brother Dainty Man, the winner of the first ever coursing Derby in 1930. Dan Walsh, a good friend of Joe's, had a connection with the winner, and that is the reason why his nephew, the ex-footballer Dr Jim Brosnan, gives his date of birth as the day that Dainty Man won the Derby.

The most famous dogs in Dingle during my early school days were Droichead Bán and Fancy Blend. Mickey Boland owned the Droichead and Jimmy McKenna, the man who captained Dingle to its first county title in 1938, owned Fancy. We looked forward to seeing the dogs being walked when going to school every morning.

There was often a greyhound in the Moriarty home, though not in recent times. Náis had a reasonable one in the early 1950s; after he won a race at the Tralee Track, he was sent to the famous trainer Tom Lynch in Dublin. His kennels were not far away from where I now live, and I was a frequent caller to plan the progress of Náis's Oran Victor. The nearest he came to a win was a good second in Shelbourne Park and another close but losing finish at Navan.

When my father had another promising one a year later I convinced him that he was worth sending to Dublin, where all the good ones raced. Joe Dowling, whose kennels were in the rural setting of Old Bawn beyond the village of Tallaght, became the trainer of White Loaf. I cycled out there a few times, and to be honest you would not meet many people in those days that far out from the city.

The trainer thought a lot of the dog, and we really fancied his chance when entered for a race at Harold's Cross. I got paid on that particular day – nine pounds for a fortnight – and my decision was to speculate half of it on the Loaf and keep the remainder for subsistence over the next two weeks. What is this the proverb says? A half a loaf is better than no bread.

I took a good price early on in the betting, but once the parade got under way I got it into my head that there was no way the Loaf would get beaten. He looked every inch the perfect champion and really on his toes with *fuadar*. I went to the rails and put on the second half of my fortnightly salary.

I survived the following two weeks with the help of an indeterminate loan from my sister Eileen.

I have had dogs of my own or in partnership in the meantime. I know I had one when I went into the Munster and Leinster Bank in Dublin's Baggot Street a long time ago to seek a loan of £100. When I had explained my case to the manager, Mr Wellwood, he asked what collateral I was offering. I said I had bloodstock, and following further discussion I clarified that the bloodstock in question was an extremely promising young greyhound. With that Mr Wellwood rested his pen on the table and informed me that in the long history of the bank there was no record of an advance against such a security. But he was willing to give the loan anyway on the honourable principle of good faith.

I told him that sportspeople in general had more good faith than the rest of the population put together.

Stevie Kelliher, with whom I ought to have got a lift from Killarney on that night of the Munster football final in 1953, had been a good friend of mine since childhood. He sat beside me in the CBS in Dingle for a while, and it would be fair to say that he took his share of punishment before declaring during a particularly hard hour that he was leaving and going to Baile Uí Shé school. In later years he kept greyhounds and a horse or pony for the local races, and he managed to sell me a greyhound or two that turned out reasonably well.

I remember one that I purchased in Tralee Track one night after he had run a race without showing any great potential to a casual eye. The dog's name was Bone Lazy, and there was something about him that I liked, but my real interest was on account of a former purchase that won a few races. It was around 1970 and I decided that £80 would be a fair price for the animal, so I approached Stevie and his brother Timmy in the bar before racing ended.

The running of Bone Lazy earlier was being spoken of in unparliamentary language until I showed an interest. Then with the bit of roguery that is in every dealer, the brothers began to extol the dog's virtues and highlight his misfortunes during the race. I asked them for a selling price, and I was told an even hundred. I offered sixty. Before long we had willing helpers and eventually we struck hands at £80.

As always Stevie had given good value, and the acquisition won over many distances on the Leinster provincial circuit without ever threatening to win a Derby.

Night at the Dogs was an RTE programme that started on Radio 1 back in the 1980s. I had spoken about the possibility of that type of programme to Maurice Quinn, then Head of Radio Sport, and he agreed to give it a try. The idea was to mix racing with music, interviews and items of interest without being too technical or going into detail that only the real faithful follower would relish.

I was the main presenter, and we had great fun doing these programmes – usually six or seven a year. Pat O'Donovan, now the General Manager of Harold's Cross, was producer most of the time. The greatest living expert on dogs, Michael Fortune, was part of the team, as was interviewer Ruth Buchanan at times also.

Producer Pat was ideal for the job as he was always willing to run with an idea no matter how crazy it sounded at first. He was a vital link in arranging the famous interview I conducted with Prince Edward of England at the Wimbledon Greyhound Track in 1990.

We both knew Patsy Byrne, an honest Kerryman from Duagh in the north of the county and a very successful building contractor in London. Gaelic football and dogs would be close together at the top of his sporting priorities. At the time in question he was co-owner with Prince Edward of a startlingly good greyhound called Druid's Johnno. The dog was long-odds favourite to win the Derby of that year, and Pat and I were planning with the cooperation of Patsy for an interview with the joint owners if the dog qualified for the final.

The star was undefeated over the early rounds of a long, drawn-out competition, and still so on semi-final night. Accordingly I journeyed across for the occasion carrying my trusty recorder. I met with a few of the security personnel that surround royalty in public places, and they assured me that the interview was on course immediately after the semi-final, provided the dog obliged. I was full of goodwill towards Buckingham Palace while the preliminary races were being run, and when the appointed time came Druid's Johnno hurtled from the traps and won more impressively than ever. I then proceeded to the relevant interview location at Patsy Byrne's table in the restaurant. I sat myself down between the co-owners, who were in a state of immense excitement and antici-pation for the final a week later. I could see that Patsy had more of the look of the traditional Gaelic football fullback than the prince. The interview then took place. The Prince mentioned the fact that winnings from the co-ownership would benefit the fund set up for the victims and relatives of the Aldershot bombing, of which he was patron. I mentioned his father Philip's luck when his dog Camira Flash won the Derby of 1968, and Edward was naturally hoping to emulate the achievement.

We spoke for a good while after the interview had been com-pleted, and I found him to be very interesting. I got the distinct impression that he would just love to be an ordinary person like Patsy and myself, free as the wind to wander anywhere as we wished. He told me that he would be willing to do another interview a week later if the favourite won.

When I came away from the interview area I was approached

by a posse of British journalists who had been refused interviews and were anxious to find out from me what the prince had said. I pleaded that I would need to ring my producer for clearance to reveal the details of the interview – not that I had any intention of doing so. I was then asked what questions I had posed to him, and again I was as vague as a Kerryman can be in such situations. A straight question followed enquiring if I had asked His Royal Highness why he thought his father was booed when his dog had won in 1968. I gave a straight answer to that one, stating that I did not even consider asking because I thought it to be totally irrelevant to the story of Druid's Johnno.

It was the only piece of information I imparted before returning home on Sunday morning in time for a match somewhere.

Unfortunately, the curse of Biddy Early must have visited the dog on final night: for once he started very poorly, and only a marvellous recovery saw him finish a close second on the line to a Tyrone dog, Slippy Blue. We did a *Night at the Dogs* programme from Wimbledon that night, and to be honest I had genuine sympathy for both the prince and Patsy, because Druid's Johnno was a class competitor.

By the way, I have often been asked why I addressed my inter-viewee as 'Prince' rather than the more formal and customary 'Your Royal Highness'. I do not know, but if you go back to the days of patronage of the arts in Ireland by the nobility of the time there are plenty of references to An Prionsa and none whatsoever to Highnesses.

The Irish way in me just keeps breaking out.

A few years ago I spent a pleasant week touring Finland in the month of May. The excuse was that our daughter Nuala was studying law in the University of Turku and spoke regularly of the beauty of the country. Helena and I decided to take her at her word and made the trip.

I like to explore the rural parts of a country more than big cities and towns, and with that in mind we hired a car and headed north in order to get within the Arctic Circle. I always bring the golf clubs everywhere as the main part of my luggage, convinced that a solid bag provides the ideal balance for a car in motion. I did not expect to find too many courses in Finland, but I was surprised and got in a bit of play whenever the car needed the recommended rest. Believe it or not there is a golf course within the Circle, and, while it might not be up to the standard of Augusta, Grange or Ceann Sibéal, the air is mighty fresh and the bunkers more snow than sand.

The greatest sporting memory I have of the country is the unique way they run greyhound racing – at least at the track where I found myself on a Sunday-afternoon outing. I got details of the meeting from the Internet and set off to find the track located north-east of Helsinki.

The first inkling that it might differ from Shelbourne Park dawned on me about 400 yards from the racing circuit. I noticed a directional sign for a dog cemetery and headed there. It was exactly as the sign had said: a dog cemetery with hundreds of well-cared-for little plots carrying names and other details of deceased but fondly remembered dogs. I had never seen such a place before, except in miniature to the left of one of the fairways of the Dundrum Golf Course in County Tipperary. I suppose it signified the great love the Finns have for their dogs – something I came to appreciate more fully the moment we arrived at the track.

Most of the spectators had a dog of one breed or other on a leash, and tender care was being lavished on them. The track and its amenities were far from state of the art, but I learned quickly that the dog was far more important than the human during the outing.

I studied the form for the first race as usual and noticed that the breeder of one of the runners was given as P. Hennessy, Irlanda. That was enough for me, as the same Paul often trained a few of my greyhounds, and I decided to have a bet on the Irlanda dog. I enquired about betting facilities and was directed to the other side of the track, where I found that the entire operation consisted of an ancient cash register placed on a small table. It worked as well as any Tote outlet I ever saw: the young lady took my few *markka*, and the register coughed out a ticket that linked it in some way to the number two on Hennessy's dog. Like a lot of his runners, this one won the race, making my first betting venture in Finland a success.

Another surprise awaited me when I went to collect my winnings: it was explained to me that winning bets were paid out in vouchers for dog food in the local supermarket, in accordance with the wishes of owners and patrons. It was yet another statement about the status of the dog, and I experienced a few more before I left. After the final race, I went to speak to the owner of a greyhound that had trailed in last a fair distance behind the others. After admiring the dog's appearance, I told the female owner in the nicest possible way that the dog had no future as a racer. Her answer, in four words with emphasis on each, dismissed my view as totally irrelevant: 'But he loves it!'

I learned then that she had travelled 200 miles to that meeting and had every intention of returning soon in order to allow the dog to carry on doing what he loved. I gave her the dog-food voucher I had won.

I believe that most sporting organizations err in not engaging in enough promotion, and it was with that in mind that Pat O'Donovan and I set about injecting more fun into the running of greyhound racing. Trainer Ger McKenna loaned us a dog which we renamed Radio Sport, and fortunately he won some excellent races on occasions when we were on air with *Night at the Dogs*.

Later on we devised the career of a greyhound called Stagalee. Patsy Byrne offered us the pick of a litter down in Duagh, and the choice was left to me. In the end it was down to one of three. I rejected one on the grounds of its fondness for laying back and resting. From the last two contenders, I finally made my choice of one on the basis that an interested third party was directing my attention as much as possible to the other.

I returned with an unnamed young greyhound of racing age and landed him in Dolores Ruth's kennels in Rathdangan, County Kildare. The plan was that his career would be monitored on Des Cahill's morning slot on 2FM once the show got on the road. The name 'Stagalee' was chosen for two reasons: there was a popular band of that name a few years earlier, and his sire's name was Hypnotic Stag. Stagalee duly qualified for racing, and the big night of his first race was well flagged on 2FM.

It was all great fun, but he was a huge disappointment in his first outing, which I recorded on tape for the morning programme. In the spirit of entertainment rather than gravity I concentrated on Stagalee's style of running and ignored the five runners that were actually ahead of him. I had Dolores primed for an interview in which she would say nothing but good about the dog, and she obliged until she thought I had finished and switched off the recorder. It was then she said, 'What a plonker!' – which I captured on tape; we let that go out on air as well.

Stagalee soon became a real star, winning good races, generating fan mail and receiving invitations to race at this track and that. We took him to Enniscorthy to take part in the main race on the card and the distinction of parading him went to Martin Storey, the famous Wexford hurler. I gave an interview that went out on the public address before the race and predicted that Stagalee would win after moving in to second place at the third bend.

Amazingly enough, that's the way it turned out.

What was not known at the time was that Stagalee had a weakness for chips, especially on the way home after racing, and we did not disappoint him that night when he spotted an American chipper on our way through Bunclody. He had done us proud in the race, and he was allowed some ketchup and vinegar as a bonus. I don't think I ever saw him happier, and I said so on radio the following morning when giving an account of the safari in Wexford.

All in all he won five good races before suffering a broken leg in a trial in Longford. He got the best of veterinary care at Danny McHenry's clinic in Newbridge, but although the leg mended perfectly he was never the same again. He retired to the kennels of a keen animal lover in Baden-Baden in Germany and had a few nostalgic runs around tracks in France, as well as making guest appearances at German dog shows.

★

In December 1998, trainer Paul Hennessy in Kilkenny put Pat O'Donovan and me in touch with an owner in Rathmore in Kerry who owned a dog that had failed to win more than one race out of his dozen starts, or thereabouts. Her name was Eileen Murphy and she agreed to the sale for a satisfactory figure. As a Bord na gCon employee Pat was no longer allowed the luxury of ownership, but there was no bar on his wife, Breda, so she and I went into partnership.

Breda's first venture was highly successful. The dog we called Unique Reward quickly got the knack of winning, and at one stage won four in a row at Shelbourne Park against top-class opposition. We had endless fun in watching him, backing him and even going on tour. He won quality races at Harold's Cross, Waterford, Cork and Limerick, where he won the Consolation St Leger final. He also won at Shawfield in Glasgow, where he reached the semi-finals of the Scottish Derby and won a Special Open Race on the night of the final. We followed him all the way.

We had promised him a weekend in London, and we did not disappoint him: he competed against the best in that city in a race at Wembley, though not as a winner.

Many of the joys of racing hinge on the eternal hope that the next venture is going to be the really memorable one. But there comes a time when such delusions come to an abrupt end.

I experienced one definite ending at Mullingar on a fine Saturday morning. I'd brought yet another promising sort along for its first trial, hoping that signals of potential greatness would be manifest. I met the late Gerry L'Estrange TD on the same mission, and he, too, was eager to find if his hopes were to be realized. As it was the first trial for both our dogs, we decided to let them run together. We did not bother putting them in traps; we just held them until the electric hare sped by, then released them. In my case it was immediate disaster with my hero showing absolutely no inclination to run. It was a terrible moment and a shattered dream as I observed him hold his ground.

Meanwhile Gerry's had actually taken off, but soon doubled

back to rejoin us three. It was not the time for a conversation, and with his political experience the TD was first to break the silence of sudden sadness. At first his remark made no sense whatsoever to me: 'Mine is worse than yours.'

I objected on the grounds that my one had not moved a millimetre and asked was there a lower level of ineptitude.

'You have it all wrong, Micheál. Your fella took one decision and stuck with it.'

That is the way of sport, and in that dog's case all the fun was in the year-long anticipation leading up to the symphony that was never composed.

But I can tell you that my next one, Dún Síon Sona, will sweep all before him!

Chapter Seventeen

I come from Kerry, a county that has won thirty-two All-Ireland football championships, but over the years I have often been invigorated by the sight of a county breaking through to win a title after decades of futility – from 1949, when the footballers of Meath broke through the barrier, to 2003, when the footballers of Tyrone did likewise.

Consider the case of hurling in 1980. Kilkenny, Cork and Tipperary had claimed seventeen of the previous twenty All-Ireland titles, and no county had won its maiden All-Ireland since Waterford in 1948. This was not a healthy situation for the GAA.

If one was to enquire about the status of Offaly hurling in the spring of 1980, the story of the Faithful County would not take that long to relate. They had appeared in the Leinster final of 1969, to be sure, but one would need to go back to 1928 to find the previous time they'd reached that stage.

It was as cold a canvas as ever, then, at the start of 1980, and if Our Lord himself had appeared on top of the monument in the square at Birr broadcasting the following message, not even St Peter – if he happened to be dropping by on his way to Dooley's – would have believed a single syllable:

> Hear ye, hear ye,
> There are twenty years left in this century of mine,
> *Fiche bliain sa Mhílaois freisin,*
> And there is no county in Ireland,
> Not even Cork, Kilkenny nor Tipperary,
> That will win more All-Ireland titles,
> Or provincial titles,
> Than you the Faithful people of Offaly.

But the miracle really did happen. Before the bells of the earth tolled the demise of the twentieth century and the second millennium, the senior hurlers of Offaly had played in eleven consecutive Leinster finals, and sixteen in all, winning seven, and adding four glorious All-Ireland titles.

I recall well the day in 1980 when Kilkenny, as All-Ireland champions, were raging favourites to take their eighth provincial title in ten years. Like everybody else I was expecting a win for the Cats, but I had got a warning two weeks earlier. I called to the Eye and Ear Hospital in Adelaide Road after the Leinster semi-finals to see a neighbour's child, Alan Waters, the son of Offaly parents.

The late Pat Carroll of Offaly had got an accidental knock the same day during the semi-final with Laois, and he, too, was taken to Adelaide Road. While there I met a pair of Offaly hurlers, Paddy Delaney and Fr Mick Kennedy, who called to enquire about Pat's welfare. We got into a hurling discussion; most of my observations related to Kilkenny, but the pair repeatedly interrupted me to note that they had won a semi-final that day as well as the Cats. 'Remember that,' said Paddy, with a gleam in his eye, as I left to go home.

Two weeks later in a fantastic game of hurling, Kilkenny scored 5–10, but still lost: the Faithful men, with a last-minute goal by comedian Johnny Flaherty, claimed the county's first Leinster title. You should see the gleam in Delaney's eye then!

As soon as the Offaly captain, Padraig Horan, had taken the massive Bob O'Keeffe Cup to the dressing room, he returned with me to the broadcasting box ready to talk about the historic achievement. Before we had finished, goalkeeper Damien Martin appeared, looking more solemn than I would have expected a veteran of many disappointments to be. He kept making signs which I failed to comprehend, but it was clear that he was trying to communicate a message that concerned Padraig. Damien called me aside the moment I had finished the interview and informed me that Padraig's sister had phoned Croke Park shortly after the match wishing to speak to him urgently. When he could not be found, she passed on the message that their father had died.

Damien wondered what should be done at that moment. As I chatted with Padraig, Damien rang the number left by the sister, but the line was engaged, and we decided there and then that Padraig should be told. Damien did so, and it was the saddest end to a glory hour that I was aware of since Michael Donnellan TD of Galway died at the All-Ireland football final of 1964, as his son John was leading the men in maroon to the first of three All-Ireland titles in a row.

I got the full details of Horan senior's death later that evening, and in one sense it was as fitting as the passing of a Roman warrior. He was a hurling man all his life, and there was none prouder than he when his son was appointed Offaly captain. He wanted to travel to the Leinster final, but due to failing health he was persuaded to stay at home and listen to the match. He did so and was content in the kitchen until the closing minutes, when the noise from children was making it difficult for him to hear the broadcast. He opted to listen to the remaining minutes in the peace of his car. As soon as the final whistle sounded, all rushed out in a state of extreme joy, only to be shocked at the sight of him collapsed in the car.

I attended the removal the following evening. The unanimous verdict was that he had died a very happy man and was storming Heaven's door, telling all Offaly saints to look down and see an Offaly man about to take hold of the Leinster Cup for the first time.

It took a brave effort from Galway to stop Offaly from reaching their first All-Ireland final when the sides met in an August semi-final. The men of the West won the September final later; however, a new force had truly arrived in Leinster also.

Offaly again won the Leinster title in 1981, and got a bye to the All-Ireland final. Galway again won their way to the final with wins over Antrim and Limerick, and were favourites to retain the McCarthy Cup. They looked the part in the first half, but Offaly were building a tradition for strong finishes and produced a late goal to snatch McCarthy from the Corrib. The goal was worked all the way from the halfback line area, with full use being made of an extra man forward as the sliotar went via Paddy Delaney, Brendan Bermingham and finally the jinking Johnny Flaherty to the Galway net.

As always there was a background to the fairy tale come true, and it could be summarized into two separate parts.

The first was the arrival of a quiet Corkman, Brother Denis, in Birr in the late 1960s. He was a hurling enthusiast and believed that teaching the proper skills to pupils in the Presentation College would yield dividends in time. By degrees the skill levels attained were transferred to the club scene, and a visionary might have been able to see light at the end of a long tunnel.

The second ingredient that led to the unheralded successes was the appointment of Dermot Healy as manager of the county hurlers for the 1980 season. He was a Kilkenny man, he had experience in management and he carried respect that made it easy to impose discipline and cultivate team spirit. He was the right man at the right time. He may have cost his native county a few All-Irelands, but the overall impact of the arrival of Offaly as a hurling power is incalculable. The game of hurling badly needs more like them.

Of Offaly's other three All-Ireland titles won before the end of the century, the 1994 win over Limerick was the most romantic and spectacular, even if a good case can be made for the sweet win over Kilkenny in 1998. It looked a long overdue success for Limerick in the final of 1994 when they led Offaly by five points with five minutes to go. It was then the fireworks started, when Johnny Dooley decided to try for a goal from a 21-yard free.

The ultra-cool Johnny was not worried, and gauged his puck to perfection for goal number one.

Joe Quaid has been blamed for rushing the puck-out, but he did leave a Limerick player in possession. I wonder what would people be saying if Ger Hegarty had managed to strike the ball over the Offaly bar? My guess is that they would be heaping praise on Quaid for his quick thinking. At any rate, it was only a timely touch by Johnny Pilkington that foiled Hegarty, and Offaly goal number two was on its way courtesy of Pat O'Connor.

The Dooleys then stepped forward once more, with five points in rapid succession from Billy and Johnny. The Limerick lead of five points had become a deficit of six in the space of four minutes and fifty-two seconds.

The gods were hard on Limerick that day. They are the county most deserving of an All-Ireland title right now, following years of great effort since their last win thirty-one years ago. One All-Ireland title over the past sixty-four years in no way reflects the true hurling status of the Shannonsiders. They have played in the finals of 1974, 1980, 1994 and 1996, and lost all four. I hope their day will come soon, and when it does it will be all the sweeter.

Since 1992, four different Ulster counties have come forward to win a senior All-Ireland football title for the first time: Donegal (1992), Derry (1993), Armagh (2002) and Tyrone (2003). No Leinster county has made the ultimate football breakthrough since Offaly did so in 1971. It is even worse in the other provinces: Roscommon in 1943 is Connacht's last first-time All-Ireland winner, and no new name from Munster has been inscribed on the Roll of Honour since Kerry in 1903.

I believe that the creation of the border between what people called Saorstát Éireann and the Six Counties back in the 1920s cannot in a strange way be divorced from the current good health of Gaelic football in Ulster. Nationalists never accepted the border, and often looked southwards for sporting solace. They looked upon events such as All-Ireland finals as belonging to the entire Irish nation on the day, not just to the two participating counties.

An old friend of mine, the late Raymie Eastwood from Belfast, put it in context for me once. He was a good man for the big gamble on horses and dogs, and had many winners in each code, including one at Cheltenham. He actually died watching a race at Leopardstown. But for him nothing compared to an All-Ireland final, and this is how he put its significance to me: 'Sometimes, I have sympathy for people from the strong counties – they think there is no All-Ireland final when they are not in it. But we have an All-Ireland every single year and we glory in it: it is a vital part of the year and we are always part of it.'

What he was saying was that it means a little bit more to Ulster nationalists, and we are witnessing the flowering of that extreme love these days. We need look no further than the 2003 All-Ireland football champions, Tyrone. The national anthem prior to the start of the final was respected by all spectators until the Artane Band had completed the last bar. The players knew the words: sessions practising the anthem were as much a part of their dry-run weekend at the City West Hotel in Dublin as tactics and logistics. After the match, the players gathered round the Sam Maguire Cup in the dressing room and sang the anthem once more.

Crossmaglen Rangers won the AIB All-Ireland club championship titles of 1997, 1999 and 2000. Is it fair to ask how many they would have won if the British Army had not commandeered a portion of their playing grounds for a long stretch of years? Manager Joe Kernan and the players might well give 'at least five' as an answer; on the other hand, the confiscation made it easier to motivate the youth to practise on what was left of their ground.

Of course the political motivation is only one of the factors that has led to the satisfactory state of Ulster football at the moment. The ongoing work in the schools and clubs would be foremost, and the ever-increasing contribution of some third-level educational establishments is encouraging.

Enthusiasm for Ulster football is not always confined to the nationalist section of the population. I was stopped once by an RUC patrol during the successful run of Crossmaglen Rangers. While searching for some form of identity, I asked the policeman where he was from.

'Crossmaglen' was the answer, and there was only one retort to that.

'Do you know Joe Kernan?'

'Big Joe, everybody knows him.'

The need to show identification evaporated at that.

The first great Ulster football breakthrough in my time was achieved by Down. In 1959, when they won their first Ulster title, but crumbled against Galway in the All-Ireland semi-final in Croke

Park, they left a lasting impression as they dared to talk confidently about change. There was a bit of show biz about the way they dashed on to the field, and my impression is that they were the first Gaelic football side to wear tracksuits.

James McCartan told me once about the journey home after that 1959 defeat.

'If you knew my father,' he said, 'you would understand the motivation that drove the team. He was waiting outside the Cusack Stand and he began to talk the minute I got into the car: Why did you do that . . . what were you trying when you did this, that and the other . . . and so on until we landed in the yard at home. I had said very little, and he spoke almost nonstop. As soon as I got out I turned to him and said: "Even if I have to steal the Sam Maguire, it will come in that gate next year."'

And it did. And nobody ever said they stole it, either.

Events of the spring of 1960 augured well when Ulster won the Railway Cup with five Down players aboard, by far the biggest representation ever from the Mourne country. The League was Down's first main target of the year, and they finished in style by beating Cavan in the final. Retention of the Ulster title was next, and for the second year in a row they beat Cavan, the most feared team in the province.

Offaly had won their first Leinster that year and surprised all experts by holding Down to a draw in the All-Ireland semi-final. There was little in it in the replay, but the Ulster men got there by two points. Meanwhile, Kerry qualified for yet another All-Ireland final, and as impressive winners a year earlier they were clear favourites. An eight-point win for the Mourne men rates as one of the biggest upsets in the history of football, and it sparked off the liveliest post-match scenes ever seen on the field. Kevin Mussen was the man who stepped forward to accept the Sam Maguire Cup, and he was the first man to carry the famous trophy across the border. Down have played in four subsequent finals without defeat: in 1961 (before 90,556 spectators, the largest crowd ever at a sporting event in Ireland), 1968, 1991 and 1994. Beating Kerry along the championship route in four of their five winning campaigns, twice in the semi-final, and twice in the final adds further lustre to Down's achievement.

The 1960–61 team ranks with the best of all time – I would rate them second to the Kerry team of the 1970s and 80s. They were particularly brilliant in attack. Centre forward James McCartan had such strength that it was almost impossible to prevent him from driving through the middle for scores or to set them up. Seán O'Neill and Paddy Doherty possessed guile and true craft. The other three forwards – the late Brian Morgan, Patsy O'Hagan and Tony Hadden – helped to comprise the best forward unit seen in years.

There will be a place for them in the most cherished halls of the GAA for ever. Their historic breakthrough against all the odds in 1960 still acts as inspiration for those that have not yet got beyond the dreaming stage.

Donegal's All-Ireland triumph of 1992 was the first of the wonders of the 1990s. Few if any would have predicted in the spring of 1992 that Sam Maguire was destined for the Donegal hills before the year was out. But as the year went on the romantic tale took shape.

Brian McEniff was the devoted and driven manager, and many of his footballers had won under-21 All-Ireland medals with the county in either 1982 or 1987. The senior CV was improving also: the team had drawn the 1989 Ulster final with Tyrone, won the title a year later and reached the final again in 1991. More notice should have been taken of them in 1992, but luckily for them that was not so, and they were rank outsiders against Dublin in the All-Ireland final.

Dublin had been very impressive all year, and I felt it would be their title when I set out to go to Donegal on the Monday before the final. The atmosphere was brilliant, with Donegal experiencing the joy of being in an All-Ireland final for the first time. I travelled around a fair bit, and on the Tuesday played a game of golf with three friends in Nairn and Portnoo, where the football talk was superb all day. I still felt that as newcomers Donegal had little chance of beating Dublin, but did not air that view openly. When I was leaving much later one of the trio said that it was likely that the four of us will never again meet. There and then I promised to be back on the first tee by ten o'clock on the following Tuesday if Donegal were All-Ireland champions by then. We shook hands on that, and I departed thinking that I would not be seeing them for some time.

The world knows that Donegal played terrific football on the Sunday, and when one examines the personnel of the team it was not surprising: there was a huge number of fine natural players on the team, and they produced their best form on the hour from goal to corner forward. Anthony Molloy proved to be a magnificent captain, as well as a fine and honourable person, and what can one say about Martin McHugh except that he showed yet again the great class he had as a player. Later that night I called to the celebrations in Malahide to congratulate the players, and while jostling through the excited throngs I got a tap on the shoulder. On turning around I recognized one of the Nairn and Portnoo friends. Although he was overcome with joy and other emotions, I understood the message he was trying to convey to me: 'Could you make that half-twelve on Tuesday?'

I travelled to the north-west ahead of the Donegal cavalcade on Monday and waited on Bundrowes Bridge outside Bundoran until the team bus arrived well into the night. An endless meandering line of cars followed the bus, crowds on foot were immense and bonfires blazed under a starlit sky. It was a scene to be savoured as Anthony Molloy and Brian McEniff alighted from the bus and walked Sam Maguire across the bridge from Leitrim and into Donegal for a historic first visit.

Anthony Molloy invited me into the bus for the remainder of the journey into the town. I always had a *grá* for the county since my Coláiste Íosagáin days and the lads from there with their musical Irish. And I made it to the first tee at half-twelve on Tuesday, and the football talk was better than ever.

Although Clare won its first All-Ireland hurling championship in 1914, the eighty-one years that elapsed before their second title qualify that 1995 team to be among the great breakthrough sides.

Every minute of the saga of 1995 was spellbinding. Manager Ger Loughnane strode the scene like a man who believed that the Red Sea, not to mention all the seas of the northern hemisphere, would open up before him if he desired to cross over into the Promised Land. He had great desire, and as with the miracle of the loaves and fishes he managed to offload helpings of it to his players.

It took a while before I believed it was for real. I paid little attention when the Feakle man declared in the month of May that Clare would win the Munster championship. The words were uttered after a nine-point defeat by Kilkenny in the League final, which made the prediction all the more difficult to fathom. Clare's last Munster title had been won in 1932. I was still not converted when they beat Cork in the Munster semi-final at the Gaelic Grounds in Limerick on the first Sunday of June. Luck had seemed to be turning against Clare when centre back Seánie McMahon picked up a shoulder injury a quarter-hour before the end. In normal circumstances he would have been replaced, but Clare had already used up the quota of three substitutes and thus posted Mac to the forward line. Cúchulainn, in another era, saved Ulster though mortally wounded, and on that June day in 1995 McMahon, unable to swing the hurley, somehow engineered a line ball for Clare in the closing seconds of the game, with Cork ahead by a point. Fergie Touhy stepped up and sent a sweet crossing cut towards the Ennis Road goal; I can still see the prancing young warhorse Ollie Baker waiting and tapping Clare into the Munster final against Limerick in Thurles.

There was a buzz around the ground for a good while after the match ended, and a few bodhráns were belted, but still I did not visualize Clare as Munster champions. After all, Limerick were the reigning provincial champions, and a backlash was expected as a result of the Offaly drama that cruelly denied them the All-Ireland title the previous September.

My conversion to Loughnane's May creed occurred in the dressing room before the Munster final. There was an unbelievable air of anticipation around the ground when I left my box to check the teams. Everything was fine in the Limerick dressing room, with an air of confidence prevailing. The Clare dressing room was empty when I got there, and I waited inside studying the programme. Then I heard sounds from outside.

Ger Loughnane was first in, walking with that jaunty stride of his. He came straight to me and in a most convincing voice spoke at me rather than to me with words that I will never forget: 'Don't say a word – just look at them. We cannot lose.'

I said nothing; I looked. A band of athletic-looking and focused young men, with chests forward and eyes straight ahead as if looking into the future, entered the dressing room and took up their places. There was something about their presence that I had not witnessed before. As I shook hands with Ger I said to myself for the first time that Clare would be winners of the Munster championship on the day.

I really enjoyed the broadcast. It was great to be there as the possibility grew by the minute that we were about to witness something historic. Defiance, confidence and excellence oozed from the Dalcassians, and long before sunset it was obvious all around Thurles and far beyond that the finest chapter of Clare's history in sixty-three years had been written in capital letters; the famous Clare Shout that had once welcomed de Valera to the county blended with the bodhrán-bashing and shrieks of wild glee.

I once said at a Clare function that I hoped they would never win a Munster title. I was quick to explain what I meant: my logic was that they looked forward so eagerly to a big day that it might not be as they imagined when it came. But I could see before the end of July 1995 that my logic made no sense: it was obvious from Loop Head to Lisdoonvarna that the real thing exceeded all expectations. It was blessed manna from heaven to a now liberated people.

I did not hear a prediction about winning the All-Ireland come from Ger Loughnane during August, but Clare played their best hurling to date when beating a good Galway team in the All-Ireland semi-final. In the run-up to the All-Ireland final it was often said that Clare did not have a first-class forward unit. In hindsight it sounds senseless because they had managed to score 2–13 against Cork, 1–17 against Limerick and 3–12 against Galway.

Their opponents in the final were All-Ireland champions Offaly, and there was no dearth of atmosphere or colour as throw-in time approached. The dressing rooms in use were the old ones at the Canal End of the Hogan Stand, with Clare on the right as you come in from the pitch. As usual I paid a visit and again got a message from Loughnane, who wore his confidence on the features of his face. As I was about to leave he placed both hands on my shoulders and said with the directness for which he is famous: 'Have no doubts, we are going to win this game.'

It was strong talk from a man who was managing a county that had not won an All-Ireland title in eighty-one years.

Clare were in arrears towards the end of the game when they were awarded a free behind midfield on the Hogan stand side of the field. It was in the territory where normally Seánie McMahon would be expected to be the striker, but captain Anthony Daly stepped forward, realizing maybe that McMahon had taken a knock a short while before.

I can easily see Daly now with his defiant stance over the ball, then hurtling it towards the Canal goal. Nobody present will ever forget what happened over the next few seconds: the bounce of the sliotar outwards off the crossbar, the presence of Éamonn Taaffe where it landed, and the stroke to the back of the Offaly net.

Clare were now leading by a single point. They pressed forward and gained a seventy or sixty-five. It was another crucial puck, and Daly volunteered once more. Ger Loughnane passed by as Daly settled himself over the ball not too far in from the sideline and down under my vantage point. I could see that Loughnane was talking, and Daly responded with a fluent swing and a peach of a point.

Soon Clare were All-Ireland champions. It was the completion of a fantastic second coming.

The whole of sporting Ireland adopted Clare as the people's champions. That was brought home clearly to me a few months later when I arranged to bring a large group of interested blind people on a visit to Croke Park. There were representatives from many counties, but a stranger could easily have suspected that all came from Clare. I acted as guide, and the first request I got was from a man who wished to stand on the spot where Anthony Daly was when he hit 'that great shot'. We all moved out on to the grass, and I gave a poor imitation of Daly's swing to people who could not see; one lady with a sense of humour said I was a fine player.

Somebody then expressed a wish to touch the net where the goal was scored, and so we walked all the way to the Canal Goal, where there were plenty of comments about the strength of the net, the width of the goal and the strength of the uprights as everything was touched.

We sat on the stand for a while, then went to the dressing rooms before having a drop of tea and a few sandwiches. I can tell you that many of them knew as much about the games as Ger Loughnane himself.

I am convinced that Clare would not have won the All-Irelands of 1995 and 1997 without his guidance and confidence-building technique – and I say so in the knowledge that he had a very fine bunch of players at his disposal. Like Mick O'Dwyer, Seán Boylan, Babs Keating and other managers, he did the GAA an enormous service, even if he ruffled official feathers now and then. He became a voice for the underdog. Mind you, I would not agree with the manner of all his actions, in particular the misleading tactic of selecting ghost players leading up to big games. Gaelic players are amateurs, and I hold that it is wrong to publish the name of a player as being selected on the team, then omit him when match day comes.

But then Ger always said that his only interest was the welfare of Clare hurling and that he was willing to do anything that would help. He and the lads gave us as fine a chapter as the GAA has ever known, and the names will live for ever: the inspiring Anthony Daly, the driven Brian Lohan, the daring, diminutive Davy Fitz, the calculating Seánie McMahon, the powering Ollie Baker, the darting Jamesie O'Connor, the poaching Ger 'Sparrow' O'Lough-lin . . . Feel free to add in all the others: I will concur.

Chapter Eighteen

So many superb hurling teams have competed over the past fifty-five years that it would be foolish to expect universal agreement with my choice of the greatest team I have ever seen.

Here goes.

I have already written about my admiration for the Wexford team of the 1950s, and I throw them into the hat right away.

They were not the first great team I saw in action. I broadcast the first game Tipperary played after winning the first of their three consecutive All-Ireland titles in 1949. It was the Oireachtas final of that year between themselves and Laois, and I remember clearly calling to the dressing rooms before the match.

They were under the old Corner Stand, and needless to say I was rather shy entering the room of brand-new All-Ireland champions. I had the temerity to approach the captain, Pat Stakelum, and he could not have been more helpful to an innocent *garsún* who knew little about his game. I often think of it when I meet Pat and especially when I hear him recite his favourite poem, 'A Hurler's Prayer'.

That was a sound and solid Tipperary team containing some very skilful hurlers, of whom Tommy Doyle was my favourite. The Kennys, Paddy and Seán, caught the eye regularly, and there was also the red-headed Phil Shanahan, who guided a horse pulling a bread van along Sundrive Road in Dublin on working days. And goalkeeper Tony Reddan was rated as the greatest ever in the position by the selectors of the century and millennium teams.

An equally good Cork team succeeded them as All-Ireland champions, and they, too, recorded three titles in a row. The legendary Christy Ring was the big name among them, but several of his team-mates also deserve mention: Tony O'Shaughnessy,

Willie John Daly, Matt Fouhy, Paddy Barry, Joe Twomey, John Lyons and many more.

Goalkeeper Dave Creedon may well have been the talisman of the team. He had retired from inter-county hurling before the Championship season of 1952 had started, but fortune and fate combined to bring him back. Regular goalkeeper Mick Cashman was injured, and neither the second choice nor third was available for selection. Dave was asked to stand in for the first game of the Championship against Limerick; the intended one-day stand was to extend over three seasons that brought him as many All-Ireland medals.

The Cork team of 1976–78, with a skilful forward division that included Charlie McCarthy, Ray Cummins, Jimmy Barry-Murphy and Seánie O'Leary, was the only other team to win three consecutive All-Irelands.

All of these sides deserve to be counted among the best. However, having spent a good deal of time trying to assess teams of different eras, I narrowed my search for the greatest hurling team I have seen down to a choice between the Tipperary team of 1958–65 and the Kilkenny one of 1969–75.

By the time the Championship of 1958 came around, all but two of Tipp's stalwarts of the early years of the decade had faded from the inter-county scene. Mickey the 'Rattler' Byrne was one, and the other was Holycross's John Doyle, who was taking his first distinctive step towards the garden of legends. So it was a new era for the Premier County. Tipperary is the only county to have won a senior All-Ireland title in each decade of the GAA's history since championships began in 1887. It is a proud record indeed and regardless of what the immediate future brings Nick English's contribution in managing yet another Tipp All-Ireland in 2001 ensures that 2019 is the soonest that the chain linking all decades can be sundered.

The 1958 team beat Limerick by double scores in the opening round of the Munster championship, survived by two points against Cork in the semi-final and beat reigning champions Waterford out the gate in the final. In the All-Ireland semi-final, a five-point win over defending champions Kilkenny gave them a place in the final against Galway.

Because of the state of hurling in Connacht, the All-Ireland final was their first Championship game of the year. The situation must have been incomprehensible to tourists from abroad taking an interest in the ancient game of hurling.

Galway had some excellent hurlers, such as the elegant Joe Salmon, Jimmy Duggan and the lanky Mike Sweeney in goal, plus outsiders such as Jim Fives from the great Cappoquin tribe, Joe Young from Dublin and Billy O'Neill from Cork, but they were outclassed. Eight of the Tipperary men who played in that final had collected four more All-Ireland medals apiece by 1965.

The octet included the notorious trio of John Doyle, Mick Maher and Kieran Carey, collectively known as 'Hell's Kitchen' on account of the ferocity with which they manned the last line of defence.

It has been said of them that dust clouds created by the pulling round the square on a fine summer's Sunday could match those whipped up by a Sahara whirlwind of maximum temperature.

Tony Wall, Theo English, Donie Nealon, Liam Devaney and the stylish Jimmy Doyle were the others who lasted the long haul. The team had a great balance of skill and physical strength. They won the National League in the spring of 1959, and being basically a young side they were the strongest of favourites to retain the All-Ireland title that year.

They beat Limerick in the opening round in Cork's Athletic Grounds, and with the same venue for the semi-final with Waterford in mid July there was little if any cause for concern. It was decided in Radio Éireann that Micheál O'Hehir would cover a game in the Connacht football championship rather than the hurling match. When a note was handed to him with the half-time score of the Munster hurling semi-final, he did not bother giving it out on air because he simply did not believe what was written down.

It read Waterford eight goals and three points, Tipperary 0–0.

Further inquiries were made, and by then the story had got worse or better, depending on where one's allegiance lay. Waterford had scored another goal, and eventually won by seventeen points.

They say that the wind blew strongly that day, but it does not fully explain the wonderful story that unfolded. Give credit to Waterford: they completed the job by winning the All-Ireland that year, and sadly it remains the county's last one to date. They won it with a very talented team, the best that ever came out of the county, led by the wiry and determined Frankie Walsh.

Certainly that 1959 defeat was a major setback to the proud Tipperary boys, but one of my yardsticks in assessing great teams is the manner in which they respond to defeat. Rarely has a team given as powerful an answer to adversity as the Tipperary hurlers of the time. They won the League of 1960, and regained the Munster title when beating Cork in a pulsating final.

Another shock awaited them in the All-Ireland final when Wexford, with a fifty-fifty balance of the old and new, played brilliantly in scoring an emphatic win. They still talk in Wexford of the display of John Nolan at left halfback when marking Jimmy Doyle, the Tipperary wing wizard. I remember it well as part of a fantastic team display, and whether it was his red hair or not that made him conspicuous I recall the solid hurling of Limerick man Séamus Quaid at wing forward for Wexford. The popular *garda* died tragically in 1980 in the course of duty and was mourned by sportspeople everywhere.

Tipperary did not waste time in self-pity, and before October was out they'd won the Oireachtas for the first time since 1949 and set the compass on the year ahead. It turned out to be a memorable twelve months for the Blue and Gold. They supplied a third of the winning Munster Railway Cup team on St Patrick's Day; they won the League title in May, retained the Munster crown in July, and took possession of the Liam McCarthy Cup on All-Ireland final day in September, when luck was with them in beating a game Dublin side. They also retained the Oireachtas Cup in October.

A fantastic year's hurling was the perfect riposte to the setbacks of 1959 and 1960. If for some reason their players had quit the game there and then, a place in history would have been assured for them. Few felt that way inclined, however, and when September 1962 came round Tipp were back in the All-Ireland final, with thirteen of those who started in the final of 1961 taking the field again.

Wexford provided the opposition this time, and a two-point surplus gave Tipp another title. The attempt at completing a hat trick of All-Ireland titles failed to Waterford in Munster in 1963, but over the following two years this versatile bunch of hurlers answered all queries about their place in the lore of Cúchulainn's game. Not alone did they win the All-Ireland titles of those years, but they supplemented them with National League and Oireachtas wins as well.

The campaign of 1964 was startling in its intensity and in Tipperary's margins of victory. It took fewer matches to win an All-Ireland then, with Galway competing in Munster and Ulster teams opting out. In Munster they had twenty points to spare over Clare in the semi-final and fourteen over Cork in the final. That gave them a permit to the All-Ireland final, and they had no difficulty in regaining the All-Ireland title with a fourteen-point win over Kilkenny.

Some new names had edged into the team by then, and they quickly measured up to the required standard: captain Mick Murphy, the stylish Mick Roche, the energetic and forceful show-jumper Larry Kiely and the twenty-year-old sensation from the football territory of Clonmel, Michael 'Babs' Keating.

The year 1965 produced another chapter of almost frightening domination of the hurling scene by a team freely spoken of as contenders for the title 'best of all time'. People sometimes pontificate on Tipp hurling prior to 1970 as being based more on physical strength than playing skills. It is true that they always hurled with the conviction that few were stronger than them, but from what I saw in those days they never lacked the real touches that make the game so attractive.

They waltzed through Munster in 1965, scoring an eleven-point win over Clare in the semi-final and walloping Cork by eighteen in the final.

They overcame Wexford by twelve points in the All–Ireland final, giving them a championship winning average of almost fourteen points.

Tipperary were similarly dominant in the League campaigns of 1964 and 1965, winning by wide margins and being tested only in the finals in New York, when the Yanks ran them close two years in a row.

Dónal O'Brien, who won All–Irelands with Tipp in 1961 and 1962, was New York's goalkeeper in 1964, and the team had several class players in those years. Pat Kirby of Clare was as good as you would find and became a world champion in handball; Mick Morrissey, a winner of three All–Irelands with Wexford, was also an emigrant; as were other fine players such as Paddy Dowling of Cork, Jim Carney of Clare and the dedicated Hennessy brothers from Kerry, Brendan and Michael.

I was in New York at the time of the 1964 League final, for the wedding of my sister Kathleen to Kilkenny man Bill Barry, who had hurled in goal for the Kilkenny minors in the All–Ireland finals of 1956 and 1957. While in New York I went along to the races one day at Aqueduct in the company of my uncle Michael, who was a regular patron.

As I wished to explore as much as possible of the vast complex we fixed a rendezvous for four o'clock, and when I asked 'where' my uncle simply said: 'At the $100 window – there won't be that many at it.'

I returned in due course, having seen a lot and heard some of the worst language ever poured forth as the jockeys set off on a furious five-furlong race on the dirt. I arrived back at the $100 window on time, and true to what the uncle had said the area was not crowded. But it had one customer, head close to the opening, as is customary with gamblers, and posterior protruding a little.

To my surprise I recognized the client when he turned to leave: it was the man from Clonmel, Babs Keating. It is well known that he has an eye for the horses, and I can verify that it had developed long before his daughter Orla married the jockey Johnny Murtagh.

Babs was part of that great Tipp team and has never lost touch with hurling or horses since.

During his days as Tipperary manager in the 1980s and 1990s he had a custom of having mass celebrated in his house in Castleknock on the Saturday evenings prior to important matches in Croke Park. I was always invited along, and I remember on one particular evening I had a strong fancy for a dog running in Shelbourne Park and felt a long mass might not be the best preamble. On explaining my predicament to the Babs, he disappeared for a while and returned with some money to be invested as a possible omen in relation to Tipperary's fortune on the real Sabbath.

Then as the celebrant, Canon O'Keeffe, appeared in full regalia in the midst of the congregation, he was informed promptly by the governor that he had a maximum of twenty minutes and that the white flag had now been raised.

The pace of the mass was good, and I was glad to report later that the dog's was equally adequate.

Of course Tipp won on the following day.

Many of the personnel of that Tipp team of 1958 continued to be involved in the association. The fiery fullback Micheál (Mick) Maher went into administration and in time became a discerning and capable chairman of both the County Board and the Munster Council. Dynamic forward Donie Nealon served as referee, selector and manager on numerous occasions and was secretary of the North Tipperary Board for eleven years before being elected Secretary of the Munster Council in 1977. He held the position until retirement in the spring of this year.

The Nealons were a real GAA family. Donie's father, Rodie, played hurling with Waterford and Kilkenny when domiciled in those places, and later gained senior and junior All-Ireland medals with Tipperary. He taught in Youghalarra National School, as did his father before him and son Donie when he retired. Needless to say, all the Nealons actively promoted Gaelic games, and Donie's family continued the tradition with Sinéad winning All-Ireland medals in camogie and Seán in hurling.

Consistent and stylish midfielder Theo English, who won six

All-Ireland medals in the position and only had the same partner for two years, acted as selector with the team that brought about the resurrection of Tipperary's fortunes in the mid 1980s. The man from Marlfield had another distinction: he was easily the best dancer of the lot and would still be a twice-weekly practitioner of the graceful art wherever a band strikes up an old-time waltz or a snappy foxtrot. Perhaps the dancing helped him to develop his baffling sidestep on the field.

But the Doyles, John and Jimmy, no relation, were the most famous among a galaxy of stars. John drew level with the immortal Christy Ring on 5 September 1965 on winning his eighth All-Ireland medal. To this day no other hurler has matched or bettered that total on the field of play. John attracted attention when winning his first in 1949, on account of his young age of nineteen as much as for his mature style of traditional Tipperary hurling. He was at corner back that day and in the same line of defence eighteen years later searching for a record ninth All-Ireland when lining out against Kilkenny in the All-Ireland final of 1967. The effort failed on a day when Kilkenny sparkled and broke a Tipperary championship hoodoo that stretched back to 1922.

Between 1949 and 1967 the Holycross giant built an enormous reputation as a tough defender and a great character. He had a mischievous eye, an enigmatic smile and a massive relish for keen competition. He was more skilful than he was ever given credit for; this was particularly apparent when he hurled in the halfback line, where he won two of his eight All-Ireland medals. He is the only hurler I ever saw who perfected the rugby tactic of foot-rushing that was then one of the features of Irish international teams. John often foot-rushed a sliotar for forty or fifty yards in order to gain swinging room from opponents in pursuit. He revelled in the chase, whether in the middle of the pack or seeking entry by means that seemed legitimate to him. He won ten National League medals, and he rarely missed a game over a long career.

He was not enthusiastic about the back-door system of re-entry to the championship when it was introduced. 'Imagine,' he said to me once as I brought up the subject, 'what it would be like to wake up on a Monday morning after beating Cork by a point the day before and discover that they were still in the Championship . . . now is there any fairness in that?'

Jimmy Doyle of Thurles Sarsfield was equally good, though entirely different in style and personality. The classy forward won six All-Ireland medals and an equal number of National Leagues, and is the only player in the history of Gaelic games to have played in four All-Ireland minor finals. He was goalkeeper in 1954 when beaten by Dublin, but up front according to God's plan when winning the next three.

I was in Hayes's Hotel in Thurles after a Munster final round about that time, and when the outcome of the senior game had been well thrashed out somebody mentioned 'that young lad from this town that everyone is talking about'. Almost immediately, that well-known singer of opera, Jim 'Tough' Barry from Cork, who trained more All-Ireland winning teams than anybody else, dismissed the new golden boy: 'Forget about him . . . he will never come to anything.'

Not much more was added, but I was curious about the reason behind the opinion and before I left approached Tough for enlightenment.

'Did you see the hurley he had out there today?' asked tailor Jim.

I informed him that I had not taken any great notice of it, and it was then he revealed his intuition by saying, 'Well, you will get plenty of opportunities to see it because he will have it until the day he retires. Give me the man who is breaking hurleys and calling for replacements often.'

He was right in one respect: I saw Jimmy win senior All-Irelands in three decades, and I cannot recall him ever breaking a stick. But he made hellish use of the one he brought with him.

I told him the story once, and all the hurling genius with the quiet and retiring disposition did was to have a good laugh.

It was entirely fitting that both Doyles were honoured with places on the GAA teams of the century and millennium.

★

It is time to look at my other finalist for the title of the greatest hurling team I have ever seen.

The only name of a hurler I heard before leaving Dún Síon was that of Lory Meagher, of Tullaroan and Kilkenny. My father used to mention the name now and then, pronouncing it as 'Lowry', rather than with the accented 'o' as used in Kilkenny.

In my early years as a broadcaster Jim Langton was a regular on Leinster Railway Cup teams, and I used to be fascinated with his ball control and unique crouched style of running that shielded sliothar and hurley. The classy Seán Clohessy came a little later, as did the prince of goalkeepers, Ollie Walsh. I first saw them win an All-Ireland in 1957, when they paraded sixteen men before the final with Waterford. The ghost player was the actor John Gregson, who was playing the lead role in a film called *Rooney* being shot at that time. (Tom Cheasty, the powerhouse of Waterford hurling then, told me one time that it was the wish of the film gurus that Rooney would parade with them, but the request was turned down.)

Kilkenny won the match by a single point, then both teams returned to Croke Park a few days later to be joined by Rooney for a bit of action for the film. 'He was not much good at the hurling – just able to tip it around,' was Cheasty's summing up of the Hollywood star's style of play.

I had seen Kilkenny win All-Irelands again in 1963 and 1967 before the best side that ever came out of the county began a good run in 1969. Naturally there was a carry-over from 1967 – six powerful defenders in Ollie Walsh, Ted Carroll, Pa Dillon, Jim Treacy, Pat Henderson and Martin Coogan, and that brilliant forward Eddie Keher – but the changes that took place outward from the halfback division from 1969 onwards lead me to view the team of those years as a new one. For a start, a man of enormous strength, skill and scattering potential appeared at midfield. His name was Frank Cummins. I first saw the Knocktopher youth as a footballer, and a right good one at that, with Belcamp OMI College of Dublin. They won the Leinster Colleges title of 1965, beat De La Salle of Waterford in the All-Ireland semi-final and drew with St Columb's of Derry in the final.

The replay was in Ballybay; I was working on the match and spoke to Frank for the first time. He was very dejected-looking that day, sitting on a sideline seat with an outstretched leg in plaster propped on another seat. He watched as the Derry side won the Hogan Cup by a point. Two years later he was a sub on Kilkenny's All-Ireland winning team and a fully fledged and influential mid-fielder by 1969.

The forward line-up was almost entirely new, and one player in particular stood out: Pat Delaney.

Offaly made a surprise appearance in the Leinster final that year, falling by just two points to Kilkenny, who had beaten All-Ireland champions Wexford in the semi-final. London were Kilkenny's opponents in the All-Ireland semi-final and fell heavily to the Leinster champions.

Winning the Munster title put Cork in the All-Ireland final and set up another meeting with Kilkenny, who had been surprisingly beaten by the Rebels in 1966. Strangely, it was only the second meeting of the hurling elite in an All-Ireland final in the space of twenty-two years. The result was different this time: Eddie Keher was the star and captain, and steered his men to a six-point victory.

For a number of years after this Kilkenny and Wexford produced some spectacular hurling in Leinster finals, with Kilkenny winning all titles between 1969 and 1975, bar 1970. The county's run of five consecutive Leinster titles between 1971 and 1975 was a record that stood until 2003, when the dashing modern men stretched it to the half-dozen.

It was Tipp and Kilkenny in that 1971 All-Ireland final, and it turned out to be a high-scoring game of changing fortunes. Eddie Keher was again outstanding, scoring 2–11 of Kilkenny's total of 5–14, but Tipp totted up 5–17.

Like the Tipp team of the 1950s and 1960s, Kilkenny's reaction to defeat was emphatic. The team reached a new peak of excellence in 1972, and after two herculean clashes with Wexford in the Leinster final took the Bob O'Keeffe Cup with a winning margin of eight points in the replay.

They inflicted a massive 27-point defeat on Galway in the

All-Ireland semi-final and faced Cork in an All-Ireland final for the third time in six years. The game has been labelled the best final of the 1970s, and a stupendous second-half rally by Kilkenny helped to stamp it thus.

Cork were the first-half masters and led by two points thanks mainly to two goals from Ray Cummins. Their lead was doubled with less than twenty-five minutes left in the game when a goal from Eddie Keher was the first signal that Cork might not win the match. He was out on the wing on the Hogan Stand side of the ground and took a good pass from Liam 'Chunky' O'Brien. He then made a bit of ground, and my mind's eye can still see the graceful transfer of weight to the left before firing an arching puck towards the Railway Goal; before anyone realized what was happening the sliothar was in the Cork net. It was as if, in road bowling terms, the viaduct had been lofted: Cork goalkeeper Paddy Barry was stranded as the ball sailed over his head and dipped into the corner.

It was anybody's game then, but in a jiffy Cork goals by Ray Cummins and Seánie O'Leary and an outrageous point from Con Roche looked like the seal on a Rebel victory. A premature invasion of the pitch by a group of jubilant Cork followers almost invented *Riverdance* before its time. From Kilkenny's point of view the rubber looked gone from their grasp.

It was then that the Black-and-Amber brigade showed their true greatness. Keher stepped forward and blasted a 21-yard free to the Cork net, admitting a ray of hope for the second time. If ever a goal was needed from a twenty-one it was then, but the Rower-Inistioge man opted to take a point in a similar situation minutes later. Some would say that the instinct of a prowler guided him in both cases, and in hindsight the decisions were the correct ones.

Strong men Pat Delaney and Frank Cummins were now in swashbuckling mode, as the former tore through the centre for a morale-boosting point on the run. A long gallop from midfield by Cummins ended in an equalizing goal. Delaney's gambit of hopping the sliothar off the ground on the run increased the excitement, and the whole team responded in a rampage that brought seven more points and a run of 2–9 in all without reply from a stunned

Cork team. I realized there and then that the Cats of that day were far more than a great team.

Patient Noel Skehan was the lucky captain. At last, after nine seasons as a substitute to his cousin Ollie Walsh, the Bennetsbridge man had added an All-Ireland medal on the field to his three from the bench.

From that day onwards I had the utmost respect for the new champions, and it was undiminished when they lost to Limerick in the All-Ireland final of 1973. Injury deprived them of Eddie Keher and Jim Treacy for the final; Éamonn Morrissey had emigrated to Australia after the Leinster final; recovery from an appendix operation required that Kieran Purcell did not take the field until the second half: the team looked like Samson in the aftermath of his haircut. Nevertheless, credit must be given to a good Limerick side that fashioned a solid seven-point win.

The team had many outstanding stars, such as Pat Hartigan at fullback and the talented Éamonn Cregan at centre back. It was not Cregan's regular position, but he was placed there for the purpose of restricting the power of the feared Pat Delaney. Cregan hurled the game of his life, and this was a major factor in the team's success. Then there was the inspiring captain, Éamonn Grimes, at midfield, whose leadership and work rate were top-class.

I recall an incident at a crucial stage in the game when he set off in pursuit of a soloing Chunky O'Brien. As he drew level with the target he managed to dispossess him and switch play the other way round very much against the odds.

Nothing surprised me about Limerick that day: I have rarely seen as confident a team as they lined up before the game to be introduced to Uachtarán na hÉireann, Erskine Childers. The thought struck me at the time that they were prepared on the day for any opposition, and that would include a full-strength Kilkenny side. All played a part in a popular victory, and it would be wrong not to mention stalwarts such as Richie Bennis, Éamonn Rea, the long-serving Bernie Hartigan, the young Joe McKenna or the tidy forwards Liam O'Donohue and Frankie Nolan.

★

Kilkenny were back with a full pack the following year and became almost an irresistible force. The forward area was manned by six-footers with an amalgam of talents. The central axis of Delaney and Purcell interchanged on cue, and chalked up many devastating scores. Twenty-year-old Billy Fitzpatrick was a wonderful scoring acquisition on the left wing, and the strong and persistent Mick Crotty was difficult to curb on the other side of Delaney.

With Eddie Keher in the left corner there were no problems, and likewise in the other corner, where Mick Cloney Brennan excelled in catching and scoring. The midfield pairing of Chunky O'Brien and Frank Cummins could more than hold its own with any opposition, and the defence was easily the best around.

The key man was Pat Henderson in the centre of the half-line. He had been on the scene for ten years and had collected three All-Ireland medals by then. He played hard and fair, and exerted an enormous influence with his capacity to read each game as it developed. Noel Skehan was a magnificent goalkeeper at the back of the defence, and there was nothing soft about the fullback trio of Phil Fan Larkin, Nicky Orr and Jim Treacy. The corner men carried as much guile and hurling know-how as any three wise men, or magi, as the men from the Gospels are to be referred to from now on.

Wing halfbacks are vital players on a hurling team; Kilkenny had a very astute and sweet striker on the right in the person of the underrated Pat Lawlor. Tom McCormack was originally pushed into the left slot at short notice, but settled in quickly and efficiently.

That fifteen made up the most effective single team that I ever saw on a hurling field, and it was as good the following year with Brian Cody in place of Jim Treacy. They won the All-Ireland title in both years and strung together a litany of impressive displays. I would say that Wexford were second best in the land in those years, and it was hard luck on them that the Cats were so powerful at the time. The teams produced a stunning Leinster final in 1974, when it took a free from a difficult angle by Eddie Keher in the last minute to give Kilkenny victory. Kilkenny then beat an improving Galway by twelve points in the All-Ireland semi-final and Limerick by the same margin in the final. Keher's tally in the All-Ireland final came to 1–11, and he was now the holder of five All-Ireland medals.

In 1975 another exciting game with Wexford in the Leinster final gave passage to the All-Ireland final. The surprises were in the other half of the draw, and Galway, League winners in May, caused a sensation by defeating a fancied Cork team to go through to the All-Ireland final.

The September meeting of Kilkenny and Galway was the first between the pair in a final and not a memorable one for the men of the West. They were miles short of the experience of the Kilkenny players, who also had the benefit of the game's greatest coach, Fr Tommy Maher. Fr Maher positioned himself in the stand and used a walkie-talkie instead of watching from the sideline like less enlightened managers.

A ten-point win for the Leinster men just about reflected their superiority; Eddie Keher was top scorer with 2–7. It was his tenth All-Ireland final, and it was to be his last. He bowed out of inter-county hurling after the Leinster final of 1977, his nineteenth season as a senior player.

By any standard he was an outstanding hurler. He had huge physical strength and real skill from frees and play. He excelled in team play, but it was noticeable that he seldom pulled on a ball with abandon in the air. I heard him explain the reasoning at a seminar: pulling in the air is not good tactical play generally because the chance of leaving a colleague in possession after contact is no more than fifty-fifty. On the other hand, a player who strikes a ball on the ground or from the hand ought be capable of giving a colleague a much better opportunity.

It sounds logical to me.

Was he the best Kilkenny hurler of all time? I know it is easy to get a seconder for the proposition. In All-Ireland finals alone he amassed the staggering total of 7–77. He was as near as makes no difference an automatic choice on the teams of the century and millennium, and was joined by his colleague Frank Cummins, holder of seven All-Ireland medals.

★

So which, in my humble opinion, was the finest hurling team I have seen – Tipperary of the era 1958–65, or Kilkenny 1969–75?

It would be easy to stay on the sideline and call it a draw, but I have expressed the opinion in public on a few occasions that the Kilkenny side was the best I have seen. I have looked at the situation again from all angles when planning this book, and I am now changing my mind and giving the verdict marginally to the Tipp side.

Let it be seen purely as the opinion of one person.

Looking at it sectionally, I would rate the Tipperary defence the better, with Kilkenny shading the issue elsewhere. In terms of overall team hurling both were near perfect, and consequently the logic of my reasoning is based on total returns. Both played in six All-Ireland finals during the time spans under review. Tipperary won five as against four for Kilkenny – nothing much in that. It was the supplementaries that swung me towards the Munster men in my latest joust with memory. They won five National Leagues and five Oireachtas Tournaments during their good run, while Kilkenny failed to win a National League title, and the 1969 Oireachtas triumph was their only one.

Do I hear somebody shout that they did not bother? And that the vaunted Tipperary backline would not hold candlelight to the Kilkenny forwards?

There is no definitive answer. But it is permissible to have opinions, and terrific 'divarsion' debating them.

Chapter Nineteen

The history of sport is littered with tales of unexpected results and bizarre incidents before, during and after games, from local novice contests to All-Ireland finals. Some of these stories bear retelling now and then.

Naturally the first of the kind that I would have heard about concerns Kerry, and I will begin with a strange incident that took place in the Kerry dressing room in Croke Park before the start of the 1931 All-Ireland final against Monaghan. The players were togged out and ready to take the field when goalkeeper Johnny Riordan was informed that he would not be playing and that substitute Dan O'Keeffe would take his place.

Johnny had won an All-Ireland junior medal in 1924 and had been Kerry's regular senior goalkeeper since 1927. He was regarded as an excellent man in the *bearna baoil* and a character on and off the field. His collection of medals at the time of his surprise demotion was impressive: two senior All-Ireland medals (and seemingly little more than an hour away from a third) to go with his 1924 junior one, three National League medals, and two Railway Cup ones.

As things worked out, Kerry had an easy win over Monaghan following the early drama of that All-Ireland final day, and completed the four-in-a-row the following year again without Johnny in goal.

Why was the decision to drop him taken in the first place? It was not a matter that the other players spoke much about. I once asked the late Purty Landers about it, and he was prepared to say no more than that Johnny 'broke training' on Saturday night. I take it that he simply had a pint or two. At any rate he never played football again, and substitute Danno went on to set all types of records.

The Fermoy-born man's haul of fourteen Munster championship

medals is an all-time high, and his seven All-Ireland medals stood as a record until 1986 when Páidí Ó Sé, Ogie Moran and Pat Spillane edged past him with eight. (Mikey Sheehy and Ger Power both collected their eighth on the same day, but each had missed one final.)

O'Keeffe's career is an example of the part that chance plays in the fortunes of sport. It is plausible to advance the theory that he might never have got senior recognition if Johnny Riordan had not broken training on that fateful Saturday night in 1931. Riordan was still a young man in his prime and in normal circumstances would be expected to remain as Kerry's goalkeeper for a number of years to come. Indeed he could well have become the first player to win eight All-Ireland medals considering that Kerry claimed the titles of 1931, 1932, 1937, 1939, 1940 and 1941.

The gods decided otherwise, and even if he had lasted another year or two the likely successor might have been a young man called Brendan Reidy. He won the first of three successive All-Ireland minor medals on the day of Johnny's nightmare, but O'Keeffe's brilliance in the Kerry goal from 1931 to 1948 meant that Reidy never got a look-in as a senior.

The All-Ireland football final of 1938 between Galway and Kerry ended in a draw, but before the replay got under way there was a sensation when Kerry fullback Joe Keohane and a few of the other panellists opted out, supposedly over a dispute concerning expenses.

Keohane often regaled audiences with the story of how he paid his way into Croke Park that day and ended up on the field as a Kerry player. He was still on the stand with his friends as the replay drew near its end, with Galway leading by three or four points. At this stage the referee blew on his whistle and immediately the pitch was invaded by jubilant Galway followers, who mistakenly assumed they had heard the final whistle. But the assumption was incorrect, and on the referee's calculation a few more minutes of play remained.

Pandemonium reigned, with frantic efforts to clear the pitch proving fruitless. The players also had taken the game as being over, and amid the chaos a subdued Kerry team returned to the dressing room. Galway remained on the field in anticipation of the presentation of the Sam Maguire Cup, but it eventually dawned on them that the game was as yet unfinished. Word was sent to the Kerry camp to return for the remainder of the game, but the matter was not all that simple: some of the players had already left for the hotel.

The selectors then looked around for likely substitutes, and Joe Keohane and a few of his friends came off the stand and played for the remaining four or five minutes. The result did not change, but Joe held the view for evermore that he was the only player in the history of the GAA who paid his way into an All-Ireland final and played.

Micheál O'Hehir was commentator that day, and I wonder if he was on air to commentate on the extra time that followed the chaotic hiatus. Sixty years later I commentated on another important match with a similar sort of ending.

The Clare hurlers were riding high in 1998 and hellbent on retaining the Liam McCarthy Cup. On 16 August they drew their All-Ireland semi-final against Offaly at Croke Park. The replay was fixed for the following Saturday, with Jimmy Cooney of Galway as referee.

With Clare leading by three points late in the game, I was amazed to see Jimmy signal that the match was over: both stopwatches that I had operating showed that he was a little more than two and a half minutes short of normal time. I mentioned the fact on air before going to Brian Carthy, who was down on the sideline ready to interview Clare's Jamesie O'Connor. I think I may have said that history was being made in having an interview with a player before the finish of a game. Meanwhile I watched as overzealous stewards appeared to whisk the referee off the pitch while linesman Aodán Mac Suibhne tried in vain to reach him. For a horrible instant the crazy notion struck me that Jimmy Cooney may have been trying to help me! I should explain.

I had been down in his territory the previous Thursday, presenting medals and certificates at the end of his brother Joe's

School of Hurling season. Among the presentations was a coaching certificate for Jimmy Cooney. In my few words before making the presentations I jokingly suggested to the referee that extra time in Saturday's replay would not suit RTE, as I was booked for a *Night at the Dogs* programme in Waterford that night.

A helicopter was on stand-by to ferry producer Pat O'Donovan and myself to Déise country as early as possible after the end of the game. So could Jimmy Cooney have been assisting me in getting airborne a little sooner? Of course anyone who knows the man understands that it was a simple mistake.

As a result of the error, the match was replayed; Offaly won the replay convincingly and went on to beat Kilkenny in the final. Did the error cost Clare the All-Ireland title of that year? They were leading by three points when the end was called, and I can still see Barry Murphy in possession in a scoring position at the moment of the premature final whistle. The odds certainly favoured Clare to hang on, but I would not have been prepared to bet much on it at the time. Assuming the average number of minutes would have been added on at the end of normal time, play would have gone on for another five minutes, and a lot can happen in a hurling match during that span. Hadn't Offaly scored 2–5 in less time four years earlier when they snatched the All-Ireland from Limerick? And against Clare they had cut a ten-point deficit to three when the gods came out to play with Cooney's whistle.

Scholars will be doing PhDs on Jimmy Cooney in a few hundred years time when the rest of us are forgotten. And I would bet that a thesis will show that the Bullán man was a fine hurler who won an All-Ireland medal in 1980; that he was an excellent coach; and that as a referee he was as good as the best and more knowledgeable than all on the rules of the game.

It was my privilege to have had many meetings over the years with Frank Burke, the Dublin dual player who won three All-Ireland football medals, at his Rathfarnham home and elsewhere. He was born in Kildare, but his family came to Dublin when he was quite young. He was sent as a boarder to Knockbeg College in Carlow in the early years of the past century, and being keen on hurling he brought his *camán* along. He was dismayed to be told that cricket was the game of the college.

Some time later, while home on holidays, he happened to spot a notice in a shop window concerning St Enda's in Rathfarnham – the school founded by Padraig Pearse. The part that mentioned that hurling was the game of the school appealed particularly to the young student. In no time at all he enrolled at St Enda's, a decision that was to have a major bearing on the course of his life.

He never severed his connection with St Enda's, where he became a teacher; he was also a member of the Irish Volunteers, of which Pearse was among the leaders. He gave me a graphic description of how he and a group of fellow Volunteers commandeered a tram in Rathfarnham and instructed the driver at gunpoint to drive directly to O'Connell Street on the morning of Easter Monday, 1916. They were soon installed in the GPO in readiness for the Rising.

On 21 November 1920 he was playing football for Dublin against Tipperary in Croke Park. There was tension in the air: early that morning, Michael Collins's unit had killed fourteen men in a coordinated assault on suspected British agents in Dublin. Frank was marking Michael Hogan of Tipperary when British forces entered the ground and opened fire; Hogan was shot dead, along with eleven spectators, on a day that became known as 'Bloody Sunday'.

The event was commemorated many times in later years when surviving members of the teams gathered close to the spot where Hogan died – where a left halfback defending the Railway goal normally stands.

Scoring the winning goal in an All-Ireland final assures immortality for the player involved, especially when it fashions a county's first title in ninety-one years. That was the story of Clare's Éamonn Taaffe in 1995 – almost stranger than fiction.

There was no talk of the Tubber man in the lead-up to the final with Offaly, and his name did not even appear on the official match programme. On my pre-match visits to dressing rooms I generally enquire if any extra names have been included in the team sheet, just in case. On this occasion, Ger Loughnane informed me himself that the name of Éamonn Taaffe had been appended and that he would wear Number 24.

Was he a secret weapon, and was it all planned? The events that unfolded later would suggest to a film scriptwriter that it was and that Loughnane should be convinced to run with the story. He intoduced his man at a critical time, with Clare trailing by two points. The sub read the situation to perfection when easing into the ideal position to slam a rebound from the crossbar to the Offaly net. The hero's mission was then complete, and he was substituted immediately.

Semple Stadium in Thurles, the cradle town of the GAA, is the country's premier hurling pitch and unquestionably the favourite venue of most hurlers. I was astounded to discover by accident in the month of March 2001 that the crossbars in both goals were in fact lower than the specified height.

The discovery had its roots in a hectic All-Ireland club hurling semi-final between Sixmilebridge of Clare and Graigue-Ballycallan of Kilkenny. The Bridge were two points in arrears as the game drew close to the finish, and the referee signalled for a penalty to the Banner side. Agile and alert goalkeeper Davy Fitzgerald began his measured run up the field, with goal in his mind sure as God is in heaven. Even though three men guard hurling goals for penalty pucks, my money would always be on Davy to get the green flag waving in such a situation. He had won the All-Ireland Poc Fada on the Cooley Mountains, and it takes power pucking to achieve that honour. In addition I had seen the two-handicap golfer hit a drive 412 yards to the middle of a fairway on the Woodstock course in Ennis, so there was no denying his knack of smacking a ball hard and on line.

A moment of truth for him had now presented itself, but alas for Corca Baiscinn his powerful blast rifled a few inches above the crossbar for a point that brought no joy. The matter rested there –

Dún Síon strand, with An Searrach in background

With my sister Kathleen at the New York World's Fair, 1964

With members of Cavan's 1947 All-Ireland winning football team: (back row)
Simon Deignan, Mick Higgins, myself, John Wilson; (front row) Tony Tighe,
the late Joe Stafford, Brendan Kelly (not a member of the 1947 team;
he played in the 1945 All-Ireland final)

With D. J. Carey in Semple Stadium

Golfing at Dún Síon, 1985, with Doireann, Éadaoin, Nuala, Neasa, Cormac, Aonghus, Niamh, Eamonn

Gathered round the Sam Maguire Cup, 1986, with (from top) Neasa, Cormac, Éadaoin, Nuala, Doireann, Aonghus, Éamonn, Helena and Niamh

At Shelbourne Park
with Stagalee and, from
left, trainer Dolores
Ruth, Des Cahill of
RTE, and joint owner
Pat O'Donovan

On the *Late Late Show* with Unique Reward, 1999

With young hurlers in Malawi

Buying the *Kerryman* – North Kerry edition –
in New York's Times Square, *c.* 2001

On the
Great Wall of
China, 2001

Millennium dawn, 1 January 2000, in Dún Síon's pre-Christian cemetery

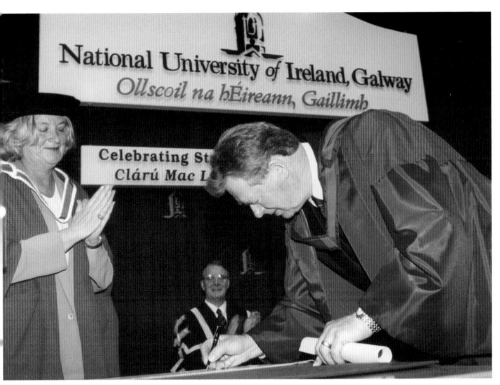

Receiving an honorary doctorate from University College Galway; also pictured are
Professor Ruth Curtis and Dr Patrick Fottrell, then president of the university

With Aonghus at Augusta National, Georgia, 2003

Helena and I with all our children: Niamh (on sofa, left), Doireann
(perched on sofa, right) and (standing) Éamonn, Cormac, Éadaoin, Neasa,
Aonghus and Nuala

With the next generation: grandchildren Tadhg (on my knee), Béibhinn,
Leonidas and Caoimhe

for all eternity it seemed – with Graigue-Ballycallan through to the St Patrick's Day final in Croke Park.

A little over a week before the Kilkenny side's date with Athenry, I decided to travel south and meet the hurlers from that pleasant part of Nore country that lies close to Ballingarry, just over the border in Tipperary. I got good directions from Eddie Keher, and I was happy to follow them even after he admitted that he had never been there himself. He alerted Denis Byrne, then a Kilkenny county player; Denis met me on arrival and brought me to the Byrne home for tea. Later he gave me one of his hurleys, before I set off to see a bit of training and meet some of the people of the area.

In the course of a chat with goalkeeper Johnny Ronan after training I jokingly remarked that it was lucky for him that Davy's Thurles shot was a little fraction on the high side.

'It wasn't,' he said, 'but thank God for the low crossbar.'

He explained then that he could not believe his luck when testing the crossbar for height during the puck-around before the game. He found it to be the most of a foot lower 'than our own or the one in Nowlan Park'.

My initial reaction was to doubt his story, and I said no more until I did a little bit of checking myself, beginning with a visit to Croke Park and a rough measuring of the height of the crossbar. I did likewise in Clones on a Saturday visit to that town before moving to Thurles on Sunday for a hurling game.

I arrived early and headed right away for the goal at the Thurles Sarsfield end of the ground, and to my amazement found that I could lay the palm of my hand on the crossbar without unduly stretching. The goal at the Killinan end was no different, and only then was I certain that my friend Johnny had a valid point: the crossbars in Semple Stadium really were well short of the required height. And maybe Davy's shot was computer-perfect after all?

Too late now for a replay!

Anyway I mentioned the fact during the subsequent commentary that day, and it brought an immediate reaction from a spectator as I was leaving the ground. He told me that he had been listening and wondered what I had been on about. I told him what I believed to be true, and we left it at that pending more examination.

When next I came to Thurles the crossbars had been raised and were once more standard height. But my friend who had been listening on my previous visit came to me again with his own version of the minor saga.

'Do you remember we were talking about those crossbars the last time we met,' said he. 'Well, I found out they were never lowered, but the ground was "rus" during development.'

For many years it was a custom that a bishop threw in the ball for the start of important GAA games. As far as I can make out it was always a bishop from the Roman Catholic Church, and the support from Archbishop Croke of Cashel and Emly at the time of the founding of the association was the likely reason for that.

The ceremony was to be seen in all its glory on All-Ireland final day. Once the parade of teams was over and defenders in place, the bishop and the President of the GAA would walk with a solemn gait until they were some ten yards inside the sideline and facing the centre of the field. Silence would descend on the crowd as they came to a halt at the exact moment that the first notes of the hymn 'Faith of Our Fathers' would pour forth from the band. Spectators and players would sing the words as fervently as massed pilgrims in St Peter's Square in Rome. It was part of the day's agenda and respected accordingly without question.

Once the singing was over, bishop and President proceeded to the centre of the field for the next part of the exercise: the kissing of the bishop's ring by the rival captains and the referee. The supplicant knelt on one knee and placed his right hand under the bishop's ringed finger before reverently kissing the symbol of divine authority.

The final ecclesiastical function on the field came with the throwing in of the ball for the start of the game. At that time sixteen players in all would line up for the throw-in – four midfielders and a dozen forwards – and a great scramble often developed from the throw. With fairness in mind the bishop would turn his back on the players and on the sound of the ref's whistle would throw the ball back over his head. The game was then on, and it was up to Church and State to get off the pitch as quickly as possible – not always with the pomp and dignity of the entrance.

It did not always work out smoothly: I remember a day when Kevin Heffernan chased hard after a short throw-in and nearly brought the Archbishop of Cashel down to earth in the process. I think it was Heffo's penchant for stopping dead as a prelude to a baffling sidestep that saved Cashel from the necessity of a canonical by-election that day. It was with that in mind that a ceremonial throw-in was introduced; once the VIPs were back on the stand the referee would handle the real throw-in.

I'm afraid the clerical throw-in was not always according to the laws of God, and I have the All-Ireland football semi-final of 1950 between Louth and Kerry specifically in mind. The aforementioned Maggie Poole, landlady to the Kerry captain Batt Garvey, had a brother, Monsignor Michael Collins, who was a big fan of Kerry football. He was stationed in America at the time, and used his summer holidays to come home every year that Kerry won the Munster championship.

Maggie's house was his base in Dublin, and regardless of his rank on the other side of the Atlantic he was always plain Mickeen to her. I have failed to find out how Mickeen was chosen to throw in the ball for the start of that 1950 All-Ireland semi-final, and I am content now with the explanation that it was the work of providence. With Batt Garvey in the house in addition to the man who had control of the ball at the start of play, it was too good an opportunity to ignore. May God forgive all Kerry people: the Monsignor was instructed to throw the ball over his right shoulder, while Batt was alerted to break from the line-up to collect the misguided ball.

The last words to the visiting cleric before he left for Croke Park that day came from his big sister Maggie: 'Mickeen, if you don't throw that ball to Batt, don't come home here for your dinner in the evening.'

Mickeen did as he was told: Batt Garvey collected, raced to the sixty-yard mark and scored the quickest point ever in an All-Ireland semi-final or final.

Justice was done in the end, however: the Wee County won the match, with goalkeeper Seán Thornton giving a masterly display.

Louth got even with Kerry in the clerical stakes as well when the counties again met in the All-Ireland semi-final two years later. Everything was going well for the Kingdom until Louth introduced a substitute named on the programme as J. McArdle. Nobody could recall McArdle earning startling headlines prior to this, and his arrival on the field did not cause any great concern to Kerry. In fact he was not McArdle at all, but champion sprinter and noted footballer Fr Kevin Connolly, who, according to some Church rule of the time, was not permitted to play football. He certainly played some brilliant football that day.

I may as well recall the day I, or rather RTE, was accused of bias.

Bad weather caused a League game to be transferred to Ballymote at short notice, and I found myself close to the sideline as I prepared to go on air out in the air. Suddenly a gentleman appeared by my side with an unusual query: 'At last I have met somebody from RTE . . . tell me, why are ye always running down the West?'

I replied by stating that I did not understand what he meant, but he was quick to give substance to his question: 'Turn on the radio or television any day and what do you hear? Rain is spreading from the West . . . Does it ever spread from where RTE is?'

My time was short, and like many a TD I promised to try to do something about the problem.

My father's brother Mickey lived in New York, where he owned a pub on 53rd Street and Third Avenue. The establishment closed for only three hours of the twenty-four, but Mickey promptly took time off every time he heard I had landed in the Big Apple.

It was during one of those trips that I wandered into Times Square. Seeing a newsagency, I ventured inwards in search of the *Kerryman*. Even when times were hard, the *Kerryman* found its way into most households in the Kingdom, and it was common enough to post it onwards to America once its contents had been well digested at home. I'm sure it meant more to Kerry emigrants, especially those with an interest in the fortunes of the Kerry football team.

There was the usual choice of material in the Times Square shop that day – *USA Today*, the *New York Times*, the *Wall Street Journal*, the *Financial Times* – and I decided to approach one of the attendants with my problem. I simply said, 'Could I have the *Kerryman*, please,' as was my wont years ago in Josie Connor's in Dingle. I was hardly prepared for the reply that came instantly from my friend: 'Do you wish to have the North Kerry edition or the South?'

Once I decided on the northern one, he went off and arrived back quickly with the cherished item.

I spoke with him for a while and learned that he was an Egyptian. He was so delighted to be helpful that I felt like telling him about the Kerry team and enquiring was there any place like Lyeracrompane in Egypt. He understood me when I said 'Go raibh maith agat' before shaking hands with him.

He replied in his own language, and I understood his sentiments.

No account of strange sporting events would be complete without a reference to Mundy Prendeville, one-time Archbishop of Perth in Western Australia.

Mundy, who came from Castleisland in County Kerry, was a member of the Kerry team that went to the All-Ireland final of 1924. However, he was back in college at All Hallows in Dublin at the time of the final and was refused permission to go the mile down the road to Croke Park.

He took 'French leave' at about three in the afternoon and arrived just in time to play on the winning team before dashing back to base once more. But the authorities refused to accept him back, and he was forced to seek ordination elsewhere.

On his elevation to high office in Perth years later, he forwarded a letter to the then President of All Hallows, quoting the following message from the Psalms: 'The stone once rejected by the builder has now become the corner-stone.'

The reply from the president was equally cryptic and divine: 'We never cease to marvel at the wonders of the Lord.'

Chapter Twenty

Of the fifteen players who hold the rare honour of winning senior All-Ireland medals in both hurling and football, four of them, all from Cork, figured on minor teams that I commentated on: Ray Cummins, Teddy McCarthy, Brian Murphy and Jimmy Barry Murphy.

Each of the Murphys completed the minor double, with Brian winning football in 1969 and hurling the following year, and Jimmy Barry winning hurling in 1971 and football in 1972. No player can match the collection of national medals won by the Kilkenny-based *garda* Brian: three senior All-Ireland hurling, one senior football, two under-21 All-Ireland hurling, one under-21 football, one minor hurling medal, one minor football, two National League hurling, one Railway Cup hurling, three Railway Cup football, four All-Ireland Club Football (with Nemo Rangers), one hurling All-Star award, and two football All-Star awards.

Jimmy Barry Murphy was seen to be special from the time he first wore the Cork jersey as a minor. He was unassuming and friendly in manner, and remained so during a glittering career as a dual player. Although he won five senior All-Ireland medals in hurling, I always felt that he was even better as a footballer. His style was natural and simple, and as a forward he had the ability to pounce for a score once the half-chance presented itself.

I recall talking to him once in the Skylon Hotel in Dublin on the morning of a minor All-Ireland semi-final. He spoke about greyhounds as well as football and hurling, and gave me a candid answer when I enquired how he felt about the Croke Park match later: 'I feel I could score three goals.'

Another person might have kept such a feeling to himself, but not Jimmy. Words from him never sounded boastful.

I used the prediction in the pre-match scene-set that afternoon by stating that the athletic youth in red being featured had the appearance of one who could score three goals. Of course I did not say that he himself had uttered words to that effect, but he did not let me down once play began; he scored two goals and a point, and if the crossbar had been a little higher than standard his prediction would have been 100 per cent correct.

He was sensational when he joined the Cork senior football team in 1973. The slim teenager sporting a crewcut was at right corner forward on a brilliant team that hit the turf at a speed of knots that season. They beat Clare by seventeen points in the semi-final of the Munster championship, and the selection of Jimmy for the Munster final against Kerry caused a stir in the days leading up to the match.

As usual Cork started as outsiders against the reigning champions Kerry, in what was to be the last final to be played in the old Athletic Grounds before the major refurbishment that yielded a fine venue renamed Pairc Uí Chaoimh by July 1976. Cork chose to say goodbye to the old with an absolutely perfect display of football. I was present but not working, and did not have the ideal viewing position at the back of the bank, but I could see most of the action. Brother Flahive, a classmate from our Dingle days, had come with me from Limerick that day, but not being over-tall he missed a good deal of the play. 'What's that for,' he asked me more than once as cheering exploded around him, and it was the same unwelcome news for him most of the time.

All I could say was, 'Another goal for Cork,' and at least on one occasion he pleaded with me, 'Are you joking, Micheál?'

I was not indeed, and before half-time Cork had recorded five goals and a half-dozen points to go with it. The game was as good as over. Kerry rallied in the second half, but a win for them was never on; Cork 5–12, Kerry 1–15 was the stark news on the board at the end. It was the most impressive performance I ever saw from a Cork football team in a Munster final, and JBM's name was to one of the spectacular goals.

The goal-scoring spree continued in a semi-final rout of Tyrone, when they registered 5–10 and earned a place in the All-Ireland final against Galway. And the strike rate was a point higher in the final, when a magnificent 3–17 gave them a seven-point win and an All-Ireland title won with flair and panache from trap to line. Jimmy scored four of the Croke Park goals and became a great favourite with the crowds. His collection of honours also measures up to the best: five senior All-Ireland hurling medals, one senior football, one under-21 hurling, one minor hurling, one minor football, two National Hurling League, one National Football League, four Railway Cup football, two All-Ireland club football (St Finbarr's), two All-Ireland club hurling (St Finbarr's), four hurling All-Star awards, and two football All-Star awards.

I rated that particular Rebel team very highly, and in another era they might have won another few All-Irelands. Their coming should not have been the surprise it was rated because Cork had won seven of the previous eight Munster minor titles (counting 1973) and brought home the All-Ireland titles from 1967 to 1969 and again in 1972. Eleven of the winning seniors of 1973 were holders of All-Ireland minor medals, and ten had possession of an under-21 one. It was a footballing side rather than grinders, and the blend was ideal. Goalkeeper and captain Billy Morgan was the best goalkeeper I've seen in action over the past fifty years; I say so conscious of the great merit of Charlie Nelligan, Páidí O'Mahony, Paddy Cullen, Johnny Geraghty, Martin Furlong and others. I nominate Billy as the best on account of the quality of forwards he had to deal with over a long career. He did not always have the best of defences in front of him, but his agility, sense of position and ability to read the minds of quick-thinking forwards such as Mikey Sheehy, John Egan, Eoin Liston, Jimmy Keaveney and many more enabled him to thwart their intentions pretty often.

That 1973 team had good balance in all sectors, but the axis of the forward line was exceptional. Centre forward Declan Barron was a fielder that could match the very best, and he was always good for a spell at midfield or halfback if needed. The tall Ray Cummins at full forward drew possession like a magnet and had the intuition to direct his passes to great effect. The other forwards fitted in like a jigsaw, and many a backline feared meeting Dave

McCarthy, Ned Kirby, Jimmy Barrett and the unique JBM when in motion. Why then, one might ask, did the Rebels of 1973 not go on to win another All-Ireland title?

It is a fair question. I have a theory that they might have added at least another if they had been stretched more in winning the 1973 crown. They may have been overconscious of their own potential in 1974, when on the surface it did not seem that there was anything great around. Kerry introduced some new faces that year, but when the Munster final was played in Killarney on a terrible July Sunday, Cork had a comfortable seven-point victory.

I often wonder how seriously Cork took Dublin in the All-Ireland semi-final of 1974. Even an iota of complacency can be fatal, and, while Dublin created great razzmatazz in a remarkable march through Leinster that year, neither manager Kevin Heffernan nor the players yet had concrete credentials for their respective roles. All that changed in the course of a memorable All-Ireland semi-final, and I will for ever maintain that the turning point was the moment when Blue Panther Anton O'Toole's rising left-footed shot hit the roof of the Cork net at the Canal End of Croke Park. It deflated Cork and gave a real birth to a Dublin football team for whom glory was beckoning.

All was not lost yet for that Cork team, as the average age was young. But the gods must have conspired against them when sending an angel to Kerry county chairman Gerald McKenna in May, urging him to appoint Mick O'Dwyer as manager. McKenna was never one to sit on a good idea.

The teams met in the Munster final in picturesque Fitzgerald Stadium in Killarney. O'Dwyer had decided to build a new team, dispensing with some players who had won All-Ireland medals and were still only in their twenties. His extremely young selection got a lucky blast-off that day when a harmless-looking kick towards the Cork goal took a deflection off Martin Doherty and ended with a green flag waving for Kerry.

It was their day, and the nucleus of the greatest football team that I have ever seen was out of the blocks. One would not blame the Cork players if they decided to leave their boots behind them in the Killarney Lakes that evening.

The atmosphere that builds in the run-up to matches is part of the attraction of sport, and the level of rivalry from the past plays its part. Few rivalries are keener or more deeply embedded than that between Dublin and Meath in football. It took root in the 1950s, and while football remains a topic of debate the four great games between the sides in the 1991 semi-final of the Leinster champion-ship will occupy a hallowed position.

It is an adage in sport that only winners are remembered, but regardless of the fact that neither ultimately won the All-Ireland title the gallant Royals and Blues of that year created memories that will be haunting for ever. What began with a gripping draw in Croke Park on 2 June ended on the 29th, by which time all of sporting Ireland had become locked in the magic of the saga. An aggregate attendance bordering on a quarter million witnessed the contests, and it would not have been fewer even if the start of each game had been timed for one o'clock in the depth of night.

I remember calling to the Meath dressing room before the start of the fourth game. Terry Ferguson began the easy chore of removing his pants with the intention of donning his playing togs, but the operation was never completed. Just as he had his right leg at half-mast his back suddenly went into spasm and it took support from those close to him to prevent a collapse. In no time at all he was on the treatment table, with the playing doctor Gerry McEntee and others working furiously on the distressed defender.

Naturally Seán Boylan ruled him out for the day, and I had the unusual story to relate on air within minutes that there was an unexpected late change on the Meath team. It was in keeping with the 'anything can happen' theme that had a four-week life span in that amazing year. The end came wrapped in delirious joy for Meath, and it could not have been any more cruel than it was on Dublin.

The Blues had looked the better side and led by three points in the dying minute of play. Meath attacked from a position deep in their own half and a bewilderingly rapid transfer of the ball brought it close to the Dublin goal, where the hairy vet Kevin Foley reappeared to score an audacious equalizing goal. The *coup de grâce* followed quickly when the suave and calculating Liam Hayes passed to Dave 'Jinxy' Beggy, and the flier who had once beaten a greyhound in Shelbourne Park raced through for the winning point.

Some say that it was a pity that Meath did not go on to win the All-Ireland title. The honour went to Down, and it was a championship that was truly won with flair and fine football. My abiding memory of the game is the impact Colm O'Rourke had on proceedings once he was introduced as a substitute in the second half. It is a mystery to me how he was able to play at all or how he was allowed to take the field. It was well known during the days preceding the final that he was ill with a heavy bout of pneumonia or something of the same ilk and unlikely to play. I was in the Meath dressing room when the players trooped in, and to my amazement the Leitrim-born Skryne man was in attendance. He looked a case for hospital to my amateur eyes and appeared to have lost a considerable amount of weight. Believing that he would take no part in the play, I informed him that it was cold outside and that in my opinion he should wear a heavy coat. He surprised me by saying that he was going to tog out with the boys, but I still did not imagine for a second that I would be talking later about his deeds on the field. His was the most heroic display I ever witnessed on a field of play.

Down, who led by four points at half-time, had stretched six ahead early in the second half when Colm appeared on the field. It looked a futile mission for some time as the Mourne men surged eleven points clear with twenty minutes to go. But O'Rourke inspired Meath to new levels. They restricted Down to a solitary point for the remainder of the match, and were only two adrift at the final whistle. There was general approval when O'Rourke was later named Texaco Footballer of the Year.

He was good as a minor in the mid 1970s but suffered a horrendous knee injury that almost ended his playing days. He battled his way back, but the late 1970s and early 1980s were bleak times for

Meath in an era dominated by Dublin and to a lesser extent Offaly. I remember attending a sports forum in Longford at the end of 1985 or early the following year when Colm was also a member of the panel. We were still talking about football when the official business was over, and it was then, over a cup of tea, that I got an insight into his football psyche.

'I am nearly twenty-nine years of age,' he said, 'and I have not a single championship medal to my credit – not even a county one. But I will keep going.'

It was true: but fortune took a decisive turn in Colm's favour late in his days, and he finished with every honour possible. He was a member of a very good Meath team that won the All-Irelands of 1987 and 1988, and went near to a few more. They had the reputation of being a physically strong and rugged side, and were not always the most popular outfit with Croke Park authorities and followers of rival teams. But they were honest and good-natured to a man and good for the game with a guarantee of excitement and 100 per cent effort every time they went out to play.

It is not always conceded, but there was a lot of skill in that team and Seán Boylan turned it to good use. The full-forward line of Colm O'Rourke, Brian Stafford and Bernard Flynn bears comparison with the best ever, and there was no shortage of quality in any sector. The team's legendary determination was visible in the demeanour of fine players such as Mick Lyons, Robbie O'Malley, Gerry McEntee, Liam Hayes, Liam Harnan . . .

By the way, I know of one section of the Dublin community that had a fondness for Meath people: the car attendants on the streets in the vicinity of Croke Park. Apparently they rate Meath people as generous when it comes to paying for minding the old banger. It was explained to me once in the following words: 'The Meath man digs his hand into the pocket and whatever comes out is yours; others take a look at what comes out and put some of it back in. Give me them big Meath men any day.'

Apart from Dublin, the main rival of that fine Meath team was Cork. Counting the replay of 1988, they played four times in

All-Ireland finals that resulted in wins for Meath in 1987 and 1988, and revenge for Cork in 1990. They were never huge admirers of each other, but the keen competitive instinct in players on both sides was the reason, rather than animosity. This was plain to all when the Meath men came in large numbers to the funeral of Cork goalkeeper John Kerins, who sadly died at a young age.

There is no question but that manager Billy Morgan was the heart and soul of that Cork team. He had a long career as Cork goalkeeper and captained the classy side of 1973 that won the All-Ireland title. As I said elsewhere, I rate him the best goalkeeper I have seen.

I was in the company of Mick O'Dwyer when the news reached us that Billy had been appointed as Cork manager late in 1986. 'That's bad for us,' Micko exclaimed. 'He knows us backwards and he has no great love for us.'

Up to the date of his appointment, Cork had never won more than two Munster titles in succession. Billy steered them to four in a row from 1987 to 1990, and Cork collected two All-Irelands in those years. He took the job at a time when football talent was plentiful in the county. Cork won six All-Ireland under-21 titles in the 1980s, but the acquisition of the former Kildare player Larry Tompkins was also crucial to the success story. It is doubtful if Cork would have won as much in Billy's time without Larry's input. He starred at centre forward in the All-Ireland final of 1989, and had assumed the captaincy when Cork retained the title a year later. He suffered a bad knee injury in that final, and his determination to get back playing again demanded sacrifice beyond the ordinary.

Purely by chance I learned of Larry's rehabilitation programme in the month of February 1991. Celebrations were still ongoing following the rare achievement of winning the All-Ireland football and hurling titles of the previous year. As part of fundraising for a trip by both teams to the famous Skydome in Toronto during St Patrick's week, a golfing event was arranged for Cork Golf Club. I was invited to take part, and who could refuse an outing at that pleasant venue? The golf was incidental, but the company was mighty, and it made for a pleasant sight when all sat down to a fine meal at day's end.

The Sam Maguire and Liam McCarthy cups adorned the top table, and leading players from other counties were welcome guests. But I noticed that the Cork football captain, Larry Tompkins, was an absentee.

He ran a pub close to the railway station at the time, and as soon as the main course was over I slipped out the side door and landed myself in Larry's hostelry. Larry was not there either, and had not been seen all day. His brother suggested that I try the gymnasium in the Silver Springs Hotel, and by ten o'clock I was at the reception desk. The person on duty was not aware of who was inside or out, and turned on the closed-circuit monitor to scan the fitness area. Who was there and plainly recognizable in a corner but Larry, working furiously with weights?

I went in and apologetically interrupted the All-Ireland winning captain, and was greeted courteously as ever by the Kildare man. He agreed to take a break, and I immediately told him where I had come from. I went as far as to say that I felt he should have been part of it as Cork captain, but he failed entirely to see my point.

'We are drawn against Kerry on June 15th in Killarney, and I want to be fully recovered from the cruciate ligament operation by then,' was his explanation for his absence from the festivities. He then related to me how he had spent the day: 'I set out in the morning to cycle to Fermoy, but I was going so well that I went as far as Mitchelstown. It was tough coming back and I had to get off twice, but I made it. I did a bit in the gym then and another little bit now.'

I could almost feel the pain myself, but I understood his motives.

I wished him well, and my parting words were that I would see him in Toronto in mid March.

'You will not – I will not be there. But with the help of God I will see you in Killarney on June 15th,' was the way he signalled his number-one priority in mid February.

One could not but admire him.

★

I have already dealt with three of the best footballing sides I have seen: the pioneering Down team of the 1960s, Kerry of the 1970s and 1980s, and Dublin of the same era.

The Galway three-in-a-row team of the 1960s is entitled to be in discussions with the trio. The achievement of winning three consecutive All-Ireland titles in football is rare; Kerry is the only county apart from Galway to have done so in the past eighty years.

Very often Galway teams produce their best football in Croke Park, and the side of the 1960s solidified that reputation. They rarely amassed staggering scoring totals, but were geniuses in retaining possession and gauging the strengths and weaknesses of the opposition. That style of play helped them to beat Kerry in the All-Ireland semi-final of 1963, but they were out of luck in the final when Gerry Davey's late goal won the title for Dublin. Dublin were awarded a line ball not far from the corner flag on the Hill 16 side of the Railway goal. The kick should have been taken from the actual spot where the ball had crossed the line, but innocently Brian McDonald dribbled the ball out to the fourteen-yard line, as would be correct in the case of a free being awarded inside the fourteen. Nobody noticed. Brian kicked from the incorrect position, Gerry Davey fisted the ball to the net and Dublin were champions.

I had not noticed the incident, and it was the same with most people until the game was well over; in fairness to Galway, they did not kick up a fuss about the innocent dribble. It might have been the making of the team, and they made no mistake the following year when they beat Kerry in the All-Ireland final.

The real drama that year occurred in the semi-final, when Galway and Meath faced each other with a Dingle man, Séamus Garvey, as referee. Pat Red Collier was one of Meath's stars at the time, and his daring style of play made him a popular figure countrywide. The sight of the barrel-chested dynamo soloing upfield with manes of flaming red hair streaming from both sides of his head was unforgettable. He was a folk hero. So when referee Garvey sent him back to retrieve a ball he had kicked away after a free had been signalled, consternation reigned as far as the Hill of Tara. The Dingle man may have acted correctly, but after all this was The

Red. Garvey's second sin, in the eyes of the Meath supporters, was the disallowing of a goal scored by the great Jack Quinn. The Kilbride man was a midfielder of note at the time who was later converted into a terrific fullback on the Meath team that won the All-Ireland title of 1967. Garvey disallowed his goal in 1964 for the simple reason that the whistle had been blown beforehand.

There was a sequel to those incidents when Meath and Galway qualified later for the final of the popular Grounds Tournament and young Garvey was again appointed as referee. Meath refused to play, and Croke Park quite rightly refused to budge. Gallant Dublin, All-Ireland champions a year earlier, stepped in to play Galway, but the show was not over yet.

I was sitting in the lower deck of the Hogan Stand with Donie O'Sullivan of Kerry when I saw Séamus Garvey scanning the scene until his eyes fell on us. He called us and mentioned that two of his umpires had failed to turn up: he was seeking substitutes. We could not let him down, and in a matter of minutes I was in a white coat, ready for duty at the Railway goal.

Noel Tierney was Galway's fullback at the time, the last stalwart of the era when strength and fearless high fielding characterized the play of the guardians of the square. Before long a Dublin player sent a real tester towards the Galway goal, tailor-made for Tierney's jumping powers, and right enough he went up and came down with the ball. He was tackled, and my judgement was that he was forced fractionally over the end line.

Showing the bravery of Garvey in the All-Ireland semi-final, I immediately shot up my right hand denoting a fifty for Dublin. My action was not pleasing to Tierney, and I learned quickly that he was a linguist, but before the matter took any other turn goalkeeper Johnny Geraghty arrived on the spot and showed the fullback a skid mark that extended beyond the line. 'That's yours, Noel. Hand over the ball and get back into the square and field the fifty.'

That settled it, and as soon as the fifty-yard free kick left its base Geraghty was roaring, 'Your ball, Noel!' As it neared the edge of the square the aggrieved fullback fielded it brilliantly and kicked what used to be described as a lusty clearance.

I learned a lot about the teamwork of Galway that day. It was educational to watch and listen to Johnny Geraghty as he controlled the area inside the fourteen-yard line with explicit directives: 'Go for it, Enda . . . Your ball, Bosco . . . Leave this to me . . . Stay down, Noel . . .' They were a team from goal to goal, and it is no wonder they won three in a row.

My umpiring career ended with that Grounds Tournament, and the GAA lost a good referee by not having the courage to appoint Séamus Garvey for subsequent matches.

And to save many from wondering how I would rank the Famous Four Football Forces of the past fifty years, I place Kerry's team of 1975–86 on top, Down of the 1960s as Tánaistí, Dublin of the 1970s in third place and Galway's team of 1964–66 in hot pursuit.

Chapter Twenty-One

I have great memories of Galway hurling from the mid 1970s onward. The county's achievements were very few at the start of that decade, numbering only two All-Ireland titles: a senior one in 1925 followed by a junior fourteen years later.

Winning the under-21 All-Ireland in 1972 triggered a new era of hope for the West, though the news that spread from Shannonside first was that the well-known Fr Paddy Mahon had taken ill at the game. He did not recover and died a few days later. How the man would have enjoyed the glories of the following years!

The real breakthrough for Galway was the winning of the National League in 1975. I was on duty when they beat Tipperary in the final in Limerick, and excitement climbed dangerously high when P. J. Qualter fired home a late goal that won the day. Elegant midfielder John Connolly was captain, and I was conscious of the presence of another Gaeltacht man, Joe McDonagh, on the right side of a powerful halfback line. His colleagues were Seán Silke and Iggy Clarke, and there are people who would swear that it was the county's best-ever combination in the area. Others put forward the unit of Pete Finnerty, Tony Keady and Gerry McInerney as the best, and I will not adjudicate on the puzzle beyond saying that they differed in style, with the white boots and flowing locks of McInerney catching many an eye as he raided upfield.

Some excellent wins, such as the All-Ireland semi-final defeat of Cork in 1975, and excruciating losses, such as losing in a replay to Wexford a year later, helped to mould the team of the 1970s into the All-Ireland-winning outfit of 1980. Only a goal separated the sides at the finish of that defeat to Wexford, and one of Wexford's goals was controversial. I was broadcasting the match in the brand-new Páirc Uí Chaoimh by the Lee, and I said at the time that the whistle had been blown by referee Mick Slattery before John Quigley gained possession and rattled the Galway net. Of course it was only an opinion, but I was asked by a Galway official a few days later would I be prepared to give evidence at the Central Council hearing that followed an objection. I declined to do so: I had merely expressed an opinion and could not attach any certainty whatsoever to it. I was a long way from the action, and hearing the sound of a whistle was out of the question on a day of a large crowd.

Some Galway players felt certain that the whistle had been blown, and there were two priests among them. But I did not hear of any of the Wexford men advance the same claim, and it was not a case of Army deafness on their part. And wasn't John Quigley on his honeymoon anyway!

The year 1980 began well for Galway when an all-Galway Connacht team beat Leinster in the semi-final of the Railway Cup and Munster in the St Patrick's Day final in Croke Park. It was the province's second title and the first since 1947; understandably, Galway players and followers celebrated in style at the sound of the final whistle.

Joe Connolly was captain, and I have never forgotten the closing words of his fine speech: 'Roll on September.' There was a daring challenge in the voice, and it augured well for Galway's hopes after the jolts of the previous years.

Galway maintained their form in the closing stages of the League, though going under in the semi-final by a goal to Cork, the eventual winners of the title. A further boost came on the 1 June when Castlegar won the All-Ireland club title with five Connolly brothers on board and Michael always a star but never an All-Star as captain.

From then on all hands were on deck, with eyes fixed on the McCarthy Cup in September. It helped that manager Cyril Farrell was not burdened with a high profile, and wins over Kildare and Leinster kings Offaly brought them a place in the All-Ireland final with Limerick.

I found during a trip to the West before the final that some followers were fearing the worst as the big day drew near. Good judges informed me that the goalkeeper was shaky on low shots, while others said they often prayed when they saw a high ball dropping towards him. I put it all down to the haunting thought that Galway had not won a hurling All-Ireland since 1923, and that was sufficient to breed a thousand doubts as the autumn tide built up momentum. But when the hour of destiny came, the big friendly goalman Mike Conneely stopped the high ones, the low ones, the hard ones and the spinning ones with a display that earned him my Man of the Match award.

The Liam McCarthy Cup was billed for a trip across the Shannon for the first time in fifty-seven years; it was a fine moment for hurling.

As I had broadcast the minor final earlier in the day I was ready to go on to the field the moment the game ended. I wanted to meet John Connolly, as I had been a great admirer of his through a long career that had brought few rewards prior to that year. He had been playing with the hurlers since the mid 1960s and had played senior football for the county also, as well as winning a Connacht championship in boxing.

As usual he greeted me in Irish when I congratulated him, and I was still on the pitch as Joe Connolly accepted the cup from GAA President Paddy McFlynn. I rate Joe Connolly's victory speech the best I've heard in any sporting forum anywhere in the world. It was delivered totally through the medium of beautiful Conamara Irish, spoken with dignity, clarity and passion. It touched all the right chords and had a wholesome sincerity.

Nár laga Dia thú, a Joe Connolly.

September had really rolled on, and Joe McDonagh was there to rock it with a hearty rendering of 'The West's Awake'. The trek home to the West the following day was most memorable, as was the sight of the Bishop of Galway, Éamonn Casey, wearing a maroon jersey.

The Galway hurlers have been in there with the best ever since. Minor and under-21 All-Irelands were won in 1983, and when another at under-21 was secured in 1986 an unprecedented era of success for the county was on hand. They were runners-up in the senior All-Ireland of 1985, having been favourites to beat Offaly.

The 1986 team was a mixture of some of the trusty men of 1980 – Sylvie Linnane, Conor Hayes, Steve Mahon and Noel Lane – and a plethora of young and skilful hopefuls. Kilkenny were the early-summer favourites following wins over Galway in the League final and All-Ireland champions Offaly in the Leinster final. Galway's display in beating Kilkenny by eleven points in the All-Ireland semi-final in Semple Stadium was the shock of the decade, and remained a talking point right up to the All-Ireland final. In terms of skill and tactics Cyril Farrell's men were fantastic, and the show gave as much satisfaction to Galway followers as any match ever played. They introduced the two-man full-forward line to great effect, and from goal to corner forward the team hummed in cohesion. Joe Cooney was the guiding genius, and his many classy strokes and deft touches matched anything that either Jimmy Doyle or Christy Ring had performed on the near-sacred pitch in their days.

There was no answer to it, even though Kilkenny had excellent players on duty. At one point during the second half I looked down from the commentary box towards Kilkenny manager Pat Henderson. His long playing career had brought him five All-Ireland medals, and he was a brilliant manager when steering the Cats to a double double of league and championship in 1982 and 1983; however, he seemed helpless there on the Thurles line that day, bibbed and broken with hands on hips and feet apart as if proclaiming that any further movement on his part would be futile. He might even have felt some pride in the game being played by Galway: there is a kinship among hurlers that is rarely found elsewhere.

As a result of that powerful display, Galway were the fancy of many to beat Cork in September's All-Ireland final. Noel Lane, one of the 1980 heroes, was captain, and utter disappointment was their lot when the final ended with the Rebels four points to the good in a high-scoring game. I remember speaking to Noel Lane during Monday's reception for both teams in the Burlington Hotel. He casually remarked that I hadn't spoken to him on my pre-match visit to the dressing room the day before. I can still see him standing in the left-hand corner of the old angled room at the end of the Hogan Stand, but I had decided that as captain he had been subjected to more talk than anybody over the preceding weeks and that it was better to leave him to his thoughts.

I related that to him, and the genial Ballindereen man said he understood, but added that as he saw me leave he said to himself that I had never before retreated without a word with him. It may have been a bad omen, but a new year had already started, and I assured Noel that I would not repeat the offence before the 1987 final, which Galway would win.

Before we realized what was happening, All-Ireland final day of 1987 was upon us. Galway had already won the Railway and National League cups. They beat Babs Keating's new-born Tipperary in the All-Ireland semi-final, and Kilkenny were their opponents in the final.

Noel Lane's role that year was that of impact substitute, and his contribution almost always included the winning goal. I nearly missed talking to him for the second year running, on account of being involved in introducing the GAA Irish Nationwide Jubilee Hurling Team of 1962 to the public before the match. But I made it in time, wished Noel well and prophesied that he would score the winning goal.

He did that almost on cue to win his second All-Ireland medal.

It was a brilliant Galway team, and they went on to win the All-Ireland of 1988 convincingly as well. I would rate that side as the best that ever came from the West.

There was real strength in the spine with John Commins in goal, the immovable Conor Hayes at fullback, the commanding Tony Keady at centre back, the durable pair of Steve Mahon and Croke Park specialist Pat Malone in the centre, the inventive Joe Cooney on the forty, and the ideal warhorse Brendan Lynskey at the edge of the square.

The flankers were equally impressive. The piercing eye of Sylvie

Linnane in defence was a deterrent in itself, and Pete Finnerty, Gerry McInerney and Ollie Kilkenny lacked nothing that top-class defenders should possess.

The forward wingers knitted in perfectly with Cooney and Lynskey, and all four – Anthony Cunningham, Michael 'Hopper' McGrath, Éanna Ryan and Martin Naughton – had blistering pace. The sight of Naughton devouring space as he hared along the left wing on fruitful solo runs is something I will not forget.

And finally the bench was ultra-strong, with the likes of Noel Lane, Tony Kilkenny and the evergreen P. J. Molloy, the only survivor from the League-winning team of 1975. And the coordinating role of manager Cyril Farrell must not be overlooked.

In a sense the team became lost after the 1988 success, and while blame can be laid elsewhere for what became known as the 'Tony Keady affair', it was partly of their own making. A trip to America where Keady played a match without having the necessary clearance was the root cause of the problem that led to suspension and some bad will. As he was Texaco Hurler of the Year at the time it could not be expected that his participation in a game would go unnoticed. What a pity that some genuinely friendly advice did not come his way beforehand. With a modicum of luck and a little bit more caution that Galway team could have won four All-Ireland finals in a row.

It's best you figure out for yourselves which four I have in mind.

Supporters' clubs abound around the country these days; they raise funds to help promote the national games in the respective counties and to cover some of the costs relating to preparing the county team. Training teams has become a very costly business, and county boards are grateful for the assistance given by supporters' clubs.

The idea was first given substance in Tipperary in the autumn of 1986. Babs Keating, ever a genial character, had been appointed manager of the county hurlers, and almost immediately supporters came to the fore with promises of financial assistance in the hope of extricating Tipperary hurling from the depths of a fifteen-year trough.

The country's first supporters' club was soon in existence, enthusiasm and hope mushroomed, and ventures including the raffling of a racehorse brought the best part of £100,000 into the training kitty. The Tipp bandwagon of 1987 was in motion before long with two more hurling legends, Theo English and Donie Nealon, joining Babs as selectors.

The supporters' club and Babs' enlightened approach brought a touch of show biz to the hurling scene, and the season was a memorable one. Tipp regained the Munster championship last held by the Premier County in 1971, and much spectacular hurling was provided. There was general delight when star players such as Nicky English, Pat Fox, Bobby Ryan and Ken Hogan made the breakthrough at last. English's kicked goal against Cork in the Munster final in Thurles gave Tipperary a draw, and anticipation was such in the county that the late Frank Patterson of Clonmel was on hand to sing 'Sliabh na mBan' in case Tipp won the title for the first time in sixteen years.

The replay in Killarney went to extra time on a day of sweltering heat, and it was baffling to see selector Donie Nealon wearing an overcoat for the duration of the game as he ran up and down along the sideline. It took me a few days to get an explanation: Donie was also Secretary of the Munster Council, and several people paid him in cash on the day for tickets sent by post in those days of non-technological means of payment. So all pockets were full of money, and the coat could not be discarded.

The win gave Tipp hurling the boost it needed at the time, and All-Ireland titles in 1989 and 1991 were just reward for a team coached to play open and exciting hurling.

There is an innate disposition in all of us to imagine that everything was better in our younger days – summers were finer, and so on. The belief sometimes extends to a view that hurlers and Gaelic footballers of old were of a higher standard; I believe this is illusory. In many ways the games are better spectacles today than in the past, though we might miss much of the high fielding that characterized football of earlier times.

I have no doubt but that the hurlers of modern times are in general as skilful as their counterparts in earlier decades, and that skill plays a much bigger part in the determination of results. Without taking in any way from the wonderful memories left by the 'big two' of the game – Christy Ring and Limerick's Mick Mackey – I have come to the conclusion that D. J. Carey would match them in all facets of the game.

From the time he first came to prominence as a member of the St Kieran's College team that won All-Ireland honours in 1988, he has thrilled followers of the game with extraordinary displays. His skills are honed to near perfection, and he has a keen understanding of teamwork at a high level. When he played on the wing, there was no more thrilling sight in sport than D. J. accelerating clear of defenders and more often than not finishing with a spectacular score. His game is built on skill, pace and quickness of thought, and he never resorts to other tactics in order to secure a score or a victory.

He is the true hurling icon of modern times. His personality is such that he feels at times that the attention he receives is to the detriment of others who deserve an equal amount of acclaim. I agree that many class players have appeared in recent times that merit as high a rating as any from the past, and in mentioning Brian Whelehan, Joe Cooney, John Fenton and Nicky English I am merely picking a handful from a plethora of worthy exponents of the great game.

During the 1990s the powerful creature known as tradition came in for incisive analysis, and the findings hinted at diminishing influence over the contests of the future. The new philosophy was that proper coaching and preparation could in reality cause champions to emerge from any quarter.

The rise of the Wexford hurlers in the middle of the decade exemplified this spirit. The love of hurling so well nourished in the 1950s and 1960s lived on in spite of poor results since 1968. As with the Cork footballers of the 1970s, the rise of an exceptional neighbouring team was the root cause of Wexford's lack of success.

Kilkenny saw to it most of the time in Leinster, and, when Wexford had the good fortune of capturing the gigantic Bob Keeffe Cup in 1970, 1976 and 1977, Cork were there to thwart them in the All-Irelands.

In 1996 optimism took hold of the followers for the first time in years, and the excitement in Croke Park on Leinster final day matched that in Semple Stadium a year earlier when Clare won Munster. Captain Martin Storey had been a popular player for years, but he became the charismatic figure of Irish sport that summer and autumn, culminating in a two-point win over Limerick in the All-Ireland final. A win after twenty-eight years of hurling famine was suitably celebrated, and the ancient art of balladry enjoyed a revival. It was good for the game.

The talk of September's glory was still in the air when Bobby Rackard, one of the Wexford legends of the 1950s, died some months later. I remember meeting Marion Rackard, daughter of Nicky, at the funeral. I had been aware that Marion generally attended Wexford's matches, but was not as passionate about the GAA as some others. Her father had developed a drink problem in his playing days, but he manfully overcame the affliction and did great work subsequently in alerting others to the dangers of alcohol.

Marion followed the fortunes of the Yellow Bellies closely during 1996. She enjoyed the whole scene and witnessed the lift the All-Ireland triumph had given the whole county: 'For the first time in my life I understood what they used be talking about.'

The crusading work of her father in relation to drink impacted on her, and she has involved herself in the same work; she is currently Chairperson of the Irish National Alliance for Action on Alcohol — a powerful body with representation from the Royal College of Physicians, the Rutland Centre and Barnardo's, among others. She believes that the GAA has not taken adequate responsibility in relation to the effects of alcohol, and should not be willing to take sponsorship from companies promoting alcoholic drinks.

★

The hype surrounding that Wexford revival in the mid 1990s bordered on show biz, and much of it could be attributed to the manager, Liam Griffin. He put a good management structure in place, which, combined with an infectious enthusiasm, created a force that was almost irresistible.

The prominence of managers represents a relatively new phenomenon in the world of the GAA: the term was rarely applied to the person in charge of a team until the arrival of Kevin Heffernan and Mick O'Dwyer in the 1970s. Prior to that they were simply trainers, and often they sought the services of an army man to devise a few simple fitness drills. Thus Jim Hehir (father of commentator Micheál) became famous as the trainer rather than manager of the Clare team that won the All-Ireland hurling title of 1914. He continued to train club teams in Dublin and had another short stint on the county scene when he took over as trainer of the Leitrim footballers in 1927.

The unusual story was told to me almost seventy years later by Tom Gannon, who was the Leitrim captain when they won the Connacht title of 1927. It was a different world then: Tom informed me that no training had been done for the matches in the West, and there was no presentation as no cup existed at the time. It was the county's first provincial title, and understandably the players were excited; when somebody suggested that the team could go further 'if only we had a trainer', the idea was taken as a good one.

As Tom was a teacher who had spent time in college in Dublin, he was given the job to go back there as soon as possible and secure a trainer. He called to see a teacher friend in Dublin, and both then headed off to O'Connell Street in the hope of finding a trainer for the new Connacht champions. They stood at the GPO for a while, and the Lord must have looked down on them because who passed by but Jim Hehir. He was still a well-known figure in Dublin thirteen years after his exploits with Clare, and the pair decided there and then to put the proposition to him. Hehir agreed, and arrangements were then made for his first visit west of the Shannon before the delegation retired to a hotel for some tea. Tom told me he was the happiest man on earth as he boarded a train later for the homeward journey; he had been sent in search of a trainer, and he had found a man who had trained a team to win an All-Ireland.

All that changed about an hour later when he looked out the window as the train pulled in to a station. He could not believe his eyes: the word 'Drogheda' was written on the wall. He was on the Belfast train!

He disembarked, but discovered that the last train back to Dublin had already left and there was no bus service at 11.30 in the night. So the Leitrim captain set off walking to Dublin through the night, and it was well bright when he reached the limits of Dublin city. He met a Good Samaritan at that point, a milkman with a horse and cart on his way to sell milk in the city, and the tired Tom took a jaunt with him as far as O'Connell Street.

The gods did not even grant the man a happy ending to the story; the trainer did his bit all right, but Kerry beat Leitrim by two points in the All-Ireland semi-final played in Tuam. There must have been terrific defences on both sides because the score line read Kerry 0–4, Leitrim 0–2.

Oddly enough, Dr Éamonn O'Sullivan had trained a Kerry team to win an All-Ireland by then. He was in charge a year earlier when the Kingdom beat Kildare, and it is almost incredible that he was still Kerry's trainer when they lost the finals of 1964 and 1965 to Galway. He was years ahead of his time in that he placed great emphasis on preparing the mind as well as the body for contest. His father, J. P. O'Sullivan, was a legendary athlete, and it is quite possible that Kerry would be a rugby stronghold today but for a quirk of fate and the presence of J. P.

Rugby was well established in the Kingdom when the GAA was founded and the new game of Gaelic football invented in 1884. There were rugby teams in most of the towns of the county, but the champions were the men of Killorglin with the powerful J. P. very much to the fore. Sometime in the late 1880s three young teachers who were conversant with the new football arrived in the Killorglin area and convinced the local champion rugby team to change codes. They did so and became Laune Rangers, with J. P. O'Sullivan as captain.

The game took off elsewhere as well, and when the Rangers won the first-ever Kerry championship in 1889 the foundation of a great tradition was laid. J. P. was commonly known as 'The Champion' on account of his prowess as an athlete, and he captained Kerry in the county's first appearance in an All-Ireland final two years later.

Nowadays the job of a team manager demands hours of work in preparation and man-management throughout most of the year. They deserve greater recognition from the governing powers of the GAA than they get.

The achievements and service of Mick O'Dwyer, Kevin Heffernan and Seán Boylan entitle them to a place of honour at any banquet, and the association is blessed that an endless number of fine people have taken up the managerial role and brought honour to it: Mickey Harte, Brian Cody, Joe Kernan, Liam Griffin, Ger Loughnane, John O'Mahony, Nicky English, Brian McEniff, Páidí Ó Sé, Babs Keating, Archdeacon Michael O'Brien and many more.

I do not intend to rank them, but I think nobody would mind if I add another name to the abbreviated list above: Eugene McGee.

The reason I do so is because it is my belief that it was concern for the state of football that brought Eugene McGee into the limelight in the first place. It is well over thirty years since I first met him in a café close to Portobello Bridge, Dublin, late one night on the way home from the dogs. He introduced himself to me and told me about his efforts in trying to create greater interest in Gaelic football among the students of UCD. He had become Club Secretary purely because nobody else showed an interest in the job, and began his career by helping the juniors. Before long he was training the College senior team, and they won the Sigerson Cup final in January 1968 – the postponed foot-and-mouth final of 1967.

The students broke new ground after winning that Sigerson when going on a trip to New York in June; the Longford-born man was making his mark.

Football prospered in UCD during the 1970s as they won six

Sigersons out of seven between 1973 and 1979. The same spell brought two Dublin championships to the College and the All-Ireland Club titles of 1974 and 1975. Still it was a surprise in football circles when McGee was appointed Offaly football manager in the autumn of 1976. A measured progression then began that brought Offaly from Division Two football that autumn to the exalted position of All-Ireland champions six years later when Séamus Darby's goal knocked a link off Kerry's five-in-a-row chain. Who could begrudge a committed and hardworking manager that moment of glory? It gave a place in history to a fine group of footballers, of whom the elegant and stylish Matt Connor was the undisputed high king.

Chapter Twenty-Two

The GAA is without question the leading community organization in the land. It has its quota of faults and weaknesses, and I will touch on those later. But there is no doubting its positive contribution to the development of this country since its foundation in 1884.

A glance through An Bráthair Liam Ó Caithnia's book *Scéal na hIomána* gives a clear picture of the extent of hurling in Ireland for centuries before the founding of the GAA. It was widely played in Leinster and Munster, in Galway and in the Glens of Antrim. It could be said that the game was part-professional for a while because it carried status with the ruling classes, and any landlord worth his salt supported a hurling team.

Matches were sometimes arranged, with amounts up to 100 guineas on offer as a prize for the winners, in addition to copious amounts of beer. Colourful playing apparel was the fashion and captaincy was deemed a great honour. Sometimes the landlord would be a non-playing captain, but in his day Viscount Desart MP was a very active hurler who played under the ordinary name of Seán A' Chaipín, Seán of the Cap. By all accounts he was a hurler of repute, and there are Irish poems lauding his deeds and mourning his death at a young age innocently caused by paint fumes as he sat for his portrait.

Football of a kind was played in Ireland over the centuries; it was known as rough-and-tumble in places, and *caid* in the Gaelic-speaking parts of Kerry. It was much closer to rugby than to the modern game of Gaelic football, which was largely invented after the founding of the GAA.

Parish against parish was the common form of competition in *caid*, with the ball being thrown in at the midpoint and the honours going to the team that brought the ball home. Folklore tells about fierce games of *caid* between Dún Síon and another village, Lios

Deargáin, six miles away as the crow flies at the foot of the beautiful Strickeen mountain. Apparently the Dún Síon team never went into action without performing a ritual dance and chant. While doing research on the matter some time ago, Lispole man Roibeárd Ó Cathasaigh, son of Billy Casey, who won five All-Irelands with Kerry, and first cousin of Brian Mullins, who won four with Dublin, unearthed the words:

> Hoo-ra-ha, Hoo-ra-ha,
> Mura gheobhair an chaid,
> Gheobhair an fear,
> Agus sé an fear a gheobhaidh é,
> Chomh maith leis an gcaid,
> Hoo-ra-ha, Hoo-ra-ha.

It bears a striking resemblance to the pre-match routine of New Zealand's All-Blacks and other Polynesian practices. The opening words of the All-Blacks' haka ritual are *Ka mate, Ka mate*, which is a threat; the same note of threat is to be found in the third line of the Dún Síon chant, *Gheobhar an fear* – we will get the man. And the opening and finishing lines of our Dún Síon one – *Hoo-ra-ha, Hoo-ra-ha* – is not a million miles from the *puhuru-huru* of the Maori version. Is it possible that some of the unfortunates transported down under in long bygone days, who carried the game of *caid* with them, also carried the Dún Síon haka?

It could be argued that the impetus that gave rise to the founding of the GAA stemmed from the Society for the Preservation of the Irish Language founded in 1876, of which Michael Cusack, founder of the GAA, was an active member. Cusack also served as treasurer of the Gaelic Union from 1882. His inspiration to found the Gaelic Athletic Association in 1884 was an offshoot of the objectives of both Society and Union.

The GAA was founded in Victorian times, and that accounts for the almost total absence of women from the movement at the beginning. Cumann Camógaíochta na nGael was not founded until

1904 and did not get around to staging inter-county championships until 1932. I have no hesitation in saying that Angela Downey of Kilkenny was the best camogie player I have seen in action; she won twelve All-Ireland titles in her time as did her sister Ann; another legend is Kathleen Mills of Dublin, who won fifteen All-Irelands back in the 1940s, 1950s and 1960s.

Ladies' football was not organized until the 1970s; now it is a trend setter for all Gaelic sports. Picking the ball straight off the ground is permitted, timing of games is done electronically, and the sin bin has been introduced. Who has been the game's best player? I would say the athletic Mary Jo Curran from Kerry.

I have been broadcasting camogie and ladies' football finals for a good number of years now and am conscious of very good levels of skill and commitment in both games. Camogie needs teams besides Cork and Tipperary challenging for All-Ireland honours, and it is a matter that requires immediate attention. I have seen some camogie and ladies' football games played as curtain-raisers to the corresponding games for men over the past two years, and I approve of the practice. It should be expanded to include some of the bigger GAA dates. I believe we will see huge developments in both camogie and ladies' football in the short- and medium-term future, especially if the process of incorporating all three Gaelic bodies in the one association is speeded up. It is encouraging that a pilot scheme is operating at the moment, but the basic idea is so logically natural that it seems to me that the amalgamation could be finalized without much further delay. It could truly be said then that the new Gaelic Athletic Association was catering for the needs of all members of the community.

A community spirit is one of the greatest assets that a locality can possess. The contribution that the GAA has made in creating that spirit throughout the parishes of Ireland is immense, and is in fact just as important as the staging of All-Ireland championships for the elite players.

The amateur ethos of the GAA, and its dependence on enormous voluntary input, is a great source of strength. I have witnessed that ethos in action in all quarters of the country through the years: the countless volunteers who coach, train and encourage the young to involve themselves in the games or other aspects of the association. Participation at any level gives GAA people the feeling that they are members of one large family. Never did I see that family bond so close to the surface as it was at the time of the death of Tyrone footballer Cormac McAnallen in March 2004. He had begun learning the game at an early age with his Eglish club, and was one of the gifted and dedicated minority who reached the promised land of All-Ireland glory. He was exceptional as a player and a person, and as such we all imagined that he belonged to us. His loss was felt by every member of the Gaelic Athletic Association. I saw many people at the funeral in Eglish on that sad March day who would be the fiercest of rivals on the field of play, but who stood shoulder to shoulder as brothers of the fallen hero.

Like many others I have given thought from time to time to the fact that Gaelic players are amateurs in a world that has many professional sportspeople. There are times when I think it is almost inevitable that the GAA will embrace professionalism, and that the association must be prepared to grapple with the problems that would ensue from such a course.

Sources external to this country, such as television networks, supply the finances necessary for Irish rugby to operate a professional wing, and Irish athletes and golfers follow international circuits in pursuit of monetary rewards. Most full-time Irish soccer players are forced to seek their fortunes abroad. But rugby, athletics, golf and soccer are international games; there is no overseas golden horizon for games that are predominantly Irish.

If a move to professionalism were dependent on commercial sponsorship, that would quickly lead to a championship for no more than a dozen teams, with the others falling by the wayside. The onset of professionalism could erode real community involvement. Loyalty would be the first casualty; in the new era small clubs could no longer expect to hold on to their star players. The GAA could do worse than engage in serious discussions with the Irish Rugby

Football Union on the merits and drawbacks of professionalism in that sport.

In my travels outside of Ireland I make a point of visiting the sporting facilities available to participants, and I have come to the conclusion that Croke Park would not exist in its current form if the GAA had not succeeded in remaining an amateur organization. It is a showpiece that holds its own with the world's best. The vast bulk of the expenditure on the reconstruction came from the association's own resources or through borrowing. I think the GAA has fallen down in not highlighting sufficiently often that the amounts paid over in VAT and PAYE as a result of the development make the government contribution look meagre. By comparison, other bodies have got more from the state for doing less. Croke Park is a symbol of the power of an organization that is not driven solely by the commercial profit motive.

Besides the paid administrators that are necessary for the professional running of a major organization, nobody makes money directly from the GAA. Of course the profile of county players enables many of them to capitalize on their fame in business or professional employment, and the very best of luck to them. I believe that the decision taken a few years ago to allow players to receive payment for endorsing certain products or performing public relations functions for commercial concerns was a positive and appropriate step.

From my contacts with GAA players I do not detect any clamour to introduce professionalism into the games. That is not to say that they do not see the need for improvements in their lot, and the existence of the Gaelic Players Association is testimony to that. By and large the players are the salt of the earth and are proud of their loyalty to the games and structures. They are willing to make sacrifices, but I do not think that they should be unduly out of pocket on account of involvement in the sport. Proper cover for loss of income due to injury should be put in place as soon as possible, as well as reimbursement for other expenses incurred. Players see the two as problems yet unsolved.

I do not think that it is appropriate in modern times to see county boards or other groups forced to organize matches or other functions to raise funds to defray expenses caused by an injury to a county player. It is time for the central authorities to put a structure in place to deal with such matters. I think it is opportune at this time also to give the GPA representation on the Central Council of the GAA. The introduction of a new voice would be invigorating, and I do not think there is any need to be suspicious of the motives of the individuals that would be put forward. It will happen at some stage – like worker representation on business boards of directors, which is now commonplace. Why delay in refreshing the councils of the GAA?

I am in favour of renting Croke Park to other sporting associations for selected special events, and I cannot visualize that this would damage the GAA in any way. Croke Park is a very valuable asset with a capacity for generating extra revenue that could be used towards games promotion, greater grants towards club development, and the various pursuits that come under the cultural arm of the association.

The function rooms of Croke Park are hired regularly for various non-GAA events, and this makes economic sense. I have attended some of these functions and could not help noticing the reaction of people who had never previously been in the stadium. It is one of amazement at the scale of the project and the special atmosphere it fosters, and it is my firm conviction that such visitors leave with respect for an organization that had the courage to follow a dream to its conclusion. The same type of effect would flow from the letting of the playing area for other sports and the exposure of the centre to worldwide audiences. If viewed from that angle, allowing international soccer and rugby matches in Croke Park could amount to a patriotic act, as it would create further awareness of Ireland abroad.

Gaelic players who travel to Australia for compromise-rules competition with Australian Rules players consider it a privilege to play in famous venues such as the Melbourne Cricket Ground. But they are ever conscious of the fact that it was the Cricket Union that pioneered the development, and would respect it accordingly and commend the ongoing improvements. Opening up Croke Park at times when it would not interfere with the GAA's own programmes would have the same effect and would be no more than a seven-day wonder.

I am conscious of the fact that many people hold a different view, and that is their right. What I have said is intended to apply mostly to Croke Park. Some of the other major GAA stadia are also underused for games, and again provided the GAA's own programme is not interfered with I would consider it prudent to let such grounds on the GAA's conditions.

I would never visualize the sharing of club grounds as being either practical or desirable. They get far more use than any of the special grounds and could not be expected to take any more. Local initiative and contributions have been largely responsible for the existence of satisfactory facilities in most of the country's 2,000-plus clubs. It is a healthy sign that the prevailing philosophy is geared towards continual upgrading.

The GAA has nothing to fear in competition from other games. Prior to the abolition of the ban on foreign games in 1971 the same fear was being traded in argument. Gaelic games are infinitely stronger now than they ever were during the ban years.

To most non-GAA people's way of thinking, the association is a conservative one, often treating proposed change with a mixture of caution and suspicion. The manner in which motions to open Croke Park to other games were ruled out of order last March is a typical example of how this notion of conservatism is nurtured. Nevertheless, the association has managed to progress on many fronts at a very acceptable pace, and under proper analysis the image of conservatism might not hold up.

In theory the organization is democratic in the extreme, and that can sometimes be a hindrance. I remember reading one time that communism offered the best vehicle for economic welfare, provided that all people were unequivocally honest. I would apply the same judgement to a democratic organization such as the GAA: its rules and procedures need honest interpretation if they are to work. To me that means giving rein to common sense and keeping the wishes of ordinary members in mind when making decisions.

That is why I was disappointed when a committee made up of past presidents of the association ruled those motions concerning the opening up of Croke Park out of order for inclusion on the agenda of the annual congress. To ordinary GAA people the move lacked the ingredient of common sense, and that is why there was an outcry.

The members of the committee are all respected figures and would not have been elevated to the eminent position of president without having contributed hugely to the association over years; this was generally accepted, and according to a strict interpretation of the rules they were correct in rejecting the motions before them. But there was a mood for debate in the air.

Until passed or rejected in line with preordained structures of voting, motions are no more than topics for debate among delegates. Debate, no matter how heated, is preferable to a prohibition on free speech. Two hours' debate at Congress would have satisfied everyone. And the verdict, as ever, would have been accepted. The cry of 'Let the games continue' could then be raised.

I have never been in favour of the ban on spectators coming on to the pitch at the end of All-Ireland finals, and the atmosphere suffers when the ban is enforced. The presentation of the Liam McCarthy Cup to D. J. Carey at the end of the 2003 All-Ireland hurling final lacked an element of excitement that only a crowd on the field can generate.

I believe that it would not be a difficult task to steward a large crowd on the field. I get a good view of proceedings on the field from my broadcasting position on the Hogan Stand, and the only danger I see is in allowing the fans to get too close to the tunnel area in front of the presentation rostrum. Surely it would be poss-ible to place a semicircular barrier of some twenty yards' radius on each side of the tunnel. It is better to control exuberance than to suppress it.

Apart from matters mentioned above, I have a brief wish list for implementation by the GAA:

a) Extend the smoking ban beyond the limits of Croke Park to other venues.

b) Take a proactive stand against one of the greatest evils in society today, the abuse of alcohol, which often dominates celebrations of sporting successes.

c) Encourage all clubs to provide and implement suitable fitness programmes for those who have ceased to be active playing members. Players are well catered for in this regard, but concern for the fitness of those beyond that stage is rarely featured.

d) Initiate a major scholarship scheme for members to third-level institutions, with academic ability as only one of several criteria for selection.

e) Expedite the pilot process that is preparing for the amalgamation of the associations catering for Gaelic football, hurling, camogie and ladies' football.

f) Encourage more participation by women in administration, refereeing, fitness programming, and other areas.

g) Embrace technology as is used in other sports when doubts exist as to the legitimacy of some scores, and ensure that a video camera is active at all inter-county senior championship matches for reference by the referee as he or she deems appropriate. Video technology is deemed a boon by referees officiating at rugby internationals; it causes little delay and in many cases aids the application of fair play.

h) Relieve referees of the responsibility for time-keeping by introducing the countdown clock; the system works very well in ladies' football.

i) Introduce a sin bin, or repentance cabin, for the temporary accommodation of offenders against fair play.

j) Encourage more use of the Irish language in the spoken form.

★

The future looks good for the GAA, and I would love to live to see the day when all counties will have experienced the ecstasy of winning the All-Ireland. That day will surely come, and I wonder now and then whether Leitrim, one of my favourites, will get there ahead of Wicklow, Carlow, Antrim and all the ever-hopeful others.

On the final day of the past millennium I was asked to envisage what the All-Ireland football final of 2020 might be like. Before committing myself to a wild guess, I cast my mind back over the preceding score years. I saw Offaly hurlers without even a Leinster title to their name at that point, yet at the death of the old millennium they were at the captain's table.

The thought that history repeats itself came to me, and thus my forecast of the 2020 All-Ireland football final involved Fermanagh and Westmeath. According to my prediction made on 31 December 1999, the scores will be level as they battle out the last minute of that 2020 final. A high ball will be heading towards midfield and the Fermanagh midfielder, Mac Dara Paisley, qualifying under the granny rule, will shout out in Irish, 'Fág fúm é, Jason,' before effecting a mighty fetch.

By then Jason Adams, qualifying under the same rule, will have raced to the wing in expectation of a well-directed left-footed pass from Mac Dara. On receiving the pass he will solo à la Seán Purcell, while the powerful Paisley will be heading goalwards.

Finally, with split-second timing, Jason will complete a perfect delivery to Mac Dara, who will drive the ball to the Westmeath net, thereby winning the match for Fermanagh.

There will be unprecedented scenes of celebration as Queen Gráinne, wife of guesting King William III, presents the Sam Maguire Cup to Mac Dara.

Go maire siad go dtí Lá Pilib a 'Chleite.

Acknowledgements

Until recently, I never seriously considered the notion of chronicling my memories, and resisted the suggestion whenever it was put to me. As I am not an organized type of person who keeps records or memorabilia, I felt I had a ready-made excuse for declining offers to write a book. But the persistence of Michael McLoughlin of Penguin Ireland eventually broke down my defence.

He wrote to me on several occasions, and we had meetings galore, usually ending with a promise from me to consider the matter further. Eventually I yielded to his request, and in hindsight I am delighted that he had the staying power to keep faith with his idea. *Gan a leithéid de dhuine, ní raibh seans ar domhan go gcuirfi mo scéal-sa ar phár – go raibh maith a Mhichíl.*

The decision to proceed brought me in touch with others in Penguin Ireland, especially Brendan Barrington, an editor of enormous patience and a capacity to accept all the worries connected with the project.

When I first announced to my family that I had agreed to write my autobiography, the idea was greeted with a mixture of incredulity and hilarity. But once I opened the laptop they joined the team as advisers and critics, with Éadaoin in particular expert in research. They quickly developed a disposition to ignore the chaos and disorder that invaded the house until the book was written and the Championship season restored normality in the month of May.

With my wife, Helena, at the helm, they became the crew that collected the photographs and filled in the gaps from the albums of my sisters Eileen, Máire and Kathleen, along with nieces Emer and Maeve Moriarty. They even arranged for ace photographer Ray McManus of Sportsfile to be present at Dublin Airport to snap the entire family, as we met on a day when some had landed and others were preparing to take to the skies.

I wrote mostly from memory, and was glad to receive confirmation or clarification of the events of my youth from Náis, Dónal, Eileen, Máire and Kathleen. And whenever my mind needed reassurance in connection with the Báile Bhuirne days, my old friend Seán Ó hAiniféin was more than willing to help.

Before I submitted the text to the publishers, my nephew Seosamh Ó Muircheartaigh, a journalist with the *Clare Champion*, read it through and offered useful advice. Of course there were others who played some part in the compilation of a story I enjoyed stitching together. *Mo mhíle buíochas do gach aon agus go bhfága Dia an tsláinte agaibh.*

Index

Hanly, Dave 108
Harnan, Liam 214
Harrington, Paddy 156–7
Harrington, Padraig 156, 157
Harte, Mickey 231
Hartigan, Bernie 193
Hartigan, Pat 193
Haughey, Charlie 118, 144
Hayes, Conor 223, 224
Hayes, Liam 213, 214
Hayes, Mick 78
Healy, Dermot 171
Hearne, Séamus 78
Heffernan, Fr Michael 133
Heffernan, Kevin 45, 63, 82,
    83, 85, 126–7, 135, 205,
    229, 231
  against Kerry in 1974 130–1,
    133
  retirement as manager 134
Hegarty, Ger 171
Hehir, Jim 229
Henderson, Pat 190, 194, 223
Hennessy, Brendan and
    Michael 186
Hennessy, Paul 163, 164, 166
Henry, Paddy 81
Hickey, David 131, 135
Higgins, Liam 122
Higgins, Michael D. 144
Higgins, Mick 28, 29, 36, 37,
    38
Hogan, Ken 226
Hogan, Michael 201
Hogan, Ted 71
Horan, Padraig 169–70

Horgan, Declan 75
Houlihan, Con 148
Hurley, Tadhg 43
Hyde, Douglas 106

Irish language 24, 141, 144
  revival of 147–8
  see also Bord na Gaeilge
Isdell, Bill 151

Jones, Iggy 39
Joy, Jimmy 81

Kavanagh, Dan 81
Kavanagh, Patrick ('PK') 23,
    59, 73, 100
Kavanagh, Séamus ('JK') 59, 70
Keady, Tony 220, 224, 225
Keane, John 118
Kearins, Mickey 128
Kearney, Jim 56
Keating, Michael ('Babs') 185,
    186–7, 224, 225, 226, 231
Keaveney, Jimmy 40, 131, 210
Keher, Eddie 190, 191, 192,
    193, 194, 195, 203
Kelleher, Robbie 131, 138
Kelliher, Kenny 52
Kelliher, Seán 50
Kelliher, Stevie 72, 159–60
Kelly, Dermot 112, 131
Kelly, Luke 60
Kemmy, Jim 115–16
Kennedy, Fr Mick 169
Kennedy, Mike 51
Kennedy, Paddy 22, 70, 89

Moriarty, Dónal (author's brother) 2, 14, 18, 62, 63, 64, 91, 95, 146, 151, 153, 154

Moriarty, Eileen (author's sister) 2, 18, 19, 62, 63, 64, 146, 147, 159

Moriarty, Ellie (author's aunt) 62

Moriarty, Joe (author's uncle) 5, 44, 46, 62, 86, 146, 155, 158

Moriarty, John (author's uncle) 62

Moriarty, Kathleen (author's sister) 2, 18, 62, 64, 186

Moriarty, Máire (author's sister) 2, 62, 63, 64, 95, 147

Moriarty, May (author's aunt) 19–21, 62

Moriarty, Michael ('Mickey'; author's uncle) 21, 62, 186, 206

Moriarty, Náis (author's brother) 2, 3, 7, 10, 14, 18, 19, 62, 64, 115, 158

Moriarty, Padraig ('Paddy'; author's brother) 2, 19, 47, 62, 63–4, 67, 85, 103, 146, 147, 151, 153, 155

Moriarty, Siobhán (author's sister) 2, 62

Moriarty, Timothy ('Thady'; author's father) 2, 114–15

Moriarty, Tom 84

Morrissey, Éamonn 193

Morrissey, Jim 78

Morrissey, Mick 79, 186

Mountjoy Prison 93–4

Moylan, Mick 82

Moynihan, Séamus 140

Mulderrig, Seán 37

Mullins, Brian 131, 136, 137

Murphy, Barry 199

Murphy, Brian 132, 208

Murphy, Eileen 166

Murphy, Jack 99, 100, 101–3

Murphy, Mick 22, 31

Murphy, Mick (Tipperary) 185

Murphy, Padraig 30, 47, 100

Murphy, Séamus 31, 88–9, 125, 137

Murphy, Seán 30, 47, 77, 84, 87, 96, 120, 122

Murphy, Tomás 31

Murphy, Tommy 90

Murray, Kieran 149

Mussen, Kevin 174

Naughton, Martin 225

Nealon, Donie 183, 187, 226

Nealon, Rodie 187

Nelligan, Charlie 135, 136, 210

Nelligan, Mikey 52

Ní Ógáin, Rois 144–5

Nic Óda, Siobhán 142

Nicklaus, Jack 153

Night at the Dogs (television programme) 160, 162, 164, 199

Pilkington, Johnny 171
Poole, Maggie 45, 205
Power, Ger 123, 126, 140, 198
Prendeville, Mundy 207
Prendeville, Ray 126
Purcell, Kieran 193, 194
Purcell, Seán 38, 39, 40, 41, 42

Quaid, Joe 171
Quaid, Séamus 184
Qualter, P.J. 220
Quigley, John 221
Quinn, Donnchadh 3, 49, 50
Quinn, Jack 218
Quinn, Máire 52, 67
Quinn, Mary 1
Quinn, Maurice 112, 160

Rackard, Billy 76
Rackard, Bobby 76, 80, 228
Rackard, Jimmy 76
Rackard, Marion 228
Rackard, Nick 76, 77, 78, 80
Radio Sport 164
Raidió na Gaeltachta 114,
    116
Railway Cup football final
    1949 Munster-Leinster 44
    1955 Leinster-Munster 78
Rea, Éamonn 193
Reddan, Tony 181
Redmond, Lorcan 133
Reenadoon 73–4
Reidy, Brendan 198
Rhatigan, Séamus 30
Richardson, Aidan 111

Ring, Christy 44, 77, 79–80,
    118, 181, 188, 227
Riordan, Con 15–16
Riordan, Johnny 197, 198
Roche, Con 192
Roche, Mick 185
Roche, Ned 85
Ronan, Johnny 203
Roscommon 172
RTE (Radio Teilifís Éireann)
    109, 206
Rustchitzko, Paddy 57
Ruth, Dolores 164, 165
Ryan, Bobby 226
Ryan, Éanna 225

St Brigid's GAA Club 148, 149,
    150
St Finbarr's School 58
St Laurence O'Toole's School
    59
St Patrick's College 33
St Vincent's GAA Club 81–2,
    83, 85, 92
Salmon, Joe 183
Saunders, John 147
Scoil Oilibhéir 141–2
Semple Stadium 118, 202, 203
Shakespeare, Joe 116
Shanahan, Phil 181
Sheahan, David 154
Sheehy, Mag 2
Sheehy, Mikey 40, 132, 138,
    139, 140, 198, 210
Sherlock, Victor 36, 37
Silke, Seán 220